WHERE TO?

How I Shed My Baggage and Learned to Live Free

Jennifer B. Monahan

Published 2019

Printed in the United States of America

Print ISBN: 978-0-578-47760-2

E-ISBN: 978-0-578-47761-9

For information, contact Spirit Evolution:

Admin@SpiritEvolution.co
www.SpiritEvolution.co

Cover photo courtesy of Pixabay.com

DEDICATION

To Penguin and Parakeet – may you live authentic lives, filled with love, joy, courage and personal power..

CONTENTS

ACKNOWLEDGMENTS

A book is never written in isolation…even if you are living in a hut in Guatemala when you are writing it! I am grateful for all the love, support and guidance I received while I was writing this book, especially from:

Everyone who came out to support the book tour for This Trip Will Change Your Life: A Shaman's Story of Spirit Evolution. You gave me the motivation to write a second book.

My many new friends in Guatemala, who opened up their homes and hearts to me. You taught me more about myself than I could have imagined.

Erin Blessing, Lane Michel and John Visconti, who gave me honest feedback on the first draft of the book. You helped me to see my story through different eyes and encouraged me when I went through the "rough patches."

444, Itzamna, Ixchel and all my spirit guides and teachers. You have continued to guide and support me on this journey, and I can't wait to see where it leads to next!

Annie Tucker, who is still the best editor I could ever ask for! You helped me create the best possible version of this book.

My mom, dad, family and friends, who have been with me through the many ups and downs of my life. You have given me wings by my knowing that the foundation of your support is always there.

INTRODUCTION

March 1, 2017 The roars of a howler monkey outside the window of my thatched-roof hut woke me up at 4 a.m. It was my second night sleeping in the jungle of El Remate, Peten, Guatemala, and I was still adjusting to all the animal noises. As I lay awake, I thought about what a blur the past two weeks had been.

I finished up my book tour for *This Trip will Change Your Life: A Shaman's Story of Spirit Evolution* in Connecticut and New Hampshire amidst the first major snowstorms of 2017. I flew home to San Francisco, packed up the last of my belongings and put everything in storage, turned in the keys for my apartment to my landlord, and then flew to Guatemala. My plan was to spend three months in Guatemala while writing my next book, and then travel around for another three months or so before returning to San Francisco.

What made me move here?

Well, in November 2014, I was hit by a minivan while walking across the street. I was out of work for a little over three months, on crutches for eight months, and wearing some form of a cast for fourteen months. My doctor didn't think I'd walk without either surgery or a crutch or brace for the rest of my life, but I happily proved her wrong, mainly because of the shamanic work I did on myself while I was healing.

Since I was stuck on my couch for about six months, I had plenty of time to think. I realized that I wanted to live life on my terms, the way I wanted to, rather than following a prescribed path

1

about how I should live, work, and be. I wanted to follow my heart and my life calling, and I knew that would require me to make some major changes to my life. In short, I wanted to live authentically.

Living authentically isn't easy. It should be, but there are so many things that hold us back. For me to get to this place, and truly know who I am, I had to do quite a bit of work over a period of several years, including:

- Releasing personas that I'd adopted in life that no longer served me
- Identifying limiting beliefs that really weren't relevant
- Discovering who I am and what makes me unique
- Figuring out my life purpose
- Learning to tap into my own personal power and trust, and
- Following my heart

Once I knew myself better, my path became clearer and I was able to move ahead…or, in this case, to Guatemala.

CHAPTER 1: JUMPING INTO THE DEEP END

July 5, 2016 I took a deep breath and picked up my cell phone. I was about to do the scariest thing I had ever done in my life.

It was a beautiful, warm sunny day in Norwood, Massachusetts. I was at a Hampton Inn, having dinner by myself on the outside patio of the hotel's restaurant. I had flown out from San Francisco that morning and was preparing for tomorrow's client meetings.

With shaky fingers and a nervous pit in my stomach, I called my boss, Ami.

Ami and I had met soon after I joined the consulting firm that we both worked for and were instantly friends. We were working together on a client engagement and bonded over late night working dinners and stress-release shoe shopping excursions. In fact, all the people I worked with at the consulting firm were enjoyable. We worked hard, but we also made time to have fun when we were together. When I came back from my three-month disability leave in February 2015 after my accident, my then-boss, Steve, worked to find me a new role within the organization that would accommodate my temporary disability requirements. Tom immediately made a home for me in his group.

In April 2016, Tom sent me to an internal meeting focused on preparing me for promotion to managing director. I came home reinvigorated and excited about my career and all of the opportunities I had in front of me at the firm. And now I was going to walk away from it.

I called Ami and, after some quick chitchat, blurted out, "I'm giving my notice. But I won't leave until the end of the month, after we wrap up this client engagement."

The silence on the other end of the phone lasted for what felt like an eternity, and then, just one word: "Why?"

Ami knew that I had a book coming out in November, and I explained that I wanted to make sure that I had the flexibility to handle all of the demands of the book launch, book tour, and any other publicity surrounding it. I hadn't ever expected to write a book, and wanted to make sure that I gave it the time it needed to be successful, rather than end up regretting not having focused on it.

"I'm not surprised that you want to concentrate on the book launch," Ami said. "I know how much work you have put into it and how important it is to you. Plus I'm sure you also want to focus on your shaman work. I'm really excited for you."

I smiled, breathed a sigh of relief, and thanked her. I went on to share that I was planning on doing my shaman work, but that I would mostly be living off of my savings during this time. I had thought about taking a leave of absence, but knew that I might need to take some independent consulting gigs to support myself, which wouldn't be possible if I were on leave.

Ami and I talked about a few other things, and then she reminded me that I needed to tell Tom as well.

Telling Tom was even more difficult than telling Ami. He spent two weeks having me explore every option available to me at the firm and trying to talk me into staying. He even brought Steve onto a call so they could both talk with me. I felt horrible about resigning. Tom and Steve had both been wonderful mentors and so accommodating to me after the accident, and I was truly grateful for them and their friendship. But my mind was made up. I promised them I would stay in touch and let them know when I was ready to come back.

This wasn't a spur of the moment decision. I had been working toward this moment for years.

It started back in 2004 at a soul quest retreat in upstate New York. We were tasked to find a sacred spot on the land and then truly get to know who we were at a soul level. I spent some time walking through fields, along streams, and in the forest, until I found a spot in the woods that called to me. I spent a few minutes meditating and looking for confirmation that this was my "sacred spot," and within seconds got my answer: a young fawn with spots walked out of the woods, over to where I was sitting, and made a complete circle around me before heading back off into the words. I was awed by the powerful sign I had just received and sat there, in gratitude, for a while before turning my attention to the tasks that the retreat guides had asked us to do. Among other things, we were to tap into our dreams for messages, look for signs around us, and see what bubbled up inside that could indicate a need for healing or greater connection to our soul's purpose.

One thing that kept coming up for me was this idea of the roles that we play in life. Because I couldn't get these ideas of roles out of my mind, I decided to make a list of the roles that I had taken on. Some of them were typical: daughter, sister, coworker. But others actually had personas attached to them. These were the roles that I had had to take on because they were necessary to help me navigate a specific life situation, but now that my life situation had changed, they were burdensome and preventing me from my true potential.

One such role was one I called the Caretaker. I had adopted this role early on in my childhood, when my parents divorced. At that time, I had two younger brothers. My mother had to work to support us, so I did the best I could to pick up responsibilities around the house, including cooking and cleaning. When I got older, and was living with my father and stepmother, that same persona took care of my two new younger brothers as well as my father.

There is nothing wrong with being a Caretaker. In fact, most of us have played that part at one point or another. However, in my case, I realized that while I was great at taking care of others, and often was the first in line to volunteer to help others, I was horrible at taking care of myself and would often push myself to work long hours, volunteer for different work and personal events, and be fully available to my friends and family members. My needs were often on the bottom of the list. To compound the issue, I would rarely let other people help me, preferring to do it all myself.

I took a good, hard look at the Caretaker persona I had adopted, and I realized that it was no longer helping me and was quite possibly even hurting me, since I was caring for others at the exclusion of caring for myself. I realized that I needed to either retire or reframe this persona so that I was healthy and in balance.

I decided to reframe Caretaker to focus first on taking care of me. This didn't mean that I was going to stop caring for others; in fact, by taking care of myself first, I later discovered that I could better care for others because I was whole and "filled up."

I started by defining the role that I wanted Caretaker to have in my life. Once I had a clear idea of what that role looked like, I walked back over to my sacred space in the woods where I had had the encounter with the fawn and held a small ceremony.

I began by envisioning Caretaker as a separate entity that was sitting across from me. I thanked Caretaker, since she had been so beneficial in my life. I outlined as many examples as I could where Caretaker taught me life lessons and helped me navigate my life and specific situations successfully. I acknowledged and fully incorporated these gifts and lessons into my heart before continuing.

"Caretaker persona," I said, "you have done so many wonderful things and helped me help others when they needed it. These are good things. However, I need you to do something for me. I need you to help me take care of myself. I need you to help me put my health and well-being first so that I am better able to help others."

And then I waited to see what bubbled up in my heart as a response to my words. It didn't take long for me to hear what Caretaker said:

"You are right. I've been with you for a long time. Now it is time for you to start living your life. The life that allows your heart to soar and be fully yourself. I will work with you to care for and balance yourself."

I thanked Caretaker for her words, and then created a symbol to remind me—and Caretaker—of our agreement.

It wasn't long after this ceremony that I made the first major change in my life. I woke up on New Year's Day 2005 and wrote down a resolution that had just popped into my head: I resolve to move someplace new and different. I had lived in New England for my entire life and wanted a change. I looked at a map of the United States and San Francisco jumped out at me. I had been there once for work and really liked it.

The next day I went into work and called the partner who headed up our West Coast offices and asked him if he had room for one more. He said yes, so I shared with my coworkers that I was going to sell my house and move to San Francisco. One of my coworkers, who had been at my house a few weeks earlier for a holiday party, immediately said that she would buy it.

I flew out to San Francisco during the house sale process and gave myself one weekend to find a place to live that would take not only me but also my dog and cat. Everyone told me that I was crazy; the housing market in San Francisco at that time was very competitive and it was virtually impossible to find an apartment. I didn't find one: I found three that met my needs. I signed a lease that weekend and a short six weeks later moved in. Everything came together smoothly and seamlessly. It was then that I realized that when I'm living in alignment with my authentic self, everything I need flows into my life easily. It was this realization that gave me the courage to call Ami and quit my consulting job and walk away from a steady salary and promising career path.

I had been getting little nudges since the accident to move away from consulting to my shamanic, coaching and author work, including having dreams where I gave notice and began living a different life, but I was still nervous about making such a drastic change. My biggest fears surfaced: *What if I fail? What if I can't make enough money and am forced to live on the streets? No, it's better to stay where I am so that I have security.*

These fears seem a bit extreme now, but isn't that how fear works? It comes up with the most far-out possible scenario and plays it in your head over and over so that you feel immobilized. At least, that's how it works for me.

And so I played it safe for about a year and a half, all the time knowing that I wasn't being true to myself. I did my coaching and shamanic work on the weekends, and spent weeknights focusing on the work needed to publish the book. As each week went by, I felt less and less connected to myself and my heart's desire. I was becoming a zombie because of my fear.

Finally one day it dawned on me: if I were to keep living my life this way, without giving the book and my shamanic work the full attention and opportunity that each deserved, I would regret it for the rest of my life. I didn't want to wake up one morning thinking, *What if I hadn't been so afraid? What if I had taken the chance and run with it? Where would I be today?*

It was the wake-up call that I needed, and I began making plans

7

to resign. Specifically, I focused on when would be the best time to do so in order to not leave my company and my client hanging while also ensuring that I had enough lead time to dedicate to the pre- and post-launch book activities.

I also told myself that I would take the month of August off so that I could recharge and transition to whatever this new life was going to be. I booked a trip to a Mexican resort for the week after my last day of work as a reward for giving my resignation.

The last few weeks of my work were challenging for several reasons. Still, I left for Mexico with mixed emotions: sadness about not working with my friends, nervousness about this next phase, and excitement about having some time off. The resort was one that I had stayed in before, in the Mayan Riviera. It's an all-inclusive adults-only resort right on the ocean, with a private beach, several swimming pools and at least seven restaurants. There are daily activities and some type of show or event each night.

I was stressed and tired when I arrived, and worried that I had somehow made the wrong decision by leaving the consulting company. I needed some type of sign that I was on the right path.

I got my sign the minute I walked up to the check in desk. The woman behind the desk told me that there was an upgraded suite available for me. If I were interested in it, they could give it to me at a greatly discounted rate. I asked to see the room and, as soon as I did I knew that it was the reassurance I needed.

The suite was two stories. The first floor was identical to the room that I had reserved. There was a large bathroom with a huge Jacuzzi bathtub that could easily fit two people, a bedroom and sitting area, and a small balcony. The second floor was a rooftop balcony with a table and chairs, a large lounger "bed," an outdoor shower and private swimming pool. The views from the rooftop faced west and took in the full panorama of the beach and ocean. I could already envision how stunning the sunset would look and how spectacular the stars would be from the lounger bed. I said yes and upgraded my room.

My first order of business was to get a relaxing massage. I made a reservation for the next day and spent the rest of the day on the beach. That night, I lay on my rooftop lounger bed and just looked at the stars. The enormity of the night sky made me feel both insignificant and awed by the vastness of the universe. I stayed there for a long time, drinking in the beauty of it all and listening to the waves on the shore.

I awoke with the dawn and did some yoga on my roof while watching the sunrise. As I walked back to my room after breakfast, I passed by two employees holding a hawk. I stopped to look, and the employees asked me if I wanted to hold the hawk. I jumped at the chance, and within seconds had put on the handling glove and had the hawk perched on my hand.

He was a beautiful dark brown color, with a lighter tan on the underside of his tail. His beak was bright yellow, tipped in grey. His brown eyes looked intently in mine, and then he lowered his head so I could pet him with my free hand. I held him for several minutes, admiring his beauty and strength.

To shamans and other indigenous healers, hawks symbolize vision, power and protection. They are also considered messengers, bringing insights into your life purpose. Hawks had shown up for me in memorable ways several times previously on my life journey, most recently on the day that I launched my shamanic practice. At that time, I viewed hawk's appearance as a confirmation on my decision to begin doing shamanic work. As I held and stroked the hawk, I realized that his coming to me today was another confirmation about the path I was taking. I silently thanked him and handed him back to his handlers.

I had every intention of spending the entire week at the resort, pampering and nurturing myself. However, I started to feel restless and decided to take a day trip to some nearby Mayan archeological sites.

The first one I went to was Muyil. Located about 90 minutes south of the resort, the Muyil ruins are adjacent to a nature preserve and a lagoon. For a few extra pesos, you can walk through the preserve to the lagoon on a raised boardwalk. As usual with these smaller sites, I was the only one at the site.

I wandered around, looking at the various buildings and ruins. I was drawn to the many Ceiba trees that had taken residence in the ruins, their roots running down the sides of temples...and most likely holding the structures together at this point. The Mayans view the Ceiba trees as a sacred living example the Tree of Life: the branches reaching up to the sky represent the Upper World, the trunk represents the Middle World, and the roots going down into the earth represent the Lower World.

Shamans work in all three worlds when they are doing their

work. The Upper World, in my experience, most closely represents how most people envision heaven. There are wispy clouds, blue skies, and sunshine. It is filled with loving, helping spirits, guides and angels, typically in human form, who want to work with and help us grow and evolve. It is a very safe place to work.

The Lower World is a beautiful nature-based world, with trees, rocks, lakes, waterfalls, the ocean and beach, flowers...Picture the most amazing places on our planet and amp them up a notch or two and you'll get an idea of what the Lower World looks like. The Lower World is also filled with loving, helping spirits and guides, however, in the Lower World, these guides are typically animals and fantastic beings such as fairies and gnomes. It, too, is a very safe place for a shaman to work in.

The Middle World is the world that we live in. In addition to the physical world that we inhabit, there is a spiritual dimension. The spiritual side of the Middle World is a mixed bag in terms of helping guides. There are some that are helpful. But there are others that do not want to help, and may actually want to harm the shaman or humans. When I work in the Middle World, I make sure that I have my power animal, a spirit guide in animal form that I call 444 that brings his unique attributes and strengths to help me when I am navigating through life or a specific challenge, and other helping guides with me to protect me from any harmful entities.

I took my time exploring the site and absorbing its magical energy. When I needed a respite from the hot sun beating down on the jungle, I slipped onto a shaded pathway. Time seemed to move more slowly here, and my body responded by moving more slowly as well.

After taking in the nearby lagoon, I began making my way back to the entrance of the site. Hearing something rustling in the jungle, I paused on the path to see what it was. Suddenly a jaguar ran out of the trees in front of me, crossed over the path and went into the jungle on the other side. It happened so quickly I didn't have any time to react or take a photo.

Jaguars have been revered by the Mayans for centuries. In ancient times, the Maya believed that jaguar was the god of the underworld. Because of jaguar's ability to be in trees as well as in water, the Mayans felt that jaguar could easily cross between the Upper, Middle and Lower Worlds as well as between daytime and nighttime. In addition, because it was the greatest hunter in the jungle, jaguar could protect shamans as they journeyed to the spirit world.

I knew this jaguar sighting was a gift and a message for me. I found it interesting that I had been thinking about the Ceiba trees and the three worlds that I work in, and here is an animal that easily crosses each world. Silently, I asked my spirit guides why jaguar was showing up on my path (literally!) at this time. I closed my eyes, paused, and waited to hear their response. It only took a minute for the words to bubble up from them:

Jaguar brings you many gifts at this time in your life. He is here to help you transition between the old world that you lived in and the new world that you are going to be living in. Much as there is a transition between daytime and nighttime, there is a transition between the life you had and the life you are going to start living. Call on jaguar at any time for help. In some ways, you are starting to show your true colors—or spots!—to the world.

I was grateful for the message and for jaguar's help, and breathed a quick thank you for the encounter.

From Muyil, I headed back north to a small Mayan site called Playacar, located within an exclusive community. The site is believed to have been the starting point for a spiritual pilgrimage women would take each year to honor the moon goddess, Ixchel, and pray for easy pregnancies and childbirth. Unfortunately, because the site is located in an exclusive community, I was only able to spend five minutes there before the security guard came and asked me to leave. While I was disappointed, I knew that I had already received what I needed to receive from my visit to Muyil.

My week in Mexico went by far too quickly, and I realized that I didn't want to leave. I had just started to relax and needed just a little bit more time. Reluctantly I boarded the plane to head home.

While the first few weeks without my daily work routine of travel, client meetings and client deliverables felt like a vacation, each day soon seemed to stretch out for far more hours than twenty-four. I did my best to keep busy, and the book launch helped. I was asked to write several articles for different online sites about the book, spirituality, and my personal interests. I'd finish them quickly, since I didn't have much else to do, and then look around, wondering what I could do next.

One day I went to the San Francisco Zoo. I had been working with one of my clients, and Vulture came forward to help with the healing work we were doing. Vulture had also come to me many times in my own healing and was physically waiting for me with his wings spread wide open to the morning sun when I was exploring a sacred Mayan site about two and a half years ago.

Vulture is associated with purification and rebirth and is the animal spirit of the CIB trecena in the Mayan spiritual calendar, the Tzolkin. Since it was the last day of the CIB trecena, I got into my car and went to the zoo to spend some time with Vulture.

The San Francisco Zoo has a condor, which is a member of the vulture family. He was tucked away in a large enclosed aviary by himself. As I walked up to his enclosure, he was standing with his back to me and his wings outstretched—an impressive sight, when you consider that the condor's wingspan is between nine and twelve feet! He turned his head, and his red eyes looked directly at me, before he went back to sunning himself.

I maneuvered around the enclosure until I was able to look at him from his side. I watched him for over half an hour, marveling at his size and presence. He became more and more beautiful the longer I spent time watching him.

He watched me as well, his eyes rarely leaving mine. I knew we had made a connection when he opened his beak, looked directly at me, and, making a hissing noise, "talked" to me. (Vultures do not have the ability to sing, they only hiss.)

I spoke softly to him, telling him that I was grateful for his healing help—both for myself and for my client. I thanked him for the work that he did on a spiritual and a physical level. I verbally admired his strength, beauty and sheer size and sent love out to him. He watched me intently while I spoke.

I looked at his feathers, and without thinking said out loud that I wished I could have one of them. As soon as I said the words, Condor twisted his head around to his wing feathers and pulled one out with his beak and placed it at his feet, before looking at me again. The message was clear—the feather was for me.

While I couldn't retrieve the physical feather in his enclosure (as much as I wanted to!), I knew that I could tap into the energy of that feather any time for my healing work. My heart was filled with gratitude and I thanked Condor for his gift.

WHERE TO?

◆ ◆ ◆

As September and October went by, I watched my savings account dwindle and began to worry about my lack of income. A friend of mine had a customer strategy consulting business and offered to staff me on a project if I could help sell it. I had worked as a business and customer strategy consultant for over 15 years and had had plenty of experience doing the project work she needed help on. I was also more than happy to help with the sales process. Usually I have a fairly high close ratio, but after three potential projects fell through, I realized that perhaps the universe didn't want me doing consulting work at all. I sat down and asked for guidance.

It is time for you to take a leap into the unknown. Walk away from restrictions and question any self-imposed rules. All the doors are open for you. You have unlimited possibilities if you put your trust in the universe. This is a time for you to be spontaneous and free. Focus on and choose a positive outlook, gratitude and abundance. Be patient. You have the support you need. The outcome will be a flow of abundance. Spend time with the masters and ancestors so you can learn from them. Connect with them and be open.

I had taken a big leap into the unknown by quitting my well-paying consulting job to focus all of my time on my shamanic and coaching business, Spirit Evolution, knowing that if I didn't at least try to live my life purpose work I would always regret it. As I reflected on my spirit guides' words, I realized that there might be more "trusting and leaping" required for me. I made a conscious decision to continue to trust and be open to the opportunities and ideas that came forward. Soon after, a curious thing happened. I started to get significantly more hits on my website by people interested in having sessions with me. While not enough to cover my monthly expenses, the extra income that was coming in helped me be more relaxed about my current financial state.

The shamanic sessions were different from ones that I had done before, and I realized that the universe was continuing my training, specifically around soul retrievals. Soul retrievals focus on finding and reintegrating parts of the soul that have left the body because of trauma or stress. What causes stress and trauma varies by individual. One small child might find a thunderstorm to be scary and traumatic, for example, while another small child might find it to be exciting and invigorating. An adult that is robbed might feel scared and victimized while another might feel angry and compelled to do something to prevent the same thing from happening to other people. Often, a person who has lost part of their soul will say things such as, "I don't feel like myself" or "I feel 'off' or broken." They may have depression, feel numb to events, or have anxiety. During a soul retrieval shamanic session, I would work with my spirit guides and power animal to search for and find the piece(s) of the soul that had left. Once found, I would help that piece of the soul recover from the stress or trauma it experienced before energetically reintegrating the soul piece(s) back into the person to fill the 'holes" that their absence had created in the person's soul. I would also ask the soul piece what gift or insight it was bringing back to the person. These gifts were as varied as each individual was, but some recent gifts for clients included experiencing joy and laughter in everyday life, bringing forward personal strength and courage to face future challenges, and seeing the inherent beauty in the self and others. In the past, I would have to go searching for these soul pieces, but now I was starting to "see" younger versions of my clients that needed healing from past events. These pieces of my clients' souls were coming forward on their own for shamanic work during the session, not only wanting to be healed and reintegrated into the client, but also bringing a gift or lesson for my clients.

One of my clients, a woman from Europe, had had a number of health issues for most of her life. She also had had an extremely traumatic experience when she was a teenager. As I started the session, two younger versions of her came forward—one from when she was in grammar school and another when she was a middle-aged adult. I worked with each to help heal them, better understand the gifts they were bringing back to my client that focused on living with a joyful heart and grounding into success, and then integrate them back into my client.

I was about to wrap up the session when a teenage version of my client came forward. And man, was she angry. She came right up into my face and began screaming about how hurt and angry she was about the trauma she experienced as a teenager. I extended the session to work with this part of my client's soul to help her release her pain and anger. I sensed immediately that she needed to be heard—something that she hadn't received at the time of the event—and gave her my full attention. Once she had said her piece, expressed a variety of emotions, and released them, I worked to help heal her energetically from the trauma. We talked about what had happened, how she was an adult now with the capability to speak and prevent the trauma from occurring again. I asked her what gift she brought back to the client, and she said, "I bring back righteous anger so that together we can take action to make things better." When I shared the experience and gift with my client, she was amazed. Her mother used to tell her when she was a teenager that she was her most powerful and motivated when she was filled with righteous anger.

Another client had a young part of himself come forward to help my client incorporate more play into his life. And yet another came forward to help my client recognize and celebrate a life transition that had been glossed over because of a family situation at the time.

In each instance, it was as if these pieces that left due to some life trauma were able to connect back to Source and love and gain some additional wisdom that would help my client at this point in his or her life. Interestingly enough, such as with my client that had the teenage trauma, the words that the soul pieces used to describe the gift were very specific and had meaning to my clients beyond just the actual message.

In addition to receiving more interest in my shamanic services, I received another affirmation from the universe that I was on the right path while recording the audiobook version of *This Trip Will Change Your Life: A Shaman's Story of Spirit Evolution* in a San Francisco recording studio.

I booked four sessions. To be honest, I didn't think that the sound engineers, both young men in their 20's would be interested in a book about a woman becoming a shaman and the messages she received during the process. I was wrong.

The first sound engineer told me at the end of the session that he was going to try to change his schedule around so he could be at all four sessions. He wanted to hear what happened. And then he shared with me what he was taking away from the book so far: he said that he realized that he didn't express enough gratitude for the many wonderful things in his life already.

The second one let me continue reading even after the studio was closed because he too wanted to hear what happened. He then talked to me for about thirty minutes after we finished recording for the day about his personal experiences with a shaman. He had grown up in Central America and had worked with a shaman for many years. After moving to the United States, he lost touch with who he was. My book made him realize that he needed to begin meditating and reconnecting with some of the teachings he had gained from the shaman.

The fact that two total strangers would not only be interested in my book, but also take something away from it to help their lives improve surprised me. Until that moment, the book had felt more like a personal writing exercise rather than something that could reach and touch people.

With the book recording done and the third potential consulting project falling through, I had time on my hands. I decided to book a trip a few weeks out to Guatemala to see Tikal, one of the major Mayan archaeological sites, as well as some other sites. I was first drawn to Mayan sites in 2013, when I went to Mexico on vacation. During that trip, I met Antonio, a Mayan shaman who introduced me to shamanism and started me on my shamanic path, and I discovered a spiritual connection with the ancient sites. Since then, I had spent significant amounts of time in Mexico, both getting my training and visiting a number of Mayan archaeological sites. I hadn't been to Guatemala and was looking forward to the trip. I ended up booking the trip for the week that coincided with the book was coming out, the Day of the Dead celebrations, and the two-year anniversary of my accident.

Let your heart govern your mind. Use this time in Guatemala to increase your frequency and power so that you can resonate at a higher level. Trust that you are on the right path and be open to receiving information on your journey. Be open to all possibilities and opportunities and live in the moment. Celebrate the joy of a new beginning and radiate your light. Let your heart be open and sing with joy. Play and have fun!

CHAPTER 2: A LAST-MINUTE TRIP

I received a message from Antonio, the Mayan shaman in Mexico who introduced me to shamanism and was instrumental in my training, a few days before my trip to Guatemala. He had been telling everyone who came to him about my book, including a man who lived just on the other side of the Golden Gate Bridge. This man was very interested in the book, and, Antonio said, would be reaching out to me.

The next day I received an email from the man. He was hoping we could meet in person and have lunch as soon as possible. We booked it for a few days before my trip.

We had a wonderful lunch and ended up talking for several hours about our individual life journeys and the impact Antonio had had on our lives. As I was driving home, however, something kept bothering me about his name. Halfway across the Golden Gate Bridge it hit me: he had the same name as the man who had hit me with his minivan while I was walking across the street almost two years prior. That accident put my life on a different course. "*Was it the same man?*" I wondered.

When I got home, I checked the police records, and, sure enough, the names matched: the man who hit me with his minivan shared the same name as the man I just had lunch with, even though they were two different people. I knew this couldn't be a coincidence—two men with the same name right around the same time as the accident. What was the significance of this?

It is the completion of a cycle. A closed loop. You started the cycle with the accident and are ending it with this meeting of the other man. It is complete now. You are now moving into your next phase and cycle. And the sign there is the name of the town you are going to stay in—it is the same as the last name of these two men. You are starting the next cycle in Guatemala and will see where you are led. You have the freedom now to follow where you are led.

I wasn't surprised by this message from my guides. I had been thinking about freedom over the past few days, and had recently come to the realization that I had been holding myself back because of my "limiting beliefs," those things that I had adhered to because I had been told, "This is the way it should be." I realized that these limiting beliefs had become ingrained in my psyche because of my family, cultural, geographical, and religious expectations. Once I became aware of them, I began questioning them and their validity.

Specifically, I had been questioning the expectation that I had to have a house or apartment to live in. (The apartment was my first break from a limiting belief. There is a societal expectation that by a certain age a person should own their home. I had owned several homes, but sold them all and chose to live in an apartment because I liked the ease and simplicity of it. To this day, I have people asking me why I don't buy a house and build equity in it.). The questions kept rattling around in my head. I decided to let them flow through to see where they would lead me.

Do I really need to have a permanent place to live? I thought. *Why couldn't I sell or store my belongings and just travel around with a carry-on suitcase to wherever I want? While I love San Francisco, there is nothing holding me here. I don't have a significant other; I don't even have any pets. I have a couple of houseplants, but I'm sure I could find homes for them.*

My shamanic, coaching and writing work can be done anywhere there is cellular and Internet access, I realized. With PayPal and other banking mobile applications, I can easily transfer money and get paid. I would miss my friends, of course, but I could always come back to San Francisco.

I checked into my heart to see how it felt about this idea and discovered a deep-seated fear. *The one thing I do have is a rent-controlled apartment, and those can be difficult to come by. I'm not sure how easy it will be to rent an apartment since I no longer have a traditional job and steady income. What if I did do this and wasn't able to find a place to live because no one would want to rent to someone without a traditional job? There it is again,* I thought. *That same fear. What if I fail and end up and living on the streets?*

I breathed through my fear and let my thoughts continue. *I like the idea of getting rid of all the excess "stuff" I've been holding onto, simplifying down to one carryon suitcase, and following my heart to wherever it leads. Last year at this time, I was in the middle of a month-long trip around the world. I called it my Victory Lap Vacation to celebrate the fact that I was alive and was down to a small brace on my foot. During the trip, I visited Mexico, England, Italy, Greece, Thailand and Japan before heading back home, and was able to stay in touch with people and manage my finances while I was on the road. I know that it can easily be done. The question is: do I have the courage to just walk away from the security of a traditional home?*

That, I realized, *is the big question that I have to answer. I don't have to make the decision today, I told myself. I can think more about it.*

I left the next morning for Guatemala. It was going to take two days to get to the jungle area where Tikal and other Mayan sites are located. In addition to serving as continued growth and learning for me, I viewed the trip as a "baby step" toward this idea of living differently and with more freedom. This trip would also be different from every other trip in that it was not a work trip and was not a break from work/vacation either. Whereas Mexico was definitely a vacation focused on taking a break from work, this trip was about travelling for the pure joy and experience of it. I resolved to be open and receptive to whatever I needed to experience, see, and learn while in Guatemala.

I landed in Flores, Peten early in the morning the next day, tired and excited to begin my trip. My room wasn't ready yet, so I wandered around Las Lagunas Boutique Hotel, the resort I would be staying in for a few days. Situated on a lagoon, the resort consisted of a number of individual cabins built over the water and had a swimming pool, a large outdoor patio, and walking trails through the jungle. I sat in one of the lounge chairs overlooking the pool and lagoon, listening to the sounds of the birds in the trees and feeling my heart swell with a sense of peacefulness that I hadn't felt before. My mind and breath slowed down and I let the energy of the jungle wash over me.

I signed up for the boat ride to Monkey Island. Monkeys had been significant to me throughout my shamanic journey. In fact, George, a man who gave me a Mayan calendar reading before my fateful trip to Mexico that led me down the shamanic path, had told me to always look for the monkeys and for the number 11, since both would be signs for me that I was on the right path for my life journey.

Monkey Island consisted of two small islands in the middle of the lagoon. The first has wild howler monkeys on it, and the second is filled with rescued howler monkeys. Poachers had captured these monkeys when they were babies and then sold them into the pet industry. Once rescued from being pets, they could not fend for themselves in the wild. They were brought to the resort, and the resort now cares for them. The boat trip fees pay for the food that is brought to the rescued monkeys daily. We saw eight or nine monkeys on the trip and watched them eat the carrots, beets, sweet potatoes and bananas that the boat operators gave them. It was fun seeing them hang upside down from their tails and reach for the food in the baskets!

When we returned, my room was ready. Each room is associated with a jungle animal. The woman at the front desk handed me my key. It had a large monkey carved into the key chain. I was staying in the Monkey Room, yet another little sign that I was where I needed to be.

My room was beautiful, with a living area, a glassed-in dining area with sweeping views of the lagoon, a sleeping area and a small balcony. It was perfect. I almost wished I could live there permanently and wondered if I could stay there for an extended time as part of the "following my heart and living out of one carry-on roller board" life I was considering. While it didn't have a kitchen and would require a car to go to the market or other restaurants, I decided to ask the manager if there was reduced rate for monthly stays while I was there.

I had asked the resort to arrange for a guide to take me to Tikal. I met him in the lobby to discuss the plans for the next day. His name was Carlos and he spoke very good English. He looked at me and said, "I work with a lot of people, tourists from all over the world. You are the first person I have seen that is happy at the beginning of vacation."

I laughed and replied, "I try to focus on the positive and choose to be happy."

We then got down to business and talked about the specifics of visiting Tikal. Carlos would be my guide, and Pedro would drive us. I've been to a number of Mayan sites in Mexico, including Chichen Itza, but when Carlos explained that tours of Tikal can take up to seven hours depending on what the visitor wants to focus on, I began to get an idea about how big the ruins were and the importance of the site. I was even more excited about seeing them tomorrow!

After we finalized the details, Carlos left and I headed out to Flores, a town located on an island on Lake Peten Itza. Roughly circular in shape, the town has a walkway that circles its perimeter, giving walkers a view of both the town's buildings and the lake. Narrow, winding cobble-stoned streets crisscross the interior of the island, with many leading up the hill to the church. Each building is painted a bright vibrant color and is tucked closely to the one next to it. The result is a riot of color that somehow works and lightens your spirits at the same time.

The exuberant colors and energy of Flores, while initially enjoyable, began to wear on me. Tourists were barhopping and talking loudly and pushing their way through the narrow streets, interrupting my thoughts and taking away from the tranquility of the lake. *I think Flores would be great for a night out,* I thought, *but I don't think I would be able to have the spiritual connection that I'm looking for here.* After a late lunch on a restaurant perched on the edge of the lake, I headed back to the hotel.

The next day I went to Tikal. It was a beautiful clear day, with an endless blue sky punctuated by white fluffy clouds. Carlos was a great guide, pointing out the history and architecture of the site, as well as various animals. We saw turkeys, toucans, spider monkeys, coati, and even a close relative of the Quetzal, the national bird of Guatemala.

We spent a lot of time walking around the ruins. I was nervous about climbing the stone steps of the first pyramid we encountered, but was pleasantly surprised that I was able to easily navigate the narrow steep steps, albeit a bit more slowly, after the accident. I felt very proud of myself as I made my way down from the top of the pyramid after admiring the view from the top.

As we entered the Great Plaza, with the Temple of the Great Jaguar on one end and the Temple of the Masks on the other, Carlos pointed to a flat stone, shaped like a circle, in the middle of the plaza. The surface was darkened from the soot of countless fires. Carlos explained that the stone was an altar, and that to this day the Mayans conducted ceremonies on the altar. I looked around to see if there were any Mayan shamans about, and was disappointed that there weren't any.

We talked as we walked, and Carlos shared with me his perspective of the world. "I have never left Guatemala. It is my home. But I am happy here. I spend my days outside in nature, in beautiful places like Tikal. So many people come here for their vacation and they are unhappy and stressed. They look at me and say, 'You are so lucky. I wish I could have the life you have.' I try to help people find happiness while they are here."

I nodded. "That's what I try to do with my shamanic sessions as well. Too many people go through their lives without realizing that happiness is within their grasp, if they stop and look for it within their hearts."

We ended up in a long grassy plaza dotted with Mayan buildings on either side. Carlos suggested that we climb up the stairs of one of the buildings, which he explained was a temple. The building had been used for Mayan ceremonies in its heyday. He took a small votive candle, some matches and some scraps of paper out of his knapsack. "Let's do a ceremony here to release our biggest problems to the Universe," he said.

Lighting the candle, he instructed me to write my problem on a piece of paper. He did the same, and then told me to roll the paper up. Once done, we invoked the helping spirits of the universe to release the problems that we had written. After expressing our gratitude for their help, we silently burned our papers. When each had been reduced to ash, we sat on the ledge of the temple and continued our conversation.

He told me about his grandfather, who was a spiritual leader in the community. His grandfather had shared a lot of wisdom with him, which Carlos then tried to share with others. He was divorced, he said, and told me that it had been difficult for him to live alone. His grandfather reminded him that sometimes you have to wait and be patient and that all things come in due time. He was hopeful that at some point he would meet the person he was meant to be with.

He asked what had brought me to Guatemala, and I told him about my shamanic work, the accident, and how I had quit my job and was starting a new phase of my life. I explained that Mayan sites felt very spiritual and sacred to me, and that I often felt like I got new insights when I visited them. I wrapped up by telling him about the book I wrote and that today was the day it launched.

Carlos was quiet for a moment, and then he looked me in the eyes and said, "I think you are going to do some very special work. You will help people understand happiness and the Mayans."

I thanked him. We sat there in silence for a while, before finally descending the steep stone steps of the temple to the grassy field below. We walked through jungle paths, back to the car, and headed out.

As we drove through a small village, Carlos mentioned that it was the village where he and Pedro lived. Since it was the Dia de los Muertos, Carlos suggested that we stop at the cemetery to see how the festivities were progressing. I was thrilled. Ever since I had been a little girl I had been fascinated by cemeteries and enjoyed looking at the tombstones and trying to envision what the lives of the people buried there were like.

The Guatemala cemeteries were completely different from those in New England, where my family members are buried. Instead of somber gray tombstones in neat lines with well-manicured grass and flowers, above ground tombs, similar to those in New Orleans, haphazardly dotted the cemetery. Each was painted a bright color: reds, blues, yellows, pinks, and greens…the entire rainbow was represented. The jungle was trying to encroach on the space; vines, leaves and wild grasses were everywhere. There were many people about, cleaning the gravesites, raking leaves, painting and decorating. It had the feeling of a party in the making.

People stared at me as I walked alongside Carlos, my red hair and fair skin a sharp contrast to their darker skin and hair. I lowered my eyes to both watch my footing on the uneven ground and avoid the stares. "Is it okay that I'm here? I don't want to be disrespectful to people and your customs," I asked. Carlos told me not to worry, and we walked around looking at the efforts of the people there. We stopped to talk to one woman who was raking leaves under a tree.

She explained that her baby had died recently and was buried under the tree. My heart went out to her. I remembered how difficult it was for my mother (and the rest of us) when my brother passed away, and know from that experience that a mother never fully recovers from the loss. She explained that she was going to decorate the gravesite with brightly colored banners and seemed at peace with her loss. I thanked her for talking with us, and Carlos and I continued walking through the cemetery. He told me the significance of the different types of tombstones and the celebration that was going to be held that evening. Seeing my interest, he invited me to join him and Pedro. I agreed.

As we left the cemetery and got back in the car, I asked if there was someplace where we could buy flowers. I wanted to put them on the grave of the baby. Carlos said that he would pick some up for me and we could bring them that night.

We continued on through the town. He pointed to a dirt road off to the right and said that Pedro's house was up that way, and then pointed out his house to me. We rode companionably back to the resort, discussed the itinerary for the next day to visit two other Mayan sites, and made plans to meet in the lobby at 8 p.m. to go to the Día de los Muertos celebration.

Unfortunately, that evening a massive thunder and lightning storm came through and the celebration was postponed until the next day.

◆ ◆ ◆

The next morning, Carlos and Pedro picked me up promptly at 8:30 a.m. In the car were the flowers I had requested. Our first order of business was to go to the cemetery to decorate the grave of the baby that had passed away. Carlos had also bought some brightly colored plastic streamers that we could use.

Before we went to the cemetery, however, Carlos asked that we stop at his house, which was on the way. He invited me to see where he lived, and showed me around. He is working with some people to convert the yard of his home into a botanical garden and a vanilla and cacao plantation. The botanical garden is filled with many beautiful orchid plants, and he pointed each out to me, along with the uses of each of the plants.

His vision is to create a space where people will want to come and stay. In a small, plant-covered outdoor alcove he is going to develop a meditation and writing area where people can relax. He pointed out another area and said that it would become the ceremonial area. And finally, there would be an area for people to camp on the grounds, if they wanted to.

We began brainstorming together about how we could

combine his botanical garden space and ceremonial knowledge that he gained from his grandfather with my shamanic and coaching skills to create Mayan-based spiritual retreats for people. The retreats could focus on helping people understand better their life purpose and find joy in living. As we talked about it, we both felt that it was much needed in today's world.

His house is also on the property. It's a simple but adequate home, perfect for one person. Next to his house is a sheltered workspace. It is here that Carlos does something that I think even more incredible than the gardens he is creating, and shows the depth of his character. He has two sewing machines, and he is teaching local women how to sew on them. Because the village is on the main road to Tikal, there are many tourists that come through, looking for authentic Guatemalan and Mayan handicrafts. His hope is that the local woman will be able to sew clothing and sell it to the tourists—and be able to earn some income for their families. In short, Carlos is empowering the local women. That resonated strongly with me. I have always believed that when women are empowered and have a hand in their personal destiny, not only the woman but also her entire family and community benefits. I began wondering how I might be able to empower more women beyond those that I reached through my shamanic and coaching work. *Perhaps I could do some type of online course or activity that could be easily accessible to women*, I thought and vowed to think more about how that could tie into the retreat idea Carlos and I had just been discussing.

We spent about half an hour adding to the decorations the baby's mother had placed for the baby. When we finished, the grave was joyfully covered in yellow and white flowers, with pink, blue and yellow streamers dangling from the tree overhead. A slight wind made them dance as we left.

We had two Mayan sites on our agenda for the day.

The first was Uaxactun, which is unique because there is a village of Mayan people still living on the site's grounds. To get to Uaxactun, you have to drive through Tikal and then follow a dirt and rock road through the jungle for about 45 minutes until you reach the village. The village is situated around a short airplane landing strip; until the dirt road was put in place, the only way to access the area was by small plane.

Today, there is a daily bus that leaves the village early in the morning and brings people to Flores and then brings them back at the end of the day. However, other than the bus and the occasional tourist, the village remains fairly isolated. In fact, Carlos explained to me that there is only one telephone in the village. When a resident wants to make a call, he or she has to walk over to the public telephone to make the call. Pigs, horses and chickens wandered around the landing strip, which served as the town center, while children played nearby.

The ruins were on either side of the village. We started by walking to the smaller part of the ruins. It was here, Carlos explained, that the astronomical complex was built. Like many Mayan ruins, Uaxactun has a set of buildings that aligned with the equinoxes and solstices. At Uaxactun, there are three buildings in a row. On the spring and fall equinoxes, the sun shines through the opening of the middle structure. For the winter solstice the sun shines through one of the structures on the side; for the summer solstice it shines through the one on the other side.

As Carlos and I talked about the buildings and their symbolism of being in balance, I began to think about how valuable a message this is to our world today. So many people live in imbalance or swing from one extreme to another. It's when we live in balance that we are most at peace—whether that balance is with our emotions, our thoughts, our physical activity, etc. We can better handle the day-to-day ups and downs from a place of peace and balance…most likely because we know that the pendulum of life always shifts back the other way. So we stop and enjoy a moment of beauty, knowing that it will fade with time. And we can make it through a difficult time or situation because we know that it will eventually pass and brighter days will come.

We walked back through the village and headed up a steep hill to the other side of the ruins. The ceremonial center was located in this part of the complex. To get to the ceremonial center, we walked along a path that had large mounds covered with grasses and small trees. These were buildings that haven't been excavated yet.

The ceremonial center building was built in phases, Carlos said. Eventually pillars and walls surrounded the altar, which was located in the center of the building. Prior to entering the altar area, the Mayans would take a sweat bath to purify their physical bodies. The sweat lodges were built right into the structure. Participants would crawl through a small opening and through a corridor to get to the sweat bath area. With the exception of the light that came through the entryway and the light of the fire, the sweat bath area would be dark. The fire and air would be enhanced with aromatic herbs.

When finished with the sweat bath, the Mayans would crawl back out. Carlos explained that the process of exiting the sweat bath symbolized being in the womb and exiting the birth canal. Upon exiting, the individual would be considered purified, reborn and transformed.

We walked through the building to the altar area. Since we were the only ones at the site, we spent some time meditating in the space. The only things that intruded on our individual thoughts were the sounds of birds and monkeys in the trees.

After a while, we decided to head back into the village and have some lunch. Carlos had arranged for us to eat at a small restaurant and lodge near the landing strip. We sat at a long wooden table and enjoyed a hearty authentic Guatemalan meal of homemade tortillas, black beans, rice and vegetables. For dessert, we had fresh oranges from a tree near the restaurant.

The owner of the lodge had built a small museum for a number of the artifacts from Uaxactun. We stopped in and looked at the painted pottery, beads and axe heads before heading out to the next site, Yaxha.

It was getting late, but both Carlos and Pedro assured me that we would be able to make it to the site well before it closed. Pedro raced down the road through the small villages. Everywhere in Guatemala are dogs. For the most part, they are a nondescript brown color, thin and just on the edge of being feral. They lounge on the sides of the road, run around with children, and are generally part of the fabric of life there. As we drove down the road, my attention was captured by a handful of dogs on the right side of the road. They were running around, playing. One dog caught my attention. He was vibrant, both physically and energetically. There was something about him that made him stand out from the other dogs.

And then, without warning, he turned and ran right under Pedro's car. It happened so quickly that Pedro didn't have time to—and couldn't—swerve to avoid the dog. There was a yelp and then silence. Pedro and I looked at each other, and I started crying.

Carlos tried to console me, but I was heartbroken. Such a vibrant happy dog! Pedro felt horrible. We rode without speaking for some time. I took several deep breaths to release the sorrow I was feeling. My mind wandered to the woman I met yesterday at the cemetery who had lost her baby. There is no rhyme or reason about death, when it will happen, and how long we will be here on Earth. Some people and living things are part of our lives for many, many years, and we have the opportunity and gift of knowing them deeply and sharing many experiences. Others come into our lives for just a brief moment, and yet our interaction with them can act as a catalyst that leaves a permanent mark on our souls and changes the course of our lives forever.

We got to Yaxha an hour before it closed. The site was deserted; we were the only ones there. After Carlos assured the security guard that we would be finished within the hour, we were granted access. Carlos rushed me through the site so I could see the highlights.

It began to rain as we walked along. Carlos asked me if I wanted to go back to the car, but I laughed it off. The rain was warm and felt so much more refreshing than the sticky humidity of the day. Plus, the many plants and trees in the jungle kept much of the rain off of us.

As we neared the main ceremonial temple, the rain stopped. We climbed the wooden stairs that the Guatemalans had so thoughtfully built on the back side of the building to the top and sat. We had an unobstructed view over the treetops of the jungle to the river. A faint mist clung to the trees, and in the distance, through the clouds, we could see the sun setting.

Carlos told me that he often comes here for sunset and he shared another ritual with me that his grandfather had taught him. He cleaned my left hand, anointed it with some peppermint oil, and had me breathe in deeply the scent with my eyes closed. Then he took my hand and we sat, meditating and listening to the jungle. We each focused on connecting to our individual hearts and then connecting to each other's. I breathed deeply, envisioning my breath going down into my heart and the energy there. The energy around my heart began to tingle, and I felt a wave of pure love pour into me. I continued breathing, using my breath to expand the love in my heart area, until my entire body was filled with it. With the next breath, I expanded out beyond my body to encompass

28

both of us, and then further and further to encompass the entire globe. I sat in my gigantic bubble of pure love, sending out good intentions to Carlos and everyone and everything on the planet.

It was nearly dark when we finished our meditation. We made our way down the stairs carefully, and worked our way through the jungle. On the jungle floor it was pitch black, so I pulled out my cell phone and used the flashlight to illuminate the rocky, root-filled path. We made it back to the parking lot at exactly the time that the site had closed. The site workers had already left, so we were truly the only ones there. We drove back to the resort in silence, each thinking about the day.

I gave Carlos and Pedro a hug goodbye when we got back to the resort. I was heading out to Guatemala City the next morning and I wouldn't see them again.

That night, as I revisited the events of the day, I began to think more about the dog. What was the purpose of his death? Why was I so attracted to him? And was there any significance to the fact that the accident occurred on the two-year anniversary of my accident? As I meditated, I received my answer.

> *There are no accidents. You were attracted to the dog because of his energy and vitality. He radiated out joy and happiness. The dog sacrificed himself to you so that you could work with its energy and use it to help others be happy and balanced. As you know, the Mayans called dog "Oc," and believed that Oc was the guardian of the material and spiritual. Oc helps us to be in balance with the spiritual and material. This is what you and Carlos have been talking about creating for others. Oc also represents loyalty, fidelity and justice, and was the secretary/writer of the Mayan spiritual guides.*

I thought about this for a while, and expressed my gratitude for the dog's gift. I sent Carlos a text, sharing the message I had received from my guides. He responded, "We must bring together our energy and vitality to help others, as the dog has done for us."

I agreed. As a shaman, I am tasked with helping others heal and live authentic lives. It is my life purpose and mission. I believe that there is something magical about the energy of the sacred places around the world, something powerful that each one of us can tap into and grow and evolve. By potentially working together with Carlos, I can do my shamanic work and introduce others to these powerful centers.

◆◆◆

The next morning I caught a morning flight to Guatemala City. I hesitated about leaving the jungle, given the affinity I felt for it while I was there, but decided to stick with my original plan. I met Roberto, the cab driver who had driven me to the airport on my flight to Flores, at the airport. He was going to drive me around for the rest of my trip.

We left early the next day for Lake Atitlan. It was a long drive—at least two and a half hours. As we left the city, the many buildings gave way to greater stretches of rolling hills and greenery. In one of the small towns we drove through it was market day. Dozens of people worked their way through the stalls and displays, bartering and making their choices. Many of the women were wearing the traditional brightly-colored Mayan clothing of a hand-woven skirt; an embroidered, square-cut blouse called a huipil; and a sash around the waist called a faha. Each town has its own design and color combination, and each family creates a variation of that design. It is said that you can identify where someone lives by the colors and style of the clothing they wear. Once they made their purchases, the women would wrap their items up in a large cloth and place the bundle on their heads.

As we neared the lake, the terrain became more mountainous. Lake Atitlan is the deepest lake in Central America, and arguably the most beautiful. Surrounded by three volcanoes, the lake is over 50 square miles and is dotted with small villages along its shores. To this day, men take small dugout boats out early in the morning to fish and women bring their laundry to the shoreline to wash it.

We hired a boat and explored a few of the towns. Each town has a dock and then the town itself perches on the side of one of the volcanoes. Narrow, winding streets bring you to town centers, where the shops and church are. From there, the views of the lake, volcanoes and mountains are stunning. We passed women in the shade, weaving fabric for clothing. They kneel and hold the loom on their laps as they work.

I stopped in one shop and purchased a traditional outfit for myself. The shopkeeper had a difficult time finding a skirt long enough to cover my knees: Mayan and Guatemalan women are much shorter than I am! However, the store didn't take credit cards, so we made arrangements for the shopkeeper, Manuela, to ride with us in the boat back to the larger town of Panajachel so I could pay by credit card.

After taking care of the financial transaction, I invited Manuela to join Roberto and me for lunch. We stopped at a small restaurant and shared a meal together, learning more about each other and our respective lives. Manuela and I hugged goodbye, and then Roberto and I were on our way back to Guatemala City.

◆ ◆ ◆

I had heard many wonderful things about Antigua, the old capital city of Guatemala, and couldn't wait to visit. Roberto and I went there the next day. It's a beautiful, albeit decaying, colonial-style city with cobblestoned streets and intricately decorated buildings. In many ways it reminded me of Merida, the capital of Yucatan, with its large town square with a cathedral on one side, and walkways and fountains in the square itself.

The city is known for its many Spanish immersion-training programs, and we saw many visitors from around the world as we walked along the streets. The international pull of the city was evident in the many different restaurants as well. Roberto and I poked around the downtown area, looking into shops, churches and hotels. We saw a display of the floats used for the Easter Passion procession. These floats are huge, heavy wooden affairs that depict the story of Jesus' passion and crucifixion and weigh several thousand pounds. They are carried down the street by a group of 80 or more strong men (or women!) on Good Friday. Because the floats are so heavy, they rotate out the people carrying them every 15 minutes or so.

Since it was right after El Día de los Muertos, Roberto and I visited the Cementerio Municipal to see how it had been decorated. The cemetery was very different from the ones I had seen in the jungle. Here, the graves are all white mausoleums. Each was beautifully maintained and decorated with flowers.

We wrapped up with a visit to the Iglesia del San Francisco, where many miracles have occurred. There is a corridor in the bottom floor of the church filled with letters, crutches and photos of people who have been cured of some type of ailment after visiting and praying at the church. I spent quite a bit of time reading the stories of these people, grateful for the healing power of love.

The next morning, a Sunday, was another beautiful sunny day, and also my last day in Guatemala. I had made plans with Roberto to go to Iximche, a Mayan archeological site located about an hour and a half outside of the city. We left early, and got there in about an hour. Because it is located in a more mountainous area, Iximche is much cooler than Guatemala City. To me, the temperature felt refreshing and reminded me of San Francisco; to Roberto it felt very cold and he put on a coat.

We hired a bilingual guide named Balam, which is Mayan for jaguar. He taught us both a lot about the site and its history. The buildings are very different from those I'd seen in other places. Built in the Post-Classical Mayan style, there are no carvings on the buildings. Many of the non-religious buildings, such as the palaces, were outlined in stones and then used wood or other materials for the walls and ceilings, rather than being built completely out of stone.

The ceremonial area is still used today by Mayans for various ceremonies. I had hoped to see a ceremony when we visited, but unfortunately we were a few minutes late. The ceremony had been completed, and all that was left were some burning candles and flowers strewn around.

The site was very peaceful and almost felt like a park. Balam explained that many of the local people would bring a lunch and come here for the day. As we left, a number of families were arriving to enjoy the sunshine and their Sunday.

The drive back took longer than out because of all the traffic. We stopped at one point because there was an exposition of about a dozen and a half handmade kites by local students. Kite flying is very popular in Guatemala. In fact, when I was visiting Uaxactun, the children there were playing with a kite they had made out of newspapers. The kites in the exposition were beautifully designed, with bright colors and local scenes depicted on them. The largest were over six feet tall. When asked, the children explained that the largest were only for decoration and would not be able to fly. But the smaller kites were flight-ready and would be flown later that day.

Roberto drove me back to the hotel, and we made

arrangements for him to bring me to the airport the next morning. I packed my bag, reflecting on my time there. *This was such a wonderful trip*, I thought. *I feel like I've connected and opened up more to myself, but almost feel as if I am cutting my growth short by leaving. I wish I had more time here, but I have to go back and do all the book launch stuff. Maybe I should come back for another vacation. Or, maybe I should come back and stay for a few months. I bet I could find a place to rent. If I did that, I would have plenty of time to visit the Mayan archeological sites and connect with the energy here. Why not? I like it here and have made a few friends. There's really nothing preventing me from doing this.*

I picked up my phone and texted Roberto and Carlos and asked them to keep an eye open for a place where I could live for a few months.

CHAPTER 3: STARTING TO MAKE CHANGES

My first full day back in San Francisco was Election Day. I spent most of the day glued to news reports, watching the results of the election. Like many other people I knew, I was shocked by the results and felt fearful about the future of the country and the basic freedoms that it was based on. I spent several days on the verge of tears, trying to avoid falling into the deep fear and anxiety I saw all around me. At this time, love and the shamanic work I do are needed more than ever.

I strengthened my resolve to go back to Guatemala for a much longer visit. There was something about the Mayan archeological sites in Guatemala and Mexico that helped me to more deeply connect with my personal and shamanic power. There was a wisdom in these sites that permeates every aspect of my being, and the sacredness of the sites touches my soul. Antonio, the Mayan shaman from Mexico who got me started on this path, had told me once that I was a Mayan shaman in a past life. While I have no way of knowing whether that is true, I do know that the sites have an impact on me and I leave them feeling more empowered.

I've also come to the conclusion that the main thing holding me back from living in my full personal power and authenticity are my limiting beliefs, such as this idea of having one place to live, which, I'm realizing more and more, is an idea that I've bought into that isn't necessarily relevant to my life or me personally. Even when I worked as a consultant and spent every week in a hotel room, I still maintained a permanent place to live in to return to. But was that really necessary?

Looking back, I realized that I could have easily not had a personal home and traveled to wherever I wanted to for the weekends and stayed in a hotel there. It would have been a lot cheaper. I wouldn't have had to come home on weekends and worried about cleaning, going grocery shopping or paying utility bills. And imagine being able to get all your belongings down to one carry on suitcase and a purse. What a stress-free existence!

Personally I think that many of us go through life with far too much physical baggage. Every item we own has a certain level of energy and responsibility associated with it. It needs to be cleaned, cared for, stored, and/or updated. Depending on the value or the level of sentimentality of the item, we may worry about it getting stolen or damaged, and may even take out some type of insurance policy on it. Unknowingly, these items add to our stress.

Now don't get me wrong. I am all for having items that bring me joy and comfort in my life. My point is that so many things don't. Instead of joy, they bring clutter, additional work, stress or unhappiness. What if I could get rid of all those things and put the rest in storage for when I'm ready to come back and have a permanent place?

Spiritually, this idea of travelling without clutter appealed to me as well. I didn't want to carry things through life that I don't like or want, such as feelings of guilt, resentment or anger. I wanted to be able to release them as soon as they tried to attach to me so that I was energetically light and able to follow my heart easily. The weight of such negative emotions would drag me down, preventing me from moving forward and connecting to my heart, so that I could shine fully. And right now my heart was saying to live as a gypsy for six months or so, starting in Guatemala. Once I was in Guatemala, I'd get clarity on where to go next.

One of the things that I really wanted to do was to put down anything that I no longer need or that doesn't serve me well—physical belongings, fears, old hurts or negative emotions that are holding me back—and walk and travel unencumbered through life.

The one hesitation I had was: would I be able to find a place to live in San Francisco when it was time to come back? I was in a rent-controlled apartment (a necessity in San Francisco given how rents have been climbing in the double digits each year) and my landlady didn't care whether or not I had a full-time, steady-income job, just so long as she got the rent money on time each month. But coming back from such a journey, I wouldn't have that type of security or job. Would someone be willing to rent to me in such a situation?

They say that the best way to eliminate a fear is to face it head on. The more I thought about it, the more I knew that I needed to do this. If I didn't, I'd regret it. And regret is a heavy burden to carry in life.

Before I could change my mind, I went up to my landlady and told her I would be moving out sometime in February, after my book tour finished. She looked like she was going to cry (I have been a very good tenant), but when I told her the reason why, she was very excited for me. With the first step complete, I turned my eye toward the belongings in my apartment.

A friend of mine was moving into a larger place in late December, so I started by inviting her over to look at everything. I knew which things I wanted to keep, so with the exception of those items, everything else was up for grabs. We went through my apartment, room by room. When all was said and done, she decided to take all my carpets, four pieces of furniture, a number of wall hangings, and everything in my kitchen cupboards that I didn't want. I told her I would pack everything up for her after Thanksgiving, and then began culling out those things that could go over to Goodwill.

While I was still taking some deep breaths and reassuring myself that everything would work out okay for me, I was a little nervous about this step. Not as nervous as quitting my job, but definitely nervous...and excited about what my future could be....and fully committed to making this life change.

I decided to get some guidance from my spirit helpers and asked them, "What do I need to keep in mind during this transitional time?"

Hold positive, loving and joyful thoughts. Write down your intentions, goals and desires so that you have clarity. We are here helping you attain what you desire. You are supported during this time. Let go of your fears and any thoughts that would hold you back. Treat yourself with love and compassion during this time. This is a time for you to go inward to understand and find your inner joy and be able to express your true essence, your true self. You are on a clear path to becoming the fullest expression of yourself. You are the creator of your own reality. Your perceptions and reality are about to change as you discover more about yourself. You will be challenged with new knowledge and insight, which will open new worlds and new possibilities for you. Define the reality you want and be open to the process of transformation. Follow your heart and see the magic that unfolds.

Follow my heart. My heart knew the type of life that it wanted to create: one that is light-filled and unburdened with negative energy; one that gives me the opportunity to travel to many places, see different things, and meet people; and one that gives me the flexibility to live my life on my terms (e.g., flexible work arrangements).

And trust. I have gotten so much better at trusting the universe and being secure in the knowledge that I am being taken care of. This message has been hammered home to me throughout my life, most recently with the accident and then quitting my job. I rarely ever questioned my intuition anymore, and found that I no longer worry about things like I used to. I trusted the universe implicitly. The key to trusting, I realized, is to not try to control the process or outcome. There are an infinite number of ways a process could unfold or an outcome could be resolved. My mind, while pretty sharp, would never be able to think of them all—and could very well not come up with the one way that could be the very best for me. The universe, in its infinite wisdom, can however.

I think that by continuing to shed these roles that I've taken on in life that no longer "fit" me, I will be able to more clearly see my true essence and self, as my guides mentioned. If taking this next leap of faith allowed me to move closer to becoming the fullest expression of myself, then I was all for it. Isn't that why we are here to begin with? To learn who we are, what our purpose is, and then let that shine out for the rest of the world to see? This change could be very exciting!

I hadn't told my mother or my family yet about my decision. My mom was coming out next week for Thanksgiving, and I figured I would tell her in person. I wasn't sure if she would be supportive or not. When I moved to San Francisco, she was upset because I was living three thousand miles away on the other side of the country. And now I'm temporarily moving to another country. She might think that I'm crazy and worry. On the other hand, she has always encouraged me to follow my dreams and do what I want to with my life. There is a chance that she will be excited for and proud of me.

◆ ◆ ◆

Thanksgiving was wonderful. I had a house full of people over and was in my glory prepping for and cooking a meal for everyone. My mom took the news of my move to Guatemala very well. I sent a note out with my holiday greeting cards that I'm moving and the reasons why I feel this is the right decision for me. So far, everyone has been very supportive. I've received messages from a number of friends and family members saying that I was living a life that they dreamed of. Several have said that they wanted to come visit me. And, quite a few have remarked on the courage it must take to do something that different with your life.

I was deep into purging things. My kitchen cabinets were practically bare and I was making daily trips to Goodwill with one or two trash bags of donations. My closets and rooms were getting emptier by the day. There was something refreshing and liberating about having all this extra space.

Although my move wasn't scheduled until February 16, I was trying to get as much packing done as possible by the beginning of January. My book tour started in mid-January and continued for a month. Between the travel for the book tour and my personal trips I was not going to be home much. The last thing I wanted to do was have to pull some all-nighters just before the movers get here.

The number of people reaching out to me for shamanic sessions continued to grow as well. The launch of the book on November 1 definitely contributed to this. My publicist had done a great job of promoting the book, and it had been featured on Buzzfeed, Brit + Co, Popsugar, MindBodyGreen, MSN, and SheKnows.com. Two weeks after publication, the book was awarded a Finalist award in American Book Fest's 2016 Best Book Awards. I've received quite a few emails from people who have read the book and either wanted a session or just wanted to tell me how much they enjoyed it. A few weeks ago I even had a new client fly out from Minneapolis for a week's worth of sessions!

With everything going on, I really needed to make sure I was taking time to care for myself and keeping my stress down. Plus I wanted to spend some time reflecting on 2017 and my resolutions and goals for the year.

CHAPTER 4: WRAPPING UP AND MOVING ON

I made only one New Year's resolution for 2017, but it was a big one: I resolve to live my life with authenticity, passion, unapologetic fierceness, courage, freedom, love and joy.

I spent some time meditating about my resolution, and asked the universe for some additional focus so that I could be as successful as possible in realizing it.

Connect to your inner strength and sacral area to bring your dreams into manifestation. This is a time of birth and rebirth for you. You are ending one cycle and beginning another, and you are moving toward the fulfillment of your dreams. You are on the right path…trust as you move forward. Follow you own inner guidance, keep your heart open, and let go of attempts to make others happy. Focus on your life purpose and all will be resolved.

If someone had told me a few years ago that this was going to be my path, I would have laughed at them. Being a shaman, quitting my job and moving to Guatemala were not on my radar screen. I had spent the past few years shedding many aspects of myself. This next phase, this move to Guatemala truly felt like a time of rebirth for me. I had no idea what I would "look like" when I come out on the other side, but I did know that I was going to focus on my life purpose and follow my own guidance.

On New Year's Eve a friend and I went hiking at the Marin Headlands. It was a beautiful sunny day. We were on a trail that didn't have many people on it. As we rounded a bend on the path, we saw a bobcat ahead of us. It was pretty large, which led me to believe that it was a male. We were close enough that we could clearly see his spots and watched him for a while—both to make sure he wasn't going to come after us and also to admire his beauty.

As a power animal, bobcat brings the gifts of new learning, trusting inner senses, and being able to see or hear what is hidden. It seems as if the appearance of bobcat mirrors the message I received today from the universe. All in all, I was excited about 2017, my resolutions, and the intentions and changes I was putting into place.

◆ ◆ ◆

Tonight was my first book tour event, at Book Passage in Corte Madera, CA. I was excited and nervous at the same time. I knew that there would be some people there, since several San Francisco friends were driving up for the event. One of my best friends, Erin, even flew out from New York to be here. I was hopeful that there would be at least 20 people there…and that I did a good job talking about the book and shamanism.

Erin and I drove up to the bookstore early so that I would have plenty of time to help with the setup, if needed. I was going to be presenting in the large back room of the store, and they had quite a few chairs set up, near stacks of my books with signs saying, "Meet the Author" posted throughout the store.

There wasn't much for me to do. I put the award stickers on the books on display, laid out my sign in sheet, and filled some bowls with chocolates. The manager readied some bottles of wine for the participants and showed me where I could wait until it was time for her to introduce me. She explained that they had allocated about 45 minutes for my talk and questions. Then people could have their books signed by me.

I needn't have worried about the attendance. There were well over 30 people at the event, including a number of people I didn't know. I looked out at the crowd of people and saw the interest in their faces. My friend Erin gave me a smile and a thumbs-up. I smiled back. To her left were my friends Tracy and Alan, who were holding their cell phones, ready to take pictures and record the event.

I took a deep breath and began. "While this book is about my personal journey to becoming a shaman, there are three core messages throughout the book that I think will resonate with anyone—whether or not that person is considering to become a shaman. They are:

1. We all have what I call "moments that change our lives forever"
2. We always have choice as to whether or not we want to act on those moments…and if we don't, we usually will get another chance later on in life
3. We are not alone. We have guides walking with us, just waiting to help us if we ask them to."

I then went on to talk more about each of these three messages and read from my book to support the points I was making. Finished with my twenty-minute presentation, I asked if anyone had any questions.

My biggest concern about the book events was that I would finish talking and the only thing I would hear are crickets because people were so bored and disinterested. That was definitely not the case with this group. Hands went up immediately, and I was inundated with questions. People asked about shamanism, what it's like to do a shamanic journey, and about specific parts of the book. In the end, the question and answer portion of the event went on for over an hour.

Those that had bought a book then lined up to have their books signed, and I found that people had even more questions that they wanted to ask me privately. One attendee happened to be with San Francisco State University and asked me if I would speak to the students there. All in all, the event lasted over two hours. The bookstore was closed when the event wrapped up, and they unlocked the doors to allow us to leave.

Each event ended up being a repeat of this first one. The San Francisco event was standing room only. In Chicago, a small group of attendees adapted to a nearly last-minute venue change and drove over an hour to the event. Because it was a smaller group, the presentation became more of a conversation, with the participants chiming in and sharing stories. In Connecticut and New Hampshire, the 30 or so participants at each event braved snowstorms and poor road conditions to attend.

In addition to the book tour and related publicity events, I continued to pack and sell belongings, conduct shamanic and coaching sessions, and spend time with friends. I took a mid-week trip up to Mt. Shasta, CA to drop my car off with my friend Arthur, who is going to start her on a regular basis. Leaving my car with Arthur really hammered home that I was about to make some major changes in my life. I took a moment to connect with myself and discovered that I felt really good about everything going on in my life. Sure, there was some stress, but overall I felt as if I were increasing in my personal power and feeling more and more empowered.

I decided to check in with the Universe to see if it had any additional insights to offer me during this period and got an answer immediately.

> *Don't forget to nurture and care for yourself during this time. Get plenty of sleep, eat healthily, and exercise when you can. Don't try to force things to happen; let things unfold. When you try to make things happen, you block the ease of manifestation. This is a time for you to learn some new life lessons that will help you help others in the future.*

The weeks flew by, and before I knew it, it was move day. It only took a few hours for the movers to load all my belongings up in their truck and bring them to the storage unit. I did one last cleaning of the apartment and then turned in the keys to my landlord. I was going to stay with a friend for a few days before heading out.

The presentation at San Francisco State University that I had agreed to at my first book event was scheduled for a couple days before my flight to Guatemala. As I rode in the cab over to the school, I looked at the rain coming down and thought, "At this time next week, I'll be in Guatemala." Wow!

There were about 25 students in the class, which focused on holistic studies. The professor had arranged for me and another person to present. After brief introductions, he asked me to start.

"I had no intention of becoming a shaman," I began. "In fact, until a few years ago, I had no idea what a shaman was. And then I took a trip to Mexico, and was literally led to a Mayan shaman there. He spent time telling me about shamanism and then proceeded to do what ended up being a four-hour shamanic session on me." I went on to explain about some of my experiences as I was trained, a few of the messages I've received to date, and the accident.

Once I finished, I turned to the woman next to me, who was a reverend at a spiritual church. She explained about the role of nature in ceremony and gave some ideas to the students about how they might incorporate ceremony in their lives.

The students had many questions, and before we knew it, the class was over. About a third of them stayed behind to talk to me individually and share their stories. I was struck by the hardships and major life events these young people had experienced so far, and, in some cases cried with them as they told me about their lives. Their wisdom and hope inspired me, and I thought about them often over the next few days as I ran around visiting friends, squeezing in a few last dance classes, and taking care of last-minute details.

On Friday morning, Eddie, my cab driver, picked me up at my friend's house and drove me to San Francisco International Airport. He gave me a hug goodbye, saying, "Have fun but be careful! Text me every once in a while so that I know you are okay." I hugged him back, promised I would, and then entered the airport.

As I looked out the plane window and watched the San Francisco skyline get smaller and smaller, I said a mental goodbye to the city that had been my home for the past eight years. My heart was filled with warring, conflicting emotions. I brushed a tear from my face, took a deep, steadying breath, and focused on the excitement in my heart about going to Guatemala fill me.

Twenty-three hours later, I landed in Flores, Guatemala. A driver was waiting to take me to the resort that I was staying at, and off we went. My plan was to spend two nights there while I looked at possible places to live. Carlos had found ten possible options and I had found one place on AirBnB.

It ended up being a very long, but fruitful, day. Carlos had borrowed Pedro's car, and we spent over seven hours driving around looking at potential hotel rooms, casitas and individual family houses that had offered a room for me. Carlos' main concern was that I needed to be in a safe location. He was also very concerned about me living alone and told me that he much preferred that I either stay with a family or in a hotel room.

I had sensed that living alone was unusual in Guatemala, especially in the more rural areas, but I didn't understand the full cultural norms and expectations until now. In Guatemala, women simply didn't live alone. In fact, men rarely lived alone either, although it was more readily accepted for a man to live alone than for a woman. I explained to Carlos that I was used to living alone, and that it was easier for me to write when I had my own place. "Sometimes," I said, "I end up writing until late in the night and then sleep late in the morning. Other times I get up very early and write. In any case, I need to have the flexibility to write when I am inspired to write, without having to worry about disturbing other people." He reluctantly conceded the discussion, but asked that we still stop and meet some of the families. I agreed.

Of all of the options we looked at, only two met my criteria.

The first was a house owned by one of Carlos' friends. It was situated right on the lake, about thirty minutes outside the city in a small village. The house was actually more of a compound with three houses on it. There was the main house, where the family stayed on weekends and where I could rent a room. There was a second house, with a family living in it. And there was a third casita with two bedrooms, a small kitchen and living area that I could stay in if I preferred. The yard was beautifully landscaped with patios scattered around with chairs and tables. We walked down the hill to the lake, where there was a large patio and cooking area. It was beautiful and definitely inspiring. My only concern was that the house was at least an hour away from where Carlos and Pedro lived, and almost ninety minutes away from Tikal and the other local Mayan archeological sites. I wasn't sure I wanted to be so far away from the few friends I did have in Guatemala. I told Carlos' friend that I really liked his home and would think about it. It was definitely on the top of the list.

The second was the AirBnB house I had found online while flying to Chicago for my book event there. We drove to El Remate, the town where the house was located and tried to call Julian, the man who owned the AirBnB house. We weren't able to reach him, but I remembered that Julian owned a restaurant in town. We found it and asked the woman working there if she knew where Julian was. She didn't, but she did, however, know where the AirBnB house was. So we all piled into Pedro's car and she guided us to the house.

The gate was locked, so we couldn't enter the yard, but we could peer through and look at the house. I had shown Carlos the pictures of the house interior and exterior from AirBnB, so we both had a good feel for what the place was like. When I had first told Carlos about the possibility of renting Julian's house, Carlos was concerned that the house was too remote and isolated...which meant, in his perspective, that it wouldn't be safe for a woman living alone.

We were pleasantly surprised to see that there were neighbors on either side of the house and two small restaurants located within a two-minute walk. The town cemetery was just past one neighbor's house, which I viewed as a plus since I like cemeteries. The lake was only a minute away and the center of town was an easy fifteen-minute walk. The hut looked solid, with a thatched-roof and a covered outdoor living room. The yard was filled with many trees—palms, coconut, banana and avocado—and a number of meandering gravel paths. Even though we couldn't get in to see it, it felt perfect.

After we finished looking at all of the options, Carlos drove me to the neighboring village of El Caoba and introduced me to Pedro's parents and one of his sisters, Maria, before we continued on to Pedro's house for a quick visit.

He and his wife, Camila, greeted us at the door. They had four children, with the youngest being about six months old. The baby was sleeping on the front porch in a hammock as we walked in.

Pedro, Camila, their young daughter, Carlos and I sat out back, visiting. The baby woke up and Camila went and got him. I asked if I could hold him, and Camila said yes. He started crying when he realized that I was a stranger and was talking to him in a different language, but then saw my hair. He was fascinated by the color and reached out to touch it. We all laughed. I handed the baby back to Camila, thanked them, and Carlos and I left.

It was nearly 6 p.m. Carlos stopped in El Remate so we could watch the sunset over the lake. The sun was a beautiful brilliant orange-red as it sunk lower in the sky and made a long line of the same color on the water. We watched the sky go from blue to pink to orange to a dark indigo and then headed back to the car.

As we got into the car, he handed me a piece of paper that listed all of the places we visited that day, with details on pricing. "Have you decided where you want to live?"

"I'm leaning toward the little thatched-roof hut, but want to think more about it tomorrow." I was planning on spending the day at the resort relaxing since the following day I was going to move into my new home. "I'll text you with what I decide." We made plans for him to pick me up Monday morning and said good night.

On Monday morning, I went to the resort restaurant to have breakfast and was happy to see Enrico there. Enrico was brother to Pedro and Maria. He was excited that I was going to be living in Guatemala and offered to take me to Santa Elena on Tuesday to a large grocery store to do some shopping. "If you need anything in the meantime, please let me know. Here's my phone number. I'll see you on Tuesday night."

Carlos arrived promptly at 11 a.m. and drove me to Julian's restaurant. I had texted him the day before letting him know that I had decided to go with the little thatched-roof hut after all. Julian loaded a big water cooler-sized bottle of water in the back of Pedro's car and we all headed over to the hut.

Julian showed me around and explained how to use the shower water heater, the Internet connection, and the washing machine. Carlos brought in my roller board and backpack and then we gave Julian a ride back to his restaurant before heading out to a local shop so that I could pick up the essentials I needed until I could go to the store with Enrico. After bringing in my purchases, Carlos gave me a hug goodbye and left. I was alone in a hut in the jungle.

My first order of business was to do a thorough cleaning. The hut had been tidied up, but I could see some cobwebs and dust. Unlike the heavy-duty cleaning I had done in San Francisco to release items I no longer needed, this cleaning allowed me to prepare the space to make the hut my home. The hut was basically a rectangle, with a half-circle at one end, which housed the bathroom. Although I couldn't be certain, it looked like the bathroom had been added on at a later date. One quarter of the rectangular part of the hut was the outside living room. There were three chairs and a couch. Low walls on the two outside walls gave structure to the room, and the open window areas allowed you to look out at the yard and its many exotic trees and plants. Full walls on the other two sides of the outside living room housed the front door and a couple windows.

The front door opened up to the sleeping area. A full-size bed, chest of drawers and trunk took up most of the space opposite the outdoor living room. To the left of the sleeping area was the bathroom. To the right was an eating area and, around the corner, the kitchen. The walls were painted bright yellows and blues and had wood trim. One wall had Mayan hieroglyphs and warriors on it.

But it was the thatched roof that really made the hut. Rising up at least two and a half stories, it had a bamboo framework that was stuffed with palm tree leaves in a beautiful symmetrical pattern. It covered the main part of the hut; in the bathroom corrugated metal formed the roof. It made the hut feel bigger than it actually was and very airy. Part of that was the sheer size and height of the roof, the other part was because where the roof met the walls of the hut there was an eight inch or so gap between the wall and the side of the roof. This allowed a lot of light—and bugs—in.

I spent several hours scrubbing down the walls and furniture, tidying up and organizing the kitchen area, and washing all of the pots, dishes and glasses. I carefully took the live frog I found living in the bookcase and put it outside and did my best not to freak out when I found a dead scorpion in a glass by the refrigerator, sincerely hoping that a previous guest had gotten it as a souvenir and forgotten it. By the time I was done, the hut was near sparkling but I was definitely not! It was getting dark so I took a quick shower. I had just finished getting dressed and was noticing all of the strange noises of the jungle night, when I heard a very welcome sound. "Hola, Jenni. Buenas noches!"

Carlos was standing outside the locked gate at the end of the driveway. Normally I don't like being called Jenni, but since it was my first night alone in a hut in the jungle AND he was bringing what looked like food, I was happy to overlook it.

He came in and noticed immediately how much nicer the hut looked. I told him that I had cleaned, but still had more to do. I had a list a mile long of things I needed to get tomorrow at the market, but was feeling more comfortable in my new home. He looked around, double-checked the mosquito netting on the bed and made sure that I was doing okay. When I replied yes, he gave me a kiss on the cheek and said, "Dulces suenos. I'll lock the gate when I go out. And I'll see you tomorrow when you go to the market."

I waved good night as he left, grateful for his visit, then locked the door and turned out all of the lights except for the one by the bed. Then I crawled into bed, adjusted the mosquito netting, and turned out the last light. It was dark. Pitch black dark. I put my hand up in front of my face but couldn't see it. In San Francisco, even when I turned out all the lights in my apartment I could still see very well since there were so many outside lights. Here there were no outside lights to cut through the darkness.

Somehow it seemed as if with the absence of light, the noises of the jungle got louder. I lay with my eyes open, listening to all the foreign noises. I recognized the screams of the howler monkeys; they sounded like something out of Jurassic Park but were harmless. It was the other noises I didn't recognize. Something was up in the roof chirping. It sounded like a bird, which relaxed me a little bit. I tossed and turned for a while, and then gave up and turned on the light.

It was a humbling and eye-opening experience to realize that whatever relationship I thought I had with Mother Nature wasn't much of a relationship at all. It had been a "sterilized" one where I spent time in and with nature on my terms, when and where I wanted, with no real exposure to the more "messy" or authentic parts of nature. When I was done being outdoors, I'd go back to my sealed apartment and not have to deal with nature.

But here in this hut in the jungle, there was no escaping Mother Nature in all her authenticity. There were no sealed edges on the roof of the hut, and pretty much anything on the smaller side could come in. There were insects everywhere, including in my hut. I had seen so many different types of bugs today that I'd never seen before. I was actually happy when I saw an ant, only because I recognized what it was!

And those things that couldn't come in did go bump in the night. Since the hut just had screens or curtains over the window openings, I could hear everything: dogs barking, roosters crowing, howler monkeys screaming and whatever it was that just ran by my window making a weird hissing and grunting noise.

It was going to take me some time to get used to living here and everything that goes along with it. I'd been in so much transition for the last few weeks that I was having a hard time realizing that I was home (at least for a few months) and nearly settled in. I closed my eyes and asked the universe, "What do I need to keep in mind to help me adapt to and be successful here?"

Don't try to force or make things happen. Just let them unfold and trust that we are with you and looking out for your best good. Things will come together in ways you couldn't have orchestrated yourself. Make sure you take time to care for yourself. Get plenty of sleep. Eat healthy foods. These things will give you the energy and focus you need to do the work you need to do here. This time is a time of spiritual growth and life lessons for you. As you grow and learn, you will be able to share your knowledge with others.

I was grateful for the reminders. I tended to put my physical needs last and ignore the very basic requirements of my body. I remembered that the last time I went through a "time of spiritual growth and life lessons" I was exhausted because of how much work energetically was required. I vowed to take better care of myself this time.

I turned out the light and tried to sleep. It was after 4 a.m. before total exhaustion took over and I fell asleep.

At 7 a.m. my neighbors were up and about. I learned very quickly that once the sun was up, everyone in the jungle gets up and starts their day. I tried to go back to sleep but wasn't able to. Giving up, I got up and began my day as well.

Enrico showed up in the afternoon with his wife Isabel, his three year old daughter Valentina, and Carlos. He introduced me to Isabel and Valentina, and we headed out to Santa Elena.

The store they brought me to reminded me of a WalMart. It had a food section, clothing, housewares and small furniture. I took my list out and began shopping. I kept Valentina entertained by having her help me pick out the items, which is why I was now the proud owner of a night light shaped like a yellow rubber duck! I quickly filled up a shopping cart with all the things I needed to make my hut a bit homier. I looked over at Enrico and asked him if he thought it would all fit in the trunk of his car. He laughed and nodded so I made my way to the checkout counter.

I quickly got into a daily routine. I'd get up in the morning and sweep the floor to remove all of the bugs that had died during the night. After showering and eating, I'd spend some time writing. At some point during the day, I would go into town and pick up some fresh bread, fruit or vegetables. Around 6 p.m. I'd head down to the dock by the lake and watch the sunset. It was a far simpler lifestyle than what I had had in San Francisco, but it appealed to me.

Within a week, I'd made some new friends as well: Marta, an expat from Holland who had lived here for nearly seven years; Felipe, a local guide who ran jungle treks; Celine, Julian's girlfriend from Switzerland; and Eduardo, who moved here a few months ago from Spain and creates ceramic art. I had met most of them at sunset, since the nightly show brought out people to the lake to watch and admire the changing colors of the sky.

The only things that were a "negative" so far were the scorpions. Unfortunately, my hope that the dead scorpion I found in a glass the kitchen was left behind by a previous renter was completely off. Scorpions, apparently, were nearly as common here as houseflies were in the United States. I'd been told that the types that had been showing up in my hut were not deadly, but that still didn't calm my fears when I'd see them. Four had worked their way into my hut this first week, and they freaked me out. My usual response was to first have a small heart attack. Then I'd get my camera to take a photo of the scorpion because one of my nephews thought they were the coolest things ever. I disagreed, but what kind of aunt would I be if I didn't at least send a photo? Finally, I would use bug spray to kill the scorpion.

I asked Marta one night how she dealt with the scorpions. After telling me how she put on a pair of pants one time with a scorpion in them (she didn't get stung), she asked me what I thought the message was from the scorpions. There had to be a reason why so many were showing up in my hut. She suggested that I journey and talk to scorpion.

I admitted that I hadn't thought of that. With other animals that show up repeatedly in my life, I do stop and tune in to see what message or gift they bring me. But with scorpion, I hadn't done that. I think my fear prevented me from even thinking about connecting with scorpion that way. There's a lesson in there: even when something scares us, we need to still pause, go within, and discover the message. It might even be more important that we do this when we are emotionally charged by a situation or sighting of an animal.

I sat down that evening and asked, "Scorpion, what message do you have for me?"

I'm showing up in your life right now to help you realize that you are in a time of rebirth. You are stepping away from things that no longer serve you in life, from things that may be poisonous to your spirit and life purpose if you don't take action. It's time for you to release this baggage and walk forward to your new life.

This message was very similar to one my friend Arthur shared with me just before I flew to Guatemala. I had had several things happen that caused me to question whether or not I should go. First, I caught a really bad cold, even though I rarely get sick. In fact, the last time I was sick was about five years ago, in 2011. Second, my credit card number was stolen. This was the first time I'd ever had anything remotely close to identity theft happen to me. Unfortunately, it was the credit card that I had set all of my recurring payments up on so I would only need to pay one bill while I was in Guatemala and traveling around. Fortunately, I caught it before I left San Francisco and was able to get a new one and re-set up the recurring payments.

I questioned if these things were signs that I shouldn't do this trip. Arthur offered to channel a message for me from his guides, and I gladly accepted.

The circumstances for Jennifer are one of straddling the belief fence. To lean in the direction of fear is to attract disruptive energies and behaviors. Jennifer is in a place of shamanic vision, sight and understanding. The journey she is taking is to reinforce that sight and the language, practices and fullness of shamanic beliefs. By that very nature, Jennifer has aligned with experiences that will provide such growth. Not all experiences are to be pleasant. Where is the learning in that type of journey? A vacation? No, not a shaman's journey. There are many who would want to explain away Jennifer's choices and behaviors, judged as weird and aberrant. There are many who are even jealous of Jennifer's seeming lack of being affected by familial controls. They do not see the emotions under the surface. They do not live the emotions that have accompanied her path. And they do not need to know or see or believe anything for Jennifer to advance in her life path and purpose.

The credit card, sickness and struggles with closing out her San Francisco home are simply part of the past story of Jennifer. How much she lets go is her journey. How much she embraces the shaman of Mayan is her choice. In all of these choices, there is no precedent for life after this journey. There is in fact no precedent for the nature of shamanism Jennifer is and will live. As you say, Arthur, "taking the ancient and making it current" is the path and work Jennifer has chosen. Jennifer is gathering more experiences, more stories and more skills as a shaman on this journey. The physical health is a sign of needing to stop and rest. Breath was short to highlight needing more harmonious breath and energy. The voice was reduced and throat restricted to bring to attention that words must change to match new intentions, which requires silence before speaking. The emotional feelings, while obvious and expected, also has a security and safety fear producing a small shock wave. The financial crisis of the credit card resulted from the shock wave as we see it. Those attracted to shifts and testing Jennifer's resolve ride the shock wave and create disruption. For this journey beginning, there is no physical accident in a crosswalk. However, there is an emotional and mental shock which Jennifer may not fully be conscious of at this point. The book tour complete, her revealing of shamanism and "woo woo" life, as well as her distance from all who she knows are her crosswalk incident this time.

While all of these negative experiences had made me feel hesitant to move, I felt better about my decision to go to Guatemala after getting this message. I thought the big takeaway from the message from Arthur's guides and from scorpion was that I would be shedding a lot of unnecessary emotional, mental and spiritual baggage that would hold me back from fully enabling and embracing my life purpose and life path.

I was noticing a difference in my shamanic work since I'd been here. I'd held eight sessions in the last two weeks, and the messages I received from my guides and the universe have been much clearer and coming to more rapidly than ever before. The messages seem to be much richer. For example, for one client, my guides gave me a beautiful crystal ball, which, when held up to the light, was filled with beautiful rainbows. The crystal ball symbolized the true essence of my client, and my guides had me integrate it into her heart energy so she could better tap into her own personal strengths and being. When I called my client back and shared this message with her, she was speechless. Then she explained to me that while I was doing the session, she was walking around the town where she lived and wandered into a crystal shop.

"I immediately gravitated to a crystal ball in the shop," she said.

"I picked it up and watched the rainbows inside shine their light. For some reason I couldn't explain, I felt compelled to hold this crystal ball throughout the entire session. I am still holding it. Now I understand why, and I think I'm going to buy it as a reminder of who I am."

I didn't know if it was because of my proximity to Tikal or because I'd started shedding some things, or a combination of both, but I was finding that the sessions were evoking more of an emotional reaction from my clients. One client started crying as I shared the messages from the session because what saying resonated with her so much. Another told me that the messages I had gotten aligned with what she had put down for her 2017 New Year's resolutions. And a third wrote me a long, beautiful email after the session detailing the impact the messages and shamanic work were having on her.

Tikal and the energy of the Mayan ruins in this area were also contributing to my spiritual growth. I had sensed the same thing when in Mexico at the ruins there, especially at Chichen Itza, where I had the wonderful experience of being at the ruins at sunrise by myself. But here, in Guatemala, I was living in close proximity to Tikal, and I was finding that the energy of the site was impacting me greatly.

For starters, I was no longer sleeping. I tried to sleep, and would maybe get one or two hours of sleep, but then the spiritual energy of Tikal and the area wakes me up. I would be up all night, until finally falling asleep around 4 a.m. It gets light here at 5:30 a.m., which is when the roosters start crowing, so that would be when I wake up. In spite of my lack of sleep, I was able to function fully. I remembered going through something similar when I first started learning about shamanism. I was learning and downloading so much that sleep was nearly impossible. But then, too, I was able to function.

I also firmly believed that the energy of the site and the universe were orchestrating things for me in my life to give me more opportunities to do my shamanic and coaching work since I had wholeheartedly said "yes" to this next transformation in my life. This week I met a woman, Renee, who was here on vacation. It turned out that Renee grew up in the same French town that I lived in when I studied in France when I was in college. Renee does channeled healing work in her free time. She invited me to France to lead some type of session and do healing work there. I explained that I was still getting settled in Guatemala and wanted to be here for a while, but that I'd love to go there in 2018. I have always wanted to do some work in France, and this seems to be my chance to do so.

I went to Tikal with Carlos this past Sunday, which happened to coincide with March's full moon. Since I had been there before and Carlos often leads tours through the site, we decided to go near the end of the day when the crowds and the heat had lessened. Specifically, we wanted to watch the sun set from one of the pyramids. We hoped that we could also watch the moon rise.

There were only a few dozen people at the site when we got there, and they all seemed to have the same intent. Carlos and I stood on the platform at the top of the Temple of the Masks, where we had a stunning view of the Grand Plaza and all the buildings and stellae to the east and the setting sun to the west.

I had felt the energy of this ancient site the last time I was there, but it was even stronger this time. There was something magical about twilight, the time between sunset and moonrise. The energy stilled, as if pausing between two deep breaths, and there was a quiet, expectant air within the site. The tallest buildings continued to vibrate with the rosy colors of the setting sun, while on the ground, in the jungle, it was already dark. Fireflies came out and lit up small areas of the darkness.

My energy slowed down and matched the energy of the site. A feeling of peaceful expectation washed over me, and I closed my eyes to savor it more. In this moment, I knew that anything was possible, and I breathed in the sacredness of it.

One by one, the stars came out in the darkening sky, and then the full moon began to rise. We watched it come up from behind the Temple of the Grand Jaguar and illuminate the entire Grand Plaza. It was so bright that we could clearly see every building as we slowly made our way out of the park and to our car, expressing our wonder, awe and gratitude for being able be at Tikal and experience its magic.

CHAPTER 5: MAKING CONNECTIONS IN THE JUNGLE

In spite of the many beautiful and magical gifts and experiences I have had here in Guatemala, there are some basic, foundational differences that reminded me of the many blessings I had—and took for granted—while living in the United States.

Here, I had to drink, cook and brush my teeth with purified water so that I didn't get sick. There was running water in my little hut for cleaning, laundry, and other purposes; however there was no guarantee that the water would be available and running when I wanted to use it. There was a back-up water supply that I had to turn on several times already.

While my house and the community had electricity, it, too, could go off at random times. I'd been here three weeks now and the electricity has gone out once. Based on the conversations I've had with people here, it went out frequently. When that happens, all you can do is wait for it to come back on. People here seemed pretty laid back about it though, and just continued on with their day.

People also seemed pretty nonchalant about all of the insects here. I still hadn't come to terms with the scorpions. I'd had eight show up in my hut, including one on the mosquito netting on my bed. Thankfully the mosquito netting did its job, but I'd much rather not have to deal with them. Since my home, like many of the homes here, was not sealed tight around windows, doors, roofs or even walls, I was going to have to get used to sharing my living quarters with them.

Carlos very nicely found an English rooster and hen for me, since they ate scorpions. They were a very pretty rust brown color, and the rooster had long black and white speckled tail feathers. I've named them Juan Carlos and Lupe and was learning how to care for them. And I was having a good laugh at the fact that a city girl now has chickens and was very grateful for them!

But there were some other differences that I wish were commonplace. For starters, people here take time to connect and focus. Everyone greets one another when passing. It was usually a simple "buenos dias," but it was genuine and enough to connect with and acknowledge the other person. The connection deepens if you asked someone how he was. In the United States, the expected response was "I'm fine" and I often sensed that the question is a throwaway question because many people don't even wait for the answer. Here in Guatemala, people would actually tell you the truth. So, if they were sick, or there was a problem in their life, or if they were celebrating something, they would tell you. The person who asked the question would listen intently and honor the conversation. I didn't know if it was because of the heat or if it was a cultural thing, but everyone moves more slowly here. Things get done, but just not at the breakneck pace that I was accustomed to. There's a level of courtesy, genuine concern and human-to-human connection that is admirable.

While I certainly haven't met everyone in Guatemala, the people that I have met would give you the shirt off their backs, even if that shirt were the only thing they owned. I've experienced a number of heartwarming and humbling acts of kindness from a group of people that seemed to have truly giving and open hearts.

When Carlos was driving me around to look at possible places to live, he took me to the home of some people who were truly destitute. He stopped by to give them some bread to help them out. The bread cost the equivalent of US 50 cents, but that was beyond the means for this family. Their home was crumbling and didn't appear to have electricity or running water. Inside was a handful of old mattresses on the dirt floor for the family to sleep on. One corner had some clothing, and there was a hammock strung from the ceiling, with a baby sleeping in it. These people truly had nothing. And yet, when Carlos gave the woman of the house the bread, she not only thanked him, but also offered to make a meal and share it with us.

In two instances I mentioned something that I was looking for, and people gave me what I wanted. One was flowers. I liked to have fresh flowers in my house, but there weren't any wildflowers growing in my yard. I hesitated picking wildflowers on the edges of other people's houses. When I went to Julian's restaurant later in the day, I noticed he had fresh flowers and I asked him about them.

"Where did you get the flowers? Is there a florist in town?"

"No, the nearest florist is in Santa Elena, about 30 minutes away," he said. "Do you need flowers for something?"

"No, I just like having them in the house. Maybe next time I go to Santa Elena I will get some. Thanks!"

The next day, when I returned from a walk, there was a bouquet of flowers waiting for me at my little hut. Julian had made a special trip to Santa Elena to get me some.

The second was a yoga mat. I had been to one store in the nearest city and didn't see any. On the night that I met Marta, we started talking about yoga. I asked her where she got her mat, since I was looking for one, and she said, "Come on over. I have a spare I can lend you."

The other thing I'd noticed was how people seem to open up their homes and time to me. In the last three weeks, I'd been invited and gone to lunch at both Enrico's house and Maria's house. They both introduced to me to their family members and have been to my house to visit. Julian invited me to a party to celebrate the two-year anniversary of his restaurant. Carlos brought me to meet his children and a shaman friend of his. Pedro lent Carlos and me his car so that we could spend the day running errands and going to Tikal. I just had to put gas in it (which I was more than happy to do). Felipe took me on two jungle hikes to teach me about the local plants and their medicinal purposes. He also gave me books on the plants here and the ruins. My sense was that people here recognize how interconnected life is and know that anything they shared with others will come back to them tenfold.

I've been trying to do my part by sharing what I have with others as well. I've invited Enrico's, Maria's and Pedro's families to my house for lunches. I made lunch for Felipe as a thank you for the time he has spent with me, and I made lunch and dinner for Carlos. I offered a free shamanic session to Marta and helped Julian with the yard work of my little hut.

And finally, I realized that people here need healing and to be listened to just as much as anywhere else. Over the last few days, I'd had a couple situations that hammered that fact home with me.

It started with a conversation with Julian. I stopped by his restaurant for breakfast and he saw me waiting and sat down to talk with me. I spent nearly an hour listening to him talk about some of the problems he was facing in his life right now, as well as discussing some of the questions he had about life. Like some of my clients, he struggled to break some of the bonds and expectations of his family and culture in general to build the life that he wanted. While no clear answers came during our conversation, I could see that just talking and having someone listen helped him immensely.

The next day, I went to Maria's house for lunch. I genuinely liked Maria – she has a ready, warm smile and just draws you in. I walked the three miles from my town to hers, and made better time than I had planned. Rather than going to her house thirty-five minutes early, I sat on a crude bench across from a small general store and started playing a game on my phone. Within five minutes, Maria walked by, on her way to the general store, and stopped in surprise.

"Why are you sitting here? Why didn't you come to my house?" she asked.

"I'm very early," I replied, "and I didn't want to disturb you."

"Why would you disturb me?" Truly puzzled by my actions, she laughed, took me by the arm to the store and then to her home. Waiting to meet me were her daughter, daughter-in-law, grandson and granddaughter.

We had a wonderful lunch and visit, but I noticed that sometimes when she laughed it didn't quite reach her eyes and that there was an air of sadness about her. I decided to ask her about it

"Are you unhappy, Maria?"

She was quiet for a moment and then nodded. "There are times when I feel sad." I nodded and squeezed her hand. She didn't say anything more about it, and I didn't press her. I sensed that she needed to feel connected to someone, so I spent time connecting with her—talking, walking arm in arm, and giving her hugs—and could see that it really helped her.

This morning, I was walking from town to my house with some chicken feed for Juan Carlos and Lupe, when a young woman called me name. I crossed the street and recognized her as Jessica, one of the workers at Julian's restaurant. I had been walking by her house and she wanted to say hello. As we talked, she started to tell me her story. She was one of seven children: five girls and two boys. At twenty-one, she was the oldest. Her mother and grandmother wanted all five girls to get professional degrees and have a career. She had graduated, against all odds, with a secretarial degree. She was married when she was going to school and became pregnant. During her last year at university, she gave birth to her now seventeen-month old daughter, but she continued her studies and would even bring the newborn baby to class with her.

Two of her sisters are at university now. Her mother went to the United States five years ago and was sending the money she made to them for school. Her father drove a taxi in Guatemala City.

"I haven't been able to get a job as a secretary, and I feel as if I have disappointed my mother and grandmother," she said. "They worked so hard for me to go to school and are working hard so my sisters can go. I don't know what to do."

"I really miss my mother," she continued, as tears welled up in her eyes. "How old are you?"

It seemed to be an abrupt conversation change, but then I realized why she was asking. "I am 51," I replied.

"Similar to my mother's age." I nodded and then did my best to be like a mom to her. I held her as she cried, while her little daughter watched with a concerned brow. Once Jessica had released her initial emotions, fear and stress, I said, "I know that your problems seem overwhelming to you right now, but often problems work themselves out in beautiful ways that we could never imagine. Trust in yourself, your family and God. You are stronger than you think."

She gave me a small, relieved smile. "Gracias."

"You're welcome. I know it is difficult for you without your mother. I live in the little yellow hut near the cemetery. Please visit me anytime."

I left with tears in my eyes. While Jessica's problems were not insurmountable, I empathized with the pain she was feeling deeply during our brief conversation. As a shaman, I often got a sense of what it is that was causing a client pain. However, in the last few weeks I'd noticed that I was actually feeling the pain that my clients felt even more strongly. I felt Julian's confusion and mind chatter that were making it difficult for him to move forward on his life path. I felt the pain that Maria had in her heart, which alerted me to the fact that Maria needed a little extra TLC. I felt the feelings that each of my clients had had this past week. And I felt the pain, loneliness and despair of Jessica. Their emotions, mental chatter, and pain sat on top of my own, like a blanket, and covered mine. I knew that I didn't experience these things with the same intensity that my client did. What I felt was a watered down version that helped me pinpoint the needs of my client, but there were times when even the watered down version could make me cry. This was one of those times.

As I walked away, I had the sense that the universe had guided me here not only to write a book and increase my personal capabilities, but also to help the people in this part of the world.

I was grateful for this increasing capability within me and knew that one of the things I wanted to do (and did) as a shaman was to help alleviate the pain that my clients have. I realized that suffering was part of life, but I also believed that many times our suffering comes from within us through our mental chatter rather than from external factors. If I could help people understand this and begin to tone down the mental chatter, I think much suffering could be eliminated or reduced.

◆ ◆ ◆

Monday is the Spring Equinox. Carlos and I are going to a local Mayan archeological site, Uaxactun, for the event. We met today to finalize our plans. I knew that the equinoxes were a big deal at Chichen Itza, but I didn't realize how important they are here as well. Carlos told me that the festivities usually go for two days, with a number of traditional musical performances; matches of the Mayan ball game, played in the ball court of the site; and a number of shamanic and other ceremonies. On the night preceding the equinox, the events go all night long and culminate with the rising sun illuminating the interior of one of the temples. I tried to imagine it all in my mind, but couldn't. I would have to wait for the actual event.

◆◆◆

On Monday, Carlos borrowed Pedro's car, and we drove through Tikal, up a winding dirt road to the village and ruins of Uaxactun. I couldn't sit still in the car and wished that it were possible to go faster. While it was only about 15 miles north of Tikal, the road to Uaxactun took us nearly an hour to navigate. The current road, a twisty, one-lane dirt road with many potholes and rocks, had been in place for only a few years. Before then, according to Carlos, the only way to get to Uaxactun was in a heavy-duty 4x4.

The sun was hanging low in the sky, nearly kissing the treetops, when we finally arrived. The village was organized around a small airstrip. A number of simple houses painted in bright colors and general stores lined the sides. When I had visited in the past, the landing strip, with its patches of grass, served as a grazing area for the many pigs and chickens. Today, the landing strip looked completely different. A large stage dominated one side of the landing strip, with dozens of green plastic chairs in front of it. The sounds of the band warming up on the stage filled the air with happy, joyful Latin music. Food stands lined the opposite side, their scents of handmade tortillas, tacos and grilled chicken intermingling and making me realize that I was hungry. Tables and chairs were placed near the food stands. Temporary thatched roofs with colorful crepe paper provided relief from the setting sun. Children ran through the area, some with kites, and I could feel their excitement over the upcoming festivities.

We went directly to the only lodging in town: a small hotel that housed a restaurant and a delightful museum of relics from the Mayan site. Since they did not have a phone and cell service was nonexistent, accommodations were available on a first-come, first-serve basis. We were too late to get a room, but the woman who ran the hotel and restaurant, offered to rent me a tent. I took her up on her offer and Carlos said he would sleep in the car.

As we were finalizing our sleeping arrangements, a trio of men walked by. Carlos excused himself and went to talk to them. It turned out that they were shamans, and were heading over to conduct a ceremony on the altar there. Carlos asked if we could attend, and they said yes.

I immediately dragged Carlos over to the hotel registration area so that we could make our way over to the ceremony site as quickly as possible. While Antonio and I had conducted a couple ceremonies together, this would be the first time that I would have seen shamans work together for a ceremony. Carlos and I finished checking in and then, with me urging him to hurry up, walked down the hill, through part of the landing strip, and turned and walked up a small hill to the part of the archeological site that housed a large altar and three temples that aligned with the solstices and equinoxes.

By the time we got there, the ceremony had already started. A fire was burning in the center of the 6-foot diameter stone altar, and a shaman was standing next to it, chanting. He was wearing cropped black pants, a red patterned sash, no shirt, and a necklace of precious stones. A small group of musicians – two marimba players and two drummers – was to the side, playing a tempo that matched the shaman's chanting. They too were dressed for the occasion, with headdresses, painted faces, cropped pants and sashes. One was wearing a hat shaped like a bat's head, with fangs and a snout nose, and a long black cape with a red lining. Scattered around the area were twenty or so Guatemalans and a couple visitors watching the ceremony.

The shaman called in the spirit of the animals in the area and made an offering to them in gratitude. The man dressed as a bat came forward to the east side of the altar. He lay prostrate in front of the altar, and then stood up. The shaman gave him a metal bucket with some of the fire from the altar in it. The bat man then danced around the altar counterclockwise, spinning and turning, while holding the fire. The shaman walked to the altar, stepped onto it, and walked counterclockwise around the fire while continuing his chanting.

After dancing around the circumference of the alter several times, the bat gave the shaman the fire, knelt and then lay prostrate on the ground before returning to his place with the musicians.

A second musician came forward, wearing brown cropped pants with fringe, brown bands on his lower arms, and a brown woven sash. On his head was the preserved head of a deer, perched on top of his scarf that covered his hair. He stood to the west side of the altar, and then he too knelt and lay prostrate in front of it. With the rhythms from the remaining musicians, the deer man began to make his way around the altar. He was holding a rattle and shook it as he danced. The musicians began playing instruments that made bird noises as the deer danced. When he finished, he closed out his dance by kneeling and lying in front of the altar.

The shaman then invited the next, and final, group of animals to dance around the fire: the humans watching the ceremony. I stood on the sidelines, trying to decide whether or not to join the other dancers. I really wanted to but felt slightly self-conscious, since nearly all of the participants were Guatemalan and I didn't want to do something that might negate the ceremony. On the other hand, I was trying to take in all the new sights and rituals, and I didn't want to miss out on anything that might happen during this last dance. Ultimately, I decided to watch rather than dance. The group danced around the altar, taking the same path that the bat and deer had. After a while, the shaman motioned for the musicians to stop and he closed out the ceremony.

I watched as people dispersed and the shamans cleared their materials from the altar area. The smell of the copal-infused fire hung in the air and I still felt the energy of the drumming and chanting running through my body. My feet felt firmly planted into the ground, almost heavy. My breathing had slowed down as well, and I felt a deep peacefulness throughout my entire being. It was an effort to move, and I realized that the ceremony had connected me more deeply with Mother Earth. This must be what it feels like to be a tree, I thought. I was completely grounded and still but vibrating with life and energy. A vision of the Tree of Life flashed through my head, and I realized that part of the ceremony was focused on linking the three worlds—Upper (branches), Middle (trunk), and Lower (roots)—so that we could have easier communication with the spirit world. I connected to my heart and let love join the peacefulness already there, meditating.

It was nearly dark before I roused myself and started walking back to the village center. As I was leaving the temple area of the site, a woman came up to me and told me in Spanish that they would be back here at 3:00 a.m. to set up the altar for the big ceremony at 4:30 a.m. "Do you need help setting up?" I asked in Spanish. "I would be happy to help." She said yes, and I thanked her for letting me know.

I looked for Carlos. He had left me at the ceremony to find

Pedro's teenage son Jorge, who was at the event as well and was going to be performing. We met at the center green and decided to go the restaurant for dinner before taking in any of the cultural events on the stage.

Carlos and I sat down at the long table that ran down the middle of the restaurant for our dinner. Several minutes later, one of the shamans came in with his wife and another woman. They sat with us and Carlos introduced me. "This is my friend Jennifer, from the United States. She is a writer. Her first book is about shamanism, her experience becoming a shaman, and Mexico. It has won three awards. She is living here in Guatemala while she writes her next book."

I cringed inwardly at Carlos' introduction of me, because I normally wouldn't tell people about the book awards…or that I was a shaman. Especially to these shamans, because I wasn't certain that they would accept me. After all, I was not from their culture and I had not been trained in the same manner as they had been. I didn't know their rituals and ceremonies. What if they thought I was a fake or somehow not acceptable? But Carlos knew Guatemalans and their culture far better than I did, and the introduction opened up the door for conversation.

The shaman began by introducing himself as Oscar. He had seen me at the ceremony earlier, and asked me in English if I was planning on going to the ceremony in the morning. I told him yes, and that I was planning on going up with all of them at 3 a.m. to help with the preparations.

"Have you ever been to a fire ceremony?" he asked. When I said no, he replied, "You are going to enjoy it."

"I'm looking forward to it," I said.

After finishing our dinner, Carlos and I walked down to the landing strip and the stage. There were thousands of stars shining in the sky, and I stopped to look at them. They stretched on an eternity and reminded me that there is a much bigger life available to each of us, if we pause to look up and remember.

We found chairs near the front of the stage as a group of local young adults began demonstrating a local, cultural dance while wearing traditional clothing. This was followed by an appearance by Pablo Collado, a Guatemalan-born musician who has traveled around the world playing the flute, and then by some more dance demonstrations. There were presentations on the significance of the Mayan ruins and on the equinoxes and solstices. Finally, local students put together short skits on Mayan culture, history and mythology. As I watched the performances, my mind wandered to my "old" life. *If I were in San Francisco right now, out with friends, we would probably be at some fancy restaurant. While each type of night out has its merits, I really prefer this one right now.*

At 10 p.m., the stage darkened and the dance party started. Carlos and I decided to forgo the dancing in favor of getting a few hours of sleep before our early wake-up to help with the preparations for the ceremony. After making sure that my tent was set up properly and that I had everything I needed, Carlos got into the car and I crawled into the tent.

I had never camped before, and being in a tent was a new experience for me. I lay on my sleeping bag and listened to the sounds of the night and the other people camping near me. I could clearly hear the sounds of the dance party, and knew that I wasn't going to be able to sleep with all the noise. It was like trying to sleep in the middle of a nightclub.

I lay there with my eyes closed and relived the day's events and conversations. My mind shifted to Carlos and our friendship. He had done a lot to help me settle in and have such memorable experiences while here in Guatemala. I was fairly certain that my experience here would not have been nearly as wonderful if Carlos had not been involved. I sent a quick prayer of gratitude to the heavens for all he had done for me.

I listened to the music until it stopped at 2 a.m. The other shamans were starting to stir from their rooms, so I got dressed, woke up Carlos, and walked with him over to the temple site.

It was dark, even with the stars and a quarter moon in the sky. We arrived first, and I breathed in the silence and the expectant energy of the space. The pyramid loomed over the altar, casting a long shadow. I could barely make out the three temples opposite the pyramid. A light flickered through the trees, and the group of shamans began making their way over to where we stood. A second group arrived behind the pyramid and parked a large van overflowing with items needed for the ceremony.

After we unpacked the van, we got to work preparing the altar. Some of the shamans created a design on the altar in sugar, and then we placed pieces of copal on top of the design. This created the spiritual foundation for the sacred fire ceremony. Once the design was covered, all the remaining areas of the top of the altar were covered with the rest of the copal. Then we spread wood chips and wood slats on top of the copal. The shamans then laid candles across the top of the wood chips, aligning the colors with the directions: red for east, white for north, black for west, yellow for south, and green and blue for the center. Along the perimeter, we then placed flower petals that aligned with the colored candles: red, white, and yellow rose petals and purple statice as a gift to the universe. Finally, we encircled the perimeter with hay.

With the altar ready, the shamans got together to discuss the best way to do the ceremony. Each expressed his or her opinion, and very quickly, the ceremony parameters were defined.

We each were given some white candles, and after lighting them, we placed them on the altar to start the fire ceremony.

One shaman took a conch shell and blew into it to call in the ancestors and guides and signal the start of the ceremony. As the fire began to take hold, another of the shamans began. He had us face east, and began chanting and calling in the spirits of the east to be with us during the ceremony. We offered our thanks and paused in reflection. Then we turned and did the same for the other directions: west, south and north. By the time we turned to face north, the fire was roaring, and I needed to take a couple steps away from it because of the intense heat it was giving off.

We all turned to face the fire, and the shaman then began speaking. Since much of the dialogue was in one of the Mayan languages, I didn't understand what he was saying, but the meaning and feeling came across to me clearly as gratitude. When he finished talking, he offered some bread and sugar to the fire.

A woman picked up where he left off. She was dressed in a traditional Mayan outfit of a white shirt with purple and deep red embroidered flowers on it and a brightly colored skirt. Her red headscarf marked her as a shaman. But it was the intensity of her petitions that caught my attention. At times crying, she prayed earnestly and sincerely. I could feel her intentions in my heart and was moved, more than once, to tears with her.

One by one, the other shamans also spoke of their gratitude for Mother Earth, the animals and food provided, for the wisdom and history of the sacred site, for the Mayans and Guatemalans, for the sun and moon, for the planet, and for each other. As each shaman finished, he or she would make an offering to the fire of candles, bread, cacao, or sugar.

The expressions of gratitude continued for nearly two hours. The same group of musicians that were at the ceremony the night before was here this morning, and they played a number of rhythms that aligned with the words being spoken. As the shamans offered their gratitude, the night sky began to gradually lighten. At first, the temple buildings were simply dark shadows in the dark grey night, then they became clearer and clearer, until finally they were easily discernable as buildings and individual details became more apparent.

I watched the sky transform from black to deep purple to a grey-blue to a pink-gold color, waiting for the moment that the sun would come up over the horizon. As the ceremony reached its climax, I and the other shamans and people around the fire were given a handful of seeds to offer. I silently expressed my gratitude for everything that had aligned in my life to bring me to this point, right here, and asked that the universe be with me and all beings as we work to achieve higher consciousness. Then I made my way to the altar and let my offering join those of the others.

Around 6 a.m., the shamans stopped their offerings and everyone turned to the east and waited for the sun to come up and illuminate the interior of the middle temple. I climbed up the pyramid, where a large group of people had gathered, to watch. Carlos had gotten there before me, and he motioned me to join him. We all stood silently, waiting.

And then it happened. The sun broke free of the horizon and began its ascent into the sky. The sky shifted from pink-gold to orange and as I watched, the sun lit up the inside of the temple. One long sunbeam shot out from the temple directly into the fire on the altar while another went straight up into the sky. It was as if the universe was saying, "We accept your offerings and your gratitude and bring them to a higher level and higher place."

I stood watching from the pyramid for another five minutes, until the sun breached over the top of the temple. Then I made my way down the pyramid and back to the altar.

The musicians started playing again, and the shamans began dancing around the altar in celebration of the equinox. Oscar waved to me and invited me to join them, which I happily did. My heart was full when the ceremony was closed. I had felt like part of a bigger community and had such feelings of gratitude flowing through me that I didn't want it to end.

With the ceremony complete, Carlos and I walked back to the hotel to get some breakfast. About twenty minutes after we sat down, we were joined by a group of the shamans from the ceremony, including Oscar. Carlos introduced me to the newcomers, reiterating about my previous book and that I was writing another one on Guatemala.

One older man to my left reached out to shake my hand. Carlos told me that his name was Danielo and he was the head shaman. Danielo spoke no English, so Carlos served as an interpreter for me to ensure that I understood everything that Danielo was saying.

"Doing the work of a shaman is good," he began, "but too many people only come to us when they are sick or need something. They do not come to us or work with us when things are going well for them or when they are healthy. And this is a mistake. It is important to work with a shaman throughout life, because the shaman can help a person connect with his spirit and with love." I nodded.

Turning and looking directly at me, he asked, "What did you feel during the ceremony?"

I responded, "I felt love and gratitude—from each of you and from myself as well. I felt the intense energy of the site and the power of the ceremony. I felt it all deep in my heart and connected to it there." As I said the words, I moved my hands over my heart to emphasize my words.

Danielo nodded. "That is the work of the shaman. To help people connect to themselves."

Oscar joined the conversation. "When we create ceremony, we do not have a book that tells us the steps to take. We connect to our hearts to determine the best steps and actions to take. We let our hearts guide the approach of the ceremony."

"In many ways, it is easier when we do a smaller, more private ceremony for, say, a family or an individual, because there are no expectations of it being a big show," added Danielo. "Often people want to see something entertaining rather than participating in a heart-driven ceremony."

I agreed with them. "I think that when ceremony becomes highly structured, with steps in a book, it loses its authenticity and meaning. Instead of reflecting what is needed for the moment, it becomes a series of mindless—and heart-less if you will—steps to be completed. It loses its power because it is not connected to the heart."

Danielo and Oscar nodded. As I had been speaking, the female shaman I had observed at the ceremony had come and sat next to them.

I turned to the woman and said to her in Spanish, "I would like to give you a hug." She seemed surprised but smiled and stood up so I could. I continued, "I did not understand the words you were saying at the ceremony, because they were in the Mayan language, but I very clearly felt your emotions as you spoke them, and your emotions moved me and my heart."

She responded. "I was honoring the wisdom of the site of Uaxactun. There is so much wisdom and powerful energy here. We had a site with this type of energy and wisdom in the village where I live, but the site is no longer there. I felt grateful to be here and to be able to connect to the energy." I gave her another hug in agreement. We formally introduced ourselves, and I learned that her name was Fatima.

Carlos spoke to me in English. "One of the reasons why you were able to help and participate in the ceremony today was because of your genuine interest in the ceremony. Danielo and the others saw your interest. They told me that most people come to this event to eat, drink and have fun. They don't often see people who are here for the ceremonial aspect of the equinox."

Fatima continued. "We are having a ceremony in my village on May 2 and 3, and we would like you to attend." My jaw nearly dropped to the table, and I'm sure that my big smile gave away my answer before I said, "I would love to attend!" She smiled in response, and I gave her my business card with my contact information on it.

"I would like to have you visit my community," said Oscar. He explained that he lived in the highlands, near Lake Atitlan. "We can share and learn from each other, and I can teach you more about ceremonies. As you know, there were some things that you could not do during the ceremony this morning because you had not been trained and prepared to do them."

I gladly accepted his invitation as well, and we exchanged email addresses. I gave him a business card and information on my book. Danielo asked for a set as well, and said he would send me an email.

I could hardly believe what had just happened. Whatever fears I had had about not being welcomed and accepted by the shamans here were completely unfounded. It brought tears to my eyes, and I realized that I would never have had this experience if I hadn't overcome some deep-rooted fears and followed my heart.

With breakfast over, we all went our separate directions. Carlos and I decided to watch the exhibition of the traditional Mayan ball game. We walked over to the ball courts, but when we got there, no one was there. I found some shaded steps on the ball court structure and sat down.

"One of the things that really impressed me about the ceremony today—besides the fact that I was able to participate—was how well the shamans worked together. And I really liked that there were female shamans. When I worked with Antonio in Mexico, he introduced me to some male shamans, but no female shamans. In fact, he told me that he doesn't usually work with female shamans," I said.

"While I think that it's a matter of preference for Antonio, I don't agree with that perspective," I continued. "I think that the world has swung too far to the masculine and in many places suppressed the feminine. Both energies are needed, and, in my opinion, it is only when they are both present and balanced that true spiritual power and connection can be achieved."

Carlos was listening intently. "But are you saying that there needs to be both a male and female shaman for all ceremonies?"

"No, not at all," I replied. "I think for the large ceremonies, yes. But often a shaman is working individually with someone. It doesn't make sense for two people to be there. However, I do think that within the shaman, the male and female energies need to be balanced—or at very least be recognized, honored and leveraged when it is appropriate."

Carlos nodded.

The energy of the ceremony was buzzing through me and, combined with the all-nighter I had pulled the night before, was making me feel tired. We headed back to El Remate. I had a late lunch, ran a couple of errands, and by 8 p.m. was in bed and did the unthinkable: I slept for eleven hours straight. I woke up feeling refreshed and alert.

CHAPTER 6: SETTLING IN

I spent the day after the Spring Equinox ceremony relaxing and watching Juan Carlos and Lupe happily walk around my yard, eating bugs. I bought some grapes and discovered that they LOVED grapes. Enough so, that both of them started eating them out of my hand. I'd never spent time with chickens before, and was surprised by how much personality they had.

Lupe was the more daring of the two. She was the first one to eat out of my hand, and she would come running when I put my hand near the ground. She would also take food out of Juan Carlos's beak if it was something that she wanted. She liked to dance and wandered into the doorway of my outdoor living room the other day and bopped along with the music that was playing.

She was also a little bit of a diva. With the grapes, she preferred that I held the grape for her while she ate it. If the grape happened to fall out of my hand onto the ground, she would give me a look that very clearly showed her disappointment in me.

Juan Carlos was a bit more standoffish, but he was slowly warming up to me...or at least to the corn and grapes that I gave him as treats. He felt compelled to announce his presence at regular intervals, but luckily not before 5 a.m.

Both of them were fascinated with my outdoor living room. They would walk up to the doorway and stick their heads in, looking around. I worked to train them to stay out of the living room. If they saw me, they might place just one foot in, while looking at me. It was almost as if they were testing me. As soon as I said their names and "no" they would step back out.

If I wasn't in the living room, they would carefully walk in, making what sound like secretive clucking noises. I imagined that they were saying to each other, "Shhhh, quiet. We don't want her to know we're in here." I could always tell when they were in the living room because they sounded different. When I caught them in the act, they wouldn't even bother to try to look apologetic, but would hightail it out.

At night, Lupe would put herself into the little chicken coop that I got and go to sleep. Juan Carlos, however, wanted to be tucked in every night. When he was ready for bed, he would come over to the living room, and I would pick him up, bring him to the coop, and put him in. If I happened to be in the house, he would march right into the house.

A few days ago, I saw the first scorpion in my hut since I got Juan Carlos and Lupe. I carefully caught the scorpion, put it in a container, and brought it out to them. You would have thought that it was Christmas morning. They were so excited! Unfortunately for them, but fortunately for the scorpion, the scorpion made it through the fence to the neighbor's yard.

We had gotten into a routine, and they knew that when I sat on the front steps, they were going to get treats. It was one of my favorite parts of the day, since I would slow down and focus solely on Juan Carlos and Lupe. As their trust in me grew, I marveled over the gift that having and caring for them gave me. I began to learn their moods and how they communicated with me and would use that information to keep them safe, healthy and entertained. In return, they gave me the gifts of peace and connection to another living thing while I was five thousand miles away from my home. Relaxing with them helped me ground and integrate everything that happened during the Spring Equinox ceremony.

The next morning I walked downtown and ran into my friend Felipe. He was very excited to see me and told me that he had a gift for me. I didn't understand the words he was saying in Spanish until he pulled something out of his pocket: two wild boar tusks. He had been up in the mountains, exploring, when he came across a dead boar. He had never seen one in the jungle before, and as he looked at it, the thought popped into his head that I needed the tusks. He didn't question the thought, and, with a quick swipe of his machete, he got them and brought them back to El Remate.

I jumped up and down. As a power animal, Wild Boar is a warrior and helps people overcome their fears and move forward courageously with their lives. This was exactly what I have been working on with this last major transition, and my sense was that the tusks were a gift and sign from the universe of the progress I have been making. I gave Felipe a kiss on the cheek and thanked him profusely.

We sat down on the benches in front of Julian's restaurant and looked more closely at them. They were covered with tartar and plaque but were roughly the same size. Julian walked by and Felipe asked him if he had any sandpaper. He did, and soon we were both cleaning the tusks. I had to chuckle. My mother is a dental hygienist, and here I was, doing her job...on boar tusks with sandpaper!

It didn't take long to restore the tusks to a creamy white color. I couldn't visit too long with Felipe because I was conducting a shamanic session for Marta that afternoon and needed to prepare for it. Felipe and I made arrangements to meet the next day to go visit a man he knew that could drill holes in them so I could string them on a necklace.

I had been doing quite a few shamanic sessions since I'd moved to Guatemala. In fact, the number of sessions I did each week had increased significantly. I didn't know whether it was because I had said "yes" to the universe or because of the book and the book tour, but I was grateful for it either way. However, today's session with Marta was the first in-person session I'd had in Guatemala. She came to my house, and we did the session there. As I had done with my remote clients, we began by talking about what was going on in her life and what she wanted the session to focus on. I then had her lie down on the bed, and I began playing the drumming track I used to journey and connect to the spirit world. Once I finished the journey, I shared with her the results from the session. With each client session, I was honored by the trust my clients put in me when they shared deeply personal aspects of their lives; with Marta, I felt even more so because she was even more vulnerable and open by being there in person with me.

It was interesting how things were unfolding. I'd been going through my days here without my usual "Type A" driven approach of setting daily goals and attacking them so that I would be able to cross them off my list. Instead, I'd set some rather broad intentions (write a book, spend time with the energy of the Mayan sites, continue to grow and expand my reach and ability to live my life purpose), and had done my best to go with the flow and see what opportunities came to me. There had been a number of times in my past when I had tried to force things to happen, or had had to work really hard to make something come together. And there had been those times when I had had things come together beautifully. I realized that in those times, I had had a different attitude and approach. I had been clear on what I wanted, but I hadn't sweated all the details. Instead, I had been open to whatever came my way and had been pleasantly surprised to see that everything fell into place without much effort. I wanted to cultivate more of that approach to life, and was using my time here in Guatemala as a testing ground.

I closed my eyes and checked in with the universe to see if there were other things for me to learn while I was in Guatemala.

> *This time here is a time for you to deepen your learning and understanding of how to trust. So much more can happen when you are open to and trust in the universe and your guides. This is a time for you to learn how to turn and give all of your concerns to a higher power so you can just relax and be in the present moment. When you are able to do that, you are able to accomplish so many things.*

The visit to Uaxactun for the Spring Equinox was a perfect example. The "Type A" version of me would have spent a lot of time trying to figure out how to make a reservation in advance, get a copy of the agenda for the event, and possibly even tried to determine who was going to be there. I would have wanted to leave for the site first thing in the morning and would have had the entire day planned with what I wanted to do, where I wanted to go, and who I wanted to meet. And then I would have worked the plan…and possibly missed out on something even better.

Instead, I forced myself to not worry about making a reservation (this was tough for me!) and told myself that whatever events I ended up going to would be the perfect ones for me. I let Carlos' schedule define when we left for the site. While it is impossible to say what would have happened if I had approached the ceremony my "old" way, I could say with certainty that I was much more relaxed when Carlos and I got to the site. I wasn't watching the clock against some predefined calendar of activities to do. And, I truly believed that by being relaxed and just being open to whatever came my way, I was able to have an experience that most have not.

◆ ◆ ◆

On Tuesday night I had Enrico, Isabel and Valentina over to my house for dinner. While Carlos and Felipe have both eaten here, this was my first "real" dinner party, and I wanted it to go well. Carlos had suggested that I make a Guatemalan meal, but I didn't want to do that. For starters, I was not familiar with Guatemalan cooking. Secondly, I was of the opinion that people like to try different foods, and part of the fun of being a foreigner was that I could make something different for them.

My biggest challenge was coming up with something that could be made in a kitchen that has two pots and one pan and four gas burners and could easily be adapted for vegetarian and meat eaters. I decided to go with a Chinese menu and made sweet and sour chicken and vegetables over rice and a simple salad with ginger dressing, followed by ice cream and fruit for dessert. They loved it and asked for the recipes so they could make it at home.

The funniest part of the evening happened while I was cooking dinner and talking to Enrico and Isabel. It was starting to get dark, and I had forgotten about Juan Carlos and his nightly routine. He wandered into the hut, looking for me, but also very nervous because of the additional people in the room. I couldn't stop what I was doing, so I told him to go outside. Of course he didn't do as I said, and instead began running around the hut, clucking and flapping his wings. Enrico decided that he would catch him, and a lively chase throughout the hut ensued, while Isabel and I laughed at Juan Carlos' antics. Enrico finally caught Juan Carlos and I told him how to put him to bed so he would stay there.

I continued to be surprised by how much people have embraced me here. I felt like I was almost part of Enrico's extended family. He was one of 13 children, of which 12 were still alive. I've met four of his siblings, their children, and his parents, and they have invited me to different family events. Next week I will be going to a wedding with Enrico's sister, Maria. The week after that I will be at a birthday party for one of the children.

Pedro, Camila and two of their children stopped by the other night to visit. And later this week, Enrico and Isabel have invited me to their house for an early birthday lunch.

I can't believe it's almost my birthday already. The last year has flown by and I've made so many changes in my life. When I look back at what my life was like a year ago versus today, every aspect of my life is different: last year at this time I was living in San Francisco, working in a high-powered consulting firm as an executive, flying all over the country for work and fun, and dating a guy that I had a lot of fun with. Today, I was living in a hut in Guatemala, working as a shaman while writing my next book, without a car or easy access to an airport, and happily single and friends with that guy. On the outside everything had changed. On the inside, I was still "me," but I felt like I had made a lot of changes internally as well. I'd learned to trust and release what I need to a higher power. I tried to start from my heart in nearly all interactions. And I felt as if I had grown in my shamanic connections and capabilities.

Given all the changes that occurred in the past year, I'm pretty excited about this next one. I decided to spend a little time meditating to see if there was anything specific I should be focusing on.

> *You will continue to strip away what you no longer need in your life and will create a life that has more freedom than you even have right now. As you make your life changes, we will support you in your quest for expansion and freedom. Continue to focus on the positive in your life. There will always be drama swirling around people, your task is to not get pulled into it. Trust your feelings and intuition, and keep coming from your heart. Let go of any doubt that you may have about yourself and your abilities.*

I definitely liked the idea of going through life even less encumbered than I was now. I liked the freedom and ease of living this way. There was so much less to worry about.

As a birthday treat to myself, I planned to spend two nights at Las Lagunas, the resort that I first stayed in last year and most recently stayed while looking for a place to live here in Guatemala, and have a massage on my actual birthday. As much as I loved my little hut, I was really looking forward to having air conditioning, a hot shower, and sleeping two nights without mosquito netting. I might even be able to sleep past 5 a.m. since Juan Carlos won't be nearby!

◆ ◆ ◆

Thursday morning I met Felipe at 6 a.m. in front of Julian's restaurant. I had hired him to take me on a day-long hike through the jungle, and we decided to start early since the temperature was expected to hit 100 degrees. I packed some snacks, water, sunblock and bug spray for us; he brought two small backpacks and two machetes, which we would use if we needed to clear a trail. Once I loaded up my backpack and slung my machete over my shoulder we started. I felt pretty badass wearing the machete, kind of like Indiana Jones.

With Felipe leading the way, we walked through the jungle along roads and trails to Ixlu, a nearby Mayan archeological site. Many of the structures in the site had not been restored. The unrestored buildings were covered with greenery—trees, shrubs and small plants—turning what was once a pyramid, temple or palace into a mound of new life. Birds of all sizes and colors were in the trees, and at one point we saw a monkey overhead. Scattered on the ground throughout the site are bits of pottery, knifepoints and bone.

We were the only ones there, and I felt the calming energy at the site. The sun worked its way through the vegetation and illuminated patches of the jungle floor with a soft golden glow. Even the birds were quiet for a moment. I stopped and let the energy of the site wash over me.

We wandered through the site and Felipe showed me where the temples, pyramids and ball courts were. We sat in the jungle on the roots of a large tree and had a snack before continuing on. As we worked our way through one clearing, I saw a man and a young boy sitting under a tree. Felipe explained to me that the man worked at the site and that I would need to sign in.

I smiled and said "hola" to the little boy and took the clipboard from the man. I looked at the other names on the sheet of paper and realized that the most recent one had signed in a week ago. This man (and possibly his child) had come to work for a week and not had any tourists visit the site. I finished signing in and handed the clipboard back. Felipe and I continued on our way.

We followed a path through the site and had started looping

back so we could begin our walk back to El Remate when something large and black ran across the trail in front of us. It was at least two feet tall, ran on four legs and had a long tail. It went by too fast for us to identify what it was, but it got me to thinking about the black jaguar that ran across my path in Mexico. I wondered if it was another jaguar and I took it as a sign that I was on the right path.

We walked a little further debating what the animal was. The sun was high in the sky, and we were both hot and sweaty. I estimated that it was at least 100 degrees. We had drunk the two bottles of water that I had brought and were now working on the gallon jug of water that Felipe had been carrying in his backpack. We decided to walk to the nearby lake, San Peten, and found a small glade at the end of the lake where we could sit, rest and have another snack.

The water looked inviting, but Felipe said that there were crocodiles in the water, so we couldn't go swimming. I suggested that we wade in the shallow area. We took off our shoes, rolled up our pants, and carefully made our way in. Felipe cautioned me to move slowly and not splash around, since the noise and movement could attract a crocodile. We waded out to about our knees. The cold water felt so refreshing that I sat down in the water in my jeans and t-shirt and let it wash away the grime from the hike. Felipe laughed at me and then joined me. We sat, submerged in the water, and explored the rocks at the bottom of the lake.

"How do you like El Remate?" he asked.

"I'm really enjoying it here. It's very different than San Francisco, but it feels like home to me. Have you ever been to the United States?"

"Yes. I used to live in Connecticut and worked painting houses," Felipe responded.

"Really? Where in Connecticut? Most of my family lives there."

"I was down in Fairfield County. I really liked it there. It was so pretty."

It was wonderful being able to talk to someone who had been to a part of the world where I had lived. Our conversation was cut short, however, when a line of bubbles formed on the surface of the water several feet away from us. That was the sign Felipe was waiting for, and we quickly got out of the water in case the bubbles were made by a crocodile swimming along the bottom of the deeper part of the lake.

Rested, cooled off and with full stomachs, we continued our trek back to El Remate. As we neared the town, we passed by an obviously vacant house. It was roughly square in shape, made out of cement with a tiled porch that ran across the front and around to one side. Pillars were spaced evenly across the porch, with cement scrolled accents hanging down between each. A corrugated metal roof covered the entire structure. Something struck me about the house, and I went to peer through the windows.

The house didn't appear to have ever been lived in, and it looked as if it was still under construction. None of the interior or exterior walls had been painted, and there were some long metal rods in the kitchen. Wires hung from the ceiling and walls where light fixtures or switches would be hung. Openings showed where appliances and sinks would eventually go. My mind immediately started imagining what the house would look like completed.

I walked from window to window, looking at each room, and, without being conscious of it, I found myself mentally arranging my furniture in the house. As soon as I caught myself, I shook my head. Having a house was not on my list of things I wanted. But even as I thought this, I was drawn back to the house like a moth to a flame.

I couldn't fathom why I was so attracted to this house, but it was undeniable. I wondered out loud to Felipe, "Do you think it is for sale?"

"Yes, I think so. I will ask around to find out for you."

I took photos of the house, and then we continued on to El Remate. I tried to think of why I would want to buy a house here, or anywhere for that matter. I had no intention of living permanently in Guatemala. I'd owned four houses in my life and had lost money on three of the four. In each instance, I felt trapped and like a slave to the house. I had vowed to never own a house again and truly enjoyed the freedom of apartment living.

And hadn't I just gotten a message about increasing my personal freedom even more this next year of my life? I couldn't see how owning a house—and one that needed more work to finish it—fit into the picture. Maybe the heat was frying my brain...

Once I got home, I sent a text to my friend Arthur asking him how crazy he thought it would be if I bought a house here in

Guatemala. He responded almost immediately, "On a scale of one to ten, about a nine. House equals roots put down and a permanent presence and relationships. It's so interesting that you are feeling that strong! Cool."

Roots. I had been more of a gypsy or nomad most of my life. I'd lived in 19 different homes in my life, which averaged out to about 2.6 years in each. And for the last 15 years or so, I had spent most of my time staying in hotels with my consulting job. I'd never really had an overwhelming desire to settle down in one place. On the contrary, I tended to get restless when I'd been in one place too long and the itch to go somewhere different hit (even if it was just changing neighborhoods in the same city). What the hell was I thinking?

"I'm not sure I'm supposed to have roots in one place," I texted back.

"I love your commitment to the journey and your spiritual roots. Maybe there is a spiritual house for roots, rather than a physical. Just heard that," he replied.

"That I could get behind," I responded. "And maybe my spiritual house will have air conditioning!"

He laughed and we texted good night to each other.

I tried to put the house out of my mind and focused on client work for the next couple of days. But it kept coming to the forefront. On Sunday, as Carlos and I were on the way to Yaxha and Topoxte, two Mayan archeological sites in the area, I told him about the house. He, of course, wanted to see it so we took a slight detour as I gave him the directions.

We walked around and looked in all of the windows, and he too felt that it was a very nice house. He much preferred the style of my little hut and had dreams of building something similar on his land, but could understand why I would like this house.

There was a young man in his late teens or early twenties in the lot next to the house, and Carlos asked him if he knew the owner of the house. The young man told Carlos that his uncle owned the house and was hoping to sell it. After a brief discussion, Carlos told me that he knew the owner very well and that the young man was going to contact the uncle and get a price for me. I had no idea what the Guatemalan housing market was like, but I did know that in San Francisco, a house like this would be out of my price range. It would be interesting to see what a house like this would go for in

Guatemala.

We got back in Pedro's car and started driving to Yaxha and Topoxte. Carlos told me about a friend of his that had a house that was on our way that had gardens of orchids and suggested that we stop. I readily agreed, and shortly thereafter we pulled over and walked a narrow path to a house tucked back from the road.

Carlos' friend was on the front porch in a hammock and got up to greet us, telling me his name was Juan. Carlos introduced me, telling Juan that my name was Jennifer. "Ahhhh," he said, "Jennifer Lopez!" I laughed and said that yes, I was Jennifer Lopez. I'd heard the joke several times already and had fun playing along.

And then Juan asked me the question that I was getting tired of answering. "Why aren't you married?"

I realized that this was a cultural difference between Guatemala and the United States, and I had experienced the same thing in Mexico. People here typically live in family units and women marry by their late teens or early 20s. Women are cared for by men, not in an oppressive way, but rather in an honorable, respectful manner. In some ways, it reminds me of the Cherokee proverb that states:

> *"A woman's highest calling is to lead a man to his soul so as to unite him with Source. A man's highest calling is to protect woman so she is free to walk the earth unharmed."*

It was rare for a marriageable-aged woman to be single, and even rarer for her to live alone. In fact, of all the people that I had met here, the only woman who was single was Marta—and she was not Guatemalan. Carlos, Felipe and Julian were all single, but there was a different standard for men. Men could live alone (but usually don't) without much concern.

I'd felt the concern for my safety and their natural desire to protect a woman from Carlos, Felipe, Enrico, Pedro and Julian. I'd been admonished to lock my door, avoid walking alone, be extra careful during Semana Santa (the week leading up to Easter) because of all the people who come to the area, and to avoid certain people or places. It went much deeper than protecting from harm from others, though. They would take my arm or hand if the road or path was uneven to prevent me from falling or open doors for me. Carlos and Felipe had both shown up at my house on several occasions with food to make sure I had enough to eat and that and didn't need anything. Julian offered me rides home on his motorbike so I wouldn't have to walk. Carlos brought over a different type of mosquito netting for me because he thought it would be better than the one I had. The list goes on…

That's not to say that I hadn't experienced this type of care or attention in the United States; I have. But there was something different about it here. There was a genuine concern for women and their wellbeing that went beyond just the women in one's immediate circle of friends and family. It was so tightly woven into the culture and fabric of everyday living here that, from my experience, it came naturally to men to think protecting women.

My experiences here led to an interesting dichotomy within me. On the one hand, I was a feminist through and through. I truly believed that all people were equal and should be treated as such, and that all people, regardless of gender, should have access the same opportunities in life. And I had a very strong "I can do it myself" independent streak in me. But on the other hand, there was something sweet and thoughtful about this treatment that allowed me to release some of the mental burdens that I'd been used to carrying by myself. I'd actually started to ask Pedro and Enrico their opinions on different things rather than just coming up with a solution myself.

I was about to give Juan my standard response of "because I haven't met the right guy" when he interrupted my thoughts and said with a big smile, "You should marry Carlos!"

The "right guy" line wasn't going to work, because I could tell that Juan would start selling Carlos' virtues to me and would most likely have the marriage ceremony scheduled before we left his house. Carlos and I had had many conversations about the fact that we were just friends, and how grateful we were for our friendship. I debated about telling Juan the truth about why I wasn't married, but Carlos spoke up first and told Juan that we were just good friends.

I hoped that Carlos' answer would deter Juan, but it didn't.

Instinctively I knew that it would be difficult for Juan to understand the deeper reason why I was single, but I decided to give it a try.

"At this point in my life I have too much work to do and don't have the time to also dedicate to a relationship. I am traveling and do not know where my work is going to take me. Relationships require a lot of work, and it wouldn't be fair of me to be in a relationship that I could not devote time to."

Juan looked at me and shook his head. It was clear that he disagreed with me and couldn't understand why someone would choose to be single.

When Carlos had asked me the same question a few weeks ago, I had explained that I truly felt that I was meant to be single for at least this part of my life so that I could have the experiences and growth opportunities that I'd been having. It was difficult enough to orchestrate all the life changes I'd been going through for one person. To get two people aligned to take on such drastic changes at the same time and agree on where to go and what to do next was near impossible in my mind. Carlos had accepted my answer, and shared that while he struggled with being single, he did like the flexibility it gave him.

In all honesty, I didn't think I would be having the experiences I'd been having if I were part of a couple.

As a single woman traveling alone, I was far more approachable than if I were with someone else. Of course, I did sometimes get some unwanted attention, but the benefits of traveling alone far outweigh the annoyance of the occasional unwanted pass. I had an elderly woman in Japan approach me in a tiny temple and we ended up talking and sharing a simple meal together. It was an experience I will never forget. In Greece I went out on a date with a local to an amazing bar that I would never have found by myself. The first time I was here, Carlos took me to meet some local people as part of the Day of the Dead celebration and I was able to hear from them the significance of the celebration and stories of their own personal losses. In Mexico, Antonio brought me to a sacred site that isn't in any tour books that helped catapult my personal healing.

At some point, I would like to have someone share my life with me, but for now, I was happy and content with my life as it was.

We left Juan's house and continued on our way. Our first stop was Topoxte, a small Mayan site located on an island in the middle of the Yaxha River and near the Mayan site of Yaxha. Carlos arranged for a boat, and we were soon on our way.

It was late afternoon, and we were the only ones there. We got out of the boat and climbed the stone steps that had been built by the Mayans. A path wound through the trees and jungle vegetation.

As we walked to the site, Carlos pointed out some of different birds, showed me where a boa constrictor lived and told me stories of experiences he had had in the past at the site.

Like many of the sites I have visited, Topoxte has only been partially excavated. We walked by a number of mounds of earth, covered with trees and brush that hid temples, buildings and pyramids. The energy here felt different though. The trees were different than others that I had seen—long branches and roots twisted around each other, creating the illusion that the trees were trying to run or reach out to something. It felt slightly eerie, and I stopped on the path and closed my eyes to feel it more deeply.

"No, it's not eerie," I thought to myself. "But more like there is an expectant waiting here, as if something is going to happen. Or that something was stopped in mid-action and is waiting for it to start up again." I wondered which it was as we walked to the ceremonial plaza.

The ceremonial plaza had been partially excavated. It was much smaller than the ceremonial plazas I had visited at other sites, but had a pyramid, temple, palace, and viewing station. Through the trees you could see the lagoon, and a constant breeze kept the temperature down. In front of the pyramid were a series of small, flat circular stones that had been used as altars by the Mayans.

Carlos decided to go take some photos of the birds on the island, leaving me alone in the plaza. Inspired by the tranquility and energy of the site, I pulled a small candle out of my purse, lit it, and placed it in the center of one of the altars. I closed my eyes and expressed my gratitude for the site, the many blessings in and aspects of my life that had brought me to this point, and my many friends and family. I then connected to my heart and worked to build up the energy there, channeling in pure love from the universe. Using a process similar to what I had done when Carlos and I were at Yaxha the previous November, I breathed into my heart, letting the energy there grow until my body was tingling with it. Once my heart energy had increased significantly, I sent it out to the planet. I breathed in and sent out love for several minutes, then opened my eyes. As I began closing out the ceremony, the wind from the lagoon blew out my candle and completed the ceremony for me.

We made our way back by boat and headed over to Yaxha, which was just a few minutes away. I had been there before, so

Carlos and I leisurely walked around the park-like grounds, looking at the various buildings. Our goal was to watch the sunset from the top of the pyramid in the main plaza. At a quarter to five, we made our way over to the pyramid and climbed the stairs to the top.

The pyramid sits higher than the jungle treetops, and from the top you have a stunning view of the entire Mayan complex and the Yaxha river. The sun was bathing everything in a pink and golden glow and reflecting off the top of the water. There were a few other people on the pyramid and we sat in silence as Mother Nature did her work to complete the day and paint the sky in a variety of colors. The sun sank lower in the sky, and Carlos pulled a flute out of his backpack. Its haunting notes filled the air as the sun disappeared beneath the horizon.

CHAPTER 7: CELEBRATING AND OPENING UP MORE

My birthday was this week. It's hard to be away from friends and family on holidays and special days, and I figured it would be a quiet, but relaxing, day. While I had many new friends here, I certainly didn't expect them to know or remember the day.

I was wrong.

On the Friday before my birthday, Isabel invited me over to her house in the afternoon. Enrico and Valentina picked me up. We stopped by Enrico's parents' house to get them and then drove the short distance to Enrico and Isabel's house.

Isabel was waiting on the front porch. After some chitchat, she motioned to me to join her in the kitchen, where she showed me a beautiful cake decorated with strawberries (one of my favorite fruits), smiled and said, "Feliz cumpleanos!" We all sat around the table, ate cake and talked.

On Sunday, Carlos had taken me to Topoxte and Yaxha and out to lunch for my birthday. He also had bought me a Snickers bar to enjoy at the top of the pyramid while we watched the sunset, but unfortunately it was too hot that day and the candy bar melted. We had a good laugh and turned our attention back to the setting sun.

Early Monday morning Marta and I went for a walk. We ended up exploring a part of the hilly area of El Remate that neither of us had been to. The views of the lake from the top of the hills were incredible, and by 6:30 a.m. we were getting hungry. We made our way to El Arbol restaurant, where Marta announced that she was buying me breakfast for my birthday.

At 6:00 a.m. on Tuesday, Julian pulled up to the front gate of my little hut and set off firecrackers. It's tradition in Guatemala to light firecrackers in front of the house of the person having a birthday on their birthday…although the tradition was to set them off at 4:00 a.m. Julian let me sleep in a little.

Later that day, I checked into Las Lagunas Boutique Hotel. The woman at the front desk remembered me from my last visit, and after greeting me by name, said, "Happy birthday! We are so glad you decided to spend your special day with us.

"Thank you!" I replied, trying to figure out how she knew it was my birthday. *Oh*, I thought to myself, *I bet it was Enrico. He works here.* She gave me the key to my bungalow and we walked over to it together, talking.

"I hear you're living in El Remate," she said. "How long will you be there?"

"About four months," I replied. "I'm writing my next book, and wanted to come to Guatemala to write it. You speak English very well. Where did you learn it?"

She explained that her family had lived in the United States for a while, and she went to school while they were living there. "But keeping up my English skills takes work. I try to read as many English books as possible so I can keep practicing."

I offered to bring her a copy of my published book, and she happily thanked me. With one last question about whether or not I needed anything, she left and I surveyed my bungalow. On the desk was a basket of fruit, with a note from the hotel manager wishing me a happy birthday. I immediately ate the strawberries.

I woke up early on my birthday and watched the sun rise over the lake, rousing the white herons that then began searching for their breakfast. Last year at this time I was in San Francisco. My mom had come out to celebrate my birthday with me. What a difference a year makes! My mind went over all the changes in my life since then, and I smiled to myself, happy with the direction my life was taking. After a leisurely hot shower and time spent responding to birthday greetings on Facebook and email, I went to the main building for breakfast. Miguel, one of the waiters that I had met when I stayed here in February, greeted me and wished me a happy birthday. I thanked him, and when he came back to take my order, requested fresh fruit and granola for breakfast.

Miguel came out of the kitchen a few minutes later, with a huge smile on his face. Instead of the granola and fruit I had ordered, he was carrying a large plate with a piece of cheesecake on it with two lit candles. He placed the plate in front of me, singing Feliz Cumpleanos to me. Written in raspberry sauce was *Happy Birthday Jennifer* on the border of the plate.

I laughed and thanked him. He asked me if I still wanted my original order, and I told him no. There was no way I was going to turn down cake for breakfast!

Enrico had told me that I needed to take the Monkey Tour again. The monkeys live on an island in the middle of the lagoon. They're spider monkeys that had been taken from the wild when they were babies and sold illegally as pets. Now rescued, they live on this island and are fed daily by the resort staff. I had taken the tour when I was at the resort in November, but this time there was something new—a three-month old baby.

As luck would have it, I was the only one on the tour. I boarded the small boat and we went to the island. Spider monkeys tended to stay in the trees and cannot swim, so the resort fed them by putting food on a wooden device that resembled a swimming pool skimmer. The food was put in the wooden basket and then extended out to the monkeys. Today's meal was carrots and beets. Since I was the only one, they let me feed them. The wooden basket was heavy, but the monkeys eagerly helped me by grabbing the basket and pulling it up to where they were in the trees.

I scanned the half dozen monkeys and saw the baby monkey clutching firmly to his mother's back. His large eyes filled his head and he missed nothing. I made sure to give the mother extra food.

While I was feeding the monkeys, one of the monkeys must have decided that I wasn't moving fast enough because she leapt from the trees onto the boat and walked over to the bucket of food. She reached in, took out two carrots, and carried them over to the seat next to me. She sat down and ate while I fed the rest. When she'd finish her carrots, she'd walk back over to the bucket, take two more, and sit back down.

Once we gave out all of the food, the monkeys in the trees retreated, but the one on the boat continued to sit there, even after the captain started it back up. Apparently she did this often, because he didn't seem concerned. The captain maneuvered the boat over alongside the vegetation hanging over the lagoon and she slowly made her way from the boat to the trees. As I watched her move, I could easily see why she was called a spider monkey—the long legs, arms and tail made her look just like a spider as she climbed up the trees.

That afternoon I went for my massage. The spa had recently opened at the resort, and rivaled any that I had been to in San Francisco. I got there early and was able to enjoy a steam sauna before my massage. I was in a state of total relaxation during the massage when a random thought popped into my head:

Can I have freedom and be in a relationship?

Where did *that* come from? My initial answer to myself was no, but I realized that I was probably limiting myself and my perspective of what a relationship could be. I decided to spend more time with the question at a later time.

That night I told Arthur about the question. We both agreed that in my massage I had gotten to the heart of what was preventing me from fully searching for and engaging in a relationship. In fact, it probably explained why I tended to gravitate toward long-distance relationships with men who weren't fully committed to being in a relationship: between the distance and the lack of commitment, I didn't have to worry about giving up my freedom.

I tried to think of an example of a committed relationship where both people were free to fully be themselves. In most of my relationships, my partner tried to change or suppress aspects of me. One didn't like it that I traveled and wanted me to change my career so that I wasn't traveling. Another felt very threatened that I earned more money than he did and made our salaries into an unhealthy competition. A third wanted to just be with me when things were going well in our lives; any time a life challenge came up, such as the death of my grandmother, he wouldn't be available to comfort me. Arthur explained to me how his relationship with his girlfriend was one where they both respect the strengths and flaws of the other person. They were fully present with each other and brought their love forward in each moment, with no expectations on the other. They also supported and encouraged each other in their individual pursuits and goals.

I would be open to a partnership like that!

◆◆◆

After two leisurely pampered days at Las Lagunas, I returned to my hut. The next afternoon Maria was coming over for some "girl time." I had gone grocery shopping the day before and then cleaned my little hut. This morning I prepared some snacks for us and figured we could walk to town and go out to either El Arbol or Las Gardenias for an early dinner so she could easily catch a bus back home.

As I sat waiting for her to arrive, I thought about the past week and all the ways the people here had shown me kindness. A pickup truck pulled up in front of my house and broke my thoughts. Maria was in the back, with about a dozen other people from her family, including her mother, Pedro, Camelia, and their children, calling out my name.

Oh, no! I thought. *It looks like the entire family is here! Did I misunderstand our afternoon and that it was going to be just the two of us? I don't have enough food!* I mentally went through the contents of my tiny refrigerator and pantry area, and knew that it was going to be impossible to offer them all something.

I was frantically trying to think of a solution when Pedro lit a string of firecrackers off the back of the pickup truck. Everyone yelled "Feliz cumpleanos!" and I realized that it was a birthday party for me. Marta, Carlos and Julian soon joined them as well.

Within minutes they had unloaded the contents of the truck, which, in addition to all the people, included a table, a bunch of chairs, a boom box and CDs, two birthday cakes, food, beverages, candy, balloons, and more firecrackers. It was truly a party in a pickup! Only a few short minutes later my house was decorated with balloons everywhere, a throne-like chair complete with palm fronds was made for me, and food and beverages were set up.

Pedro pulled me aside and told me about a couple Guatemalan birthday traditions that he knew from living in the United States for a while were different than what I was familiar with.

My friends were lining up for the first tradition. They had me remove my shoes and stand next to the table with the birthday cakes, but far enough away that I couldn't reach the table. They all sang a birthday song, and as they did they poured pitchers of water over my head. By the time they were done, I was laughing and drenched from head to toe while they clapped and cheered.

I dried off and got changed for the second tradition: as they sang I had to put my face into one of the cakes so I would get frosting all over it. I looked at Pedro with some skepticism, and he chuckled and pulled out his phone. His birthday had been a couple weeks prior, and he showed me the video of him with frosting on his face.

I told him that I thought they had the order wrong—they should put the frosting on the face first and then give the bath. He laughed and gave me the instructions for what I was to do. My friends sang the birthday song again and when it was time, I did a light face plant into one of the cakes. With everyone cheering, I then began to cut the cakes and the party began in earnest.

By the time the party ended, my face hurt from all the smiling and laughing. I sat in my now-empty hut and replayed the afternoon in my mind. *Everyone has really welcomed me here and made me part of their family. I felt some happy tears well up in my eyes and I knew without a doubt that I was exactly where I was supposed to be for my birthday.*

◆ ◆ ◆

My final birthday gift came on Sunday. Renee, the woman from France that I had met about a month ago when she was here on vacation, and I had decided to trade services. I had given her a complimentary shamanic session a few weeks back, and today was my turn. She channels messages from the spirit world and was going to give me some more details over the phone on both my romantic life and life path.

She started by talking about romance and an intimate partnership. "There are romantic partners out there for you, but you need to change the energy in the relationships. You had to be grown up at a very young age and care for others. You became like a mother, and developed a very limited perception of what a mother is. You need to bring more woman energy into the equation. You have to change the fundamental energy within yourself to change the types of romantic partners you are attracting."

She began working on my solar plexus area to help transmute and change the polarity of the energy there so that my "woman energy" would increase. "Part of the problem," she said, "is that you are so powerful that you easily take on the charge and energy of the other person. This is a good skill to have as a shaman, and it helps you in that work, but it is not good for intimate relationships. If you keep doing that, you will be dead very soon, because all the energy you take on will hurt and then kill you."

Renee continued to work on my energy centers and explain what she was doing. "In all of your experiences with men, there hasn't been much clarity about the relationship. With your powerful energy, you make the focus of the relationship on the other person so he can transform, but instead you should exert the energy for yourself."

"It is time for you to fully enter into your own energy. You are a powerful shaman and an unlimited woman. You know this is true in your heart. But you have to be open to it. You have a lot of armor around you."

As she was working to remove the armor, an animal came forward to work with me. This animal, who requested that I not share his identity said, "I will take care of you. You don't need to wear your armor. You don't need to be a rigid person or someone who needs protection, because I will protect you."

Renee kept on working to release the energy that I needed to release and help transmute it so that I would be fully immersed in my powerful feminine energy. "Your leaving your home in San Francisco was your first step to transmute your energy. The energy of your home there was too heavy for you. It was very good that you got rid of a lot of things and moved. Your home represented armor for you, and had all sorts of obligations that weighed you down. It is a miracle that you had the strength to move."

"Please understand that you are looking for a partner in life, not a child to take care of," she went on. "You need someone with an equal amount of power so that you can grow together. For now, it is important for you to fix your reflexes so that you stay in your power instead of doing things like you have in the past."

"With your own energy, you will be able to create and manifest this man from your personal, unlimited power. A capability of your power is to create because you are a channel and know how to care for people. One of your energy essences is creation. To create this man, get some clay and sculpt a form. Not of a man, but something that represents the love to be between you and your partner. Be careful to not make this sculpture the only symbol of what a successful relationship looks like to you —its purpose is to help you create, not limit what you create."

Renee shared with me the color of my creative power and cautioned me to keep it private. Then she said, "When you think of this color, you open the door of your personal energy. This energy's house is in your head area. It is sleeping here and is quiet. When you want to activate it, open the door of the sixth chakra. That will help the energy move down to the heat and ultimately down to the first chakra, which is your seat of security and roots."

"It is very easy for you to be of the sky," she stated. "It is important that you spend time with and connect to the Earth. Focus on the roots and your first chakra to ground. If you go into the sky you have to have good roots. Imagine a cross. The horizontal and vertical lines have to be the same distance."

"San Francisco is a good town for you. When you are ready to return from your trip, it is the place for you to go. But create your house before you go. This house will not have armor. It will be a nest. You will be supported and secure but can go in and out. The nest is not something that is closed. It is open. You can go in and out, and energy can do the same thing. It is open but secure."

I breathed a mental sigh of relief. I loved San Francisco and had been harboring a concern that it would be difficult for me to find a place to live when I returned from this trip.

About an hour had passed, and Renee asked me if I had any questions. I did. "You have talked about me coming into my woman energy. 'Woman' has so many different meanings. What do you mean by 'woman' for me?"

Renee was quiet for a moment, and then started talking. "I am being shown a beautiful tree, but the focus is on the roots. The tree has a lot of roots that go out in all directions. You are the woman who knows how to get nourishment and how to give nourishment. You know where to find nourishment and you share what you find. You know that you are you and that you are the others. In French we say, tu es l'autre. You know that there is no limit between you and the others, but that you are separated to receive from and forgive others."

"As a woman, you are aware of the two worlds: the material and

94

the spiritual. In the material world, people are separate. In the spiritual world, they are not separate. You are like a bridge between the two worlds, but you are much more than just a bridge. It is your way for creation. You take nourishment in the spirit world and bring it to the material world to share with others. You take the food from the material world and bring it to the spirit world."

"You are like an alchemist," she continued. "You transport and take something from one world and bring to another world. Your structure is strong to do this. When you transport these things, you permit and support the transformations. You allow the processing of the material and can be the light. The transporting from one world to another world is also the essence of the mother, who transports a soul from the spirit world to the material world as a baby."

"This is the reason why you travel a lot and are always on the road. You are transporting. You need a nest. You are always in movement because it is deep in your nature to transport and move. For a man, it is a special way to be in a relationship with you. Some men may be afraid of this. Have you heard of the Apache? They are here with us during this session because the Apache are always in movement."

"Even when you are living in the same place for four months, they say that when you are leaving, your heart and breath are always in movement. When your heart and breath are in the same rhythm, you ARE. You can be still and in movement at the same time. Especially when you are with a romantic partner, they want you to remember that you can be still and in movement with your heart and breath. This is important for you."

"You know," I said, "I had an interesting thought come to me the other day." I told her about how the question about being in a relationship and having freedom had come to me during my massage.

"The Apache believe that nobody belongs to anybody," she replied. "Nothing belongs to anybody. Animals, people, stones…all are free. Apache energy is going to work with you. There is a man, and behind him are lots of people, the entire tribe. But first, you will work with the chief/king of the Apache."

Wow. Everything Renee said resonated with me. I knew that I took on the energy of others and helped them grow and transform, especially in my personal relationships. It was very helpful in my shamanic work, but in personal relationships it put me in an odd position. I would end up feeling somewhat like a caretaker. While I enjoyed helping others, I realized that by taking on this role it limited the relationship, made it somewhat unbalanced, and prevented a true partnership. That might also explain why I have resisted being cared for by others and sometimes even bristle at how confined it makes me feel. I had been so deeply entrenched in my role as caretaker that I had been unable to accept care from anyone else and viewed it as a loss of freedom.

And then the lightning bolt, "aha" moment hit me. Freedom in a relationship for me means that I could wholeheartedly do my life-path work—transporting, healing, traveling, and being in movement—with the full support of my significant other while having the security (nest?) of a relationship where he and I were true partners to each other and I didn't get burdened down with the caretaker role. By removing the caretaker weight from the relationship, I could be free.

I needed to spend more time with this thought. It felt like a breakthrough for me, but right now I was exhausted. The energy work that Renee did wore me out and I needed a nap so I could be rested for the wedding that Maria invited me to tonight.

Later that night, at the wedding, I watched the bride and groom through the lens of my new personal insight. I realized that my insight and needs most likely were very different from the newly married couple's needs, but it helped me to look for examples of partnership vs. caretaker.

I now knew that I had some recalibrating to do so that I was ready to be in woman partnership mode, instead of caretaker mode, for my next relationship. I also needed to really think through what partnership and love looked like to me so I could sculpt it and recognize it when I see it.

The big question I was wrestling with was: how do I open fully into my woman energy and stop automatically going into the caretaker or mother mode? I had made some progress on this, since it had been something that I'd been aware of for some time, but, as with everything, there are layers and it felt like it was time for me to go another layer deeper with this. What was the life lesson for me with this?

I tuned in and asked the universe my questions.

WHERE TO?

The life lesson for you is that you can create in so many ways. You do not have to limit creation to the womb. You are much bigger and more powerful than you can even imagine. What drives this power, what gives it strength, is love. You learned love at an early age and share it with all you come in contact with.

People feel this love in you and respond to it. Some think it is romantic love and misinterpret your love that way. Some want more of it and do what they can to be around you as much as possible because it helps them feel good. Some just bask in the glow of it and give it right back. And some are afraid of it or want to destroy it. In any event, this love is what gives you power as a Woman and shaman.

You can still love without taking on the Caretaker energy. You can send limitless love to all, treat all as equals and valuable, stop and listen to others and share your gifts.

And you can create! Tap into love for direction and manifestation. That's all you need to do. You know how to take action and can create anything—your work, programs, home, relationships—without any fear.

Everything you have been seeing on this trip is here to serve as a mirror and life lesson for you. Each relationship that you have seen—Pedro and Camila, Enrico and Isabel, Maria and her husband—each is designed to help you better see the role of Caretaker or Mother. Here the culture is different. Here the woman's role is clearly defined, and it is that of Caretaker. The women here care for the man and care for the children. They excel at it, and many enjoy it. You however, need to break out of it. You are not here to stay at home and care for others, as admirable a task that is. You are here to work with others and help them heal. But to truly succeed at that, you need to come fully into your power. You will need this inner strength and knowing as you go through life and work with others.

Start by watching those around you and notice the Caretaker in each of them. Is this all there is to them, though? Can you look deeper to see the woman that exists there? It is the same with you. Watch yourself and see when you are doing the Caretaker role and when you are being Woman. See yourself through the eyes of the Woman you want to be. As you begin to see this, old patterns will drop away and will be replaced by new experiences as Woman.

And while Renee gave you an accurate description of "Woman" for you, there is so much more than what she said. You are a transporter, but you are much more than that as a Woman. You are a creator—of everything else on the planet. You are love. You are communication between the two worlds and between men and woman. You are laughter and joy. Bring these things to the forefront.

As you open up more to who you really are as Woman, you will attract to you the partner you desire.

As I thought about this message, it became clear to me what my sculpture of love between my life partner and me needed to look like. The next day I walked into town and bought some clay. Using the colors of the rainbow, I sculpted a tree with a solid root base and branches reaching up into the sky. The colors swirled into each other, creating a riot of color that practically shimmered. This tree represented me.

Then I took some gray clay and sculpted another tree. I purposely chose gray for the second tree and my life partner because I didn't want to suppose what his energetic color scheme looked like. I created an equally large tree with a solid root base and branches reaching up into the sky. I took small bits of colored clay and outlined the tree trunk in the colors of the rainbow. I may not know what his energy looks like, but I expected that my life partner would have a similarly vibrant energy around him.

Finally, I put the two trees next to each other. I entangled some of the roots from each tree with the other, leaving other roots free and independent of the other tree. The two trunks stood solidly and separately, but next to each other. And like the roots, some of the tree branches tangled up in each other while others were independent. This was my ideal relationship. My life partner and I would have a solid foundation (roots) and would be connected to each other. We could and did stand independently of each other (trunks) but were close enough to each other that we knew we could lean on the other if needed as we went through life. We each had our own interests and passions (branches), but some of them overlapped and we shared them. We both were reaching for the sky (spirituality) and were firmly grounded in the earth at the same time. And we were both vibrant, loving, alive people.

I carried that vision with me on Tuesday, when I went to Maria's house to help her prepare for her daughter's birthday party. Maria was one of twelve children. Her siblings were all married with children (and in some cases grandchildren), so any family gathering is large. Maria was expecting about fifty people to show up for the party.

There was a small team of us doing the cooking, including Maria's mother, Maria, Camila, Pedro, Maria's daughter-in-law and one of Maria's sisters-in-law. The menu consisted of tamales, which Maria had made the day before, barbecued chicken, rice, black beans, a vegetable and potato salad, nachos and homemade salsa. While there was a lot of work to be done, it went by quickly as we talked and laughed.

I was surprised when Camila asked my opinion on the flavors and textures for the traditional Guatemalan dishes we were preparing, but I realized that we were moving from a "foreign guest" to a "friend" relationship. I had also brought handmade cards for each of them to thank them for my birthday party and gifts, and I think that helped us connect more as well. Maria actually cried when she read the card I gave her.

I smiled as I watched Pedro and Camila cook together. They were adding spices and dressings to the salad and were debating and testing different approaches. It was obvious that they were longtime collaborators in the kitchen and complemented each other well. I realized that it was a great symbol for partnership, with each person bringing his or her own spice and opinion to the relationship.

Pedro went outside to check on the chicken. Camila took advantage of it just being women in the kitchen and looked at me and said, "I don't understand. You are intelligent, pretty, a good worker and obviously love children. Why don't you have a husband and children?"

Would I ever stop hearing this question? I wondered. Last week I fielded a nearly exactly worded query from Juan and Carlos on this topic. But I realized that something had shifted in me about this question. There were many times when I was asked this question that it made me feel sad or as if I didn't quite fit in. When Isabel had asked me a similar question a month ago, I gave her a vague answer and then went home and cried. Maria had also asked me this question when we were out shopping a few weeks ago, and I had given her one of my standard responses about how my work made it difficult for me to meet people.

Before I could answer, Maria piped up and repeated the reason I had shared with her previously. I nodded, and then added, "I haven't found the right man yet." As I said the words, I realized that I didn't feel sad about it. I pictured my sculpted trees in my mind, and knew that it was worth waiting for the right man and the type of partnership I desired. With a smile, I added, "At this point, I don't think I will be having children, since I'm getting too old to have them."

Maria's daughter-in-law spoke up. "A woman in my family had a child at fifty-two. There's no reason why you couldn't have one, with God's help."

"And," continued Camila, laughing, "there will be a lot of men here tonight. You could meet one tonight and make a baby tomorrow." We all had a good laugh at that, and then laughed even harder when I pointed out that all of the men that were going to be there tonight were bringing their wives with them.

As our laughter died down to smiles, and we went back to our cooking, something opened up within me. I realized that I was opening up to being "woman" and having a true partnership.

◆ ◆ ◆

The week flew by in a blur. I had a number of client sessions, which kept me busy. Marta was coming for dinner on Friday night and I had quite a bit of prep work for the Moroccan meal I was planning. It was also Semana Santa (Holy Week), and El Remate was overrun with visitors from Guatemala and around the world. My sleepy little town had a very different energy, and I choose to spend most of my time at my hut. I didn't even go to the dock at sunset because of the crowds at the lake.

By Saturday morning, though, I couldn't stand being stuck in the house, so I texted Carlos to see what he was doing. We decided to meet in Santa Elena and then head over to Flores to visit the zoo there.

I walked down to the center of town and took the bus to Santa Elena. Carlos and I took care of a few errands I had and then we hailed a tuk tuk, a small vehicle that reminds me of the red plastic Little Tykes Coupes that little children ride around in.

WHERE TO?

The zoo was small but situated on an islet in Flores. Carlos is an avid photographer, so we took our time walking around so he could get the best shot of each animal. After a late lunch, we headed over to Flores before making our way back to our respective homes.

CHAPTER 8: SPREADING MY WINGS

I realized that I really wanted to explore the area more. As much as I had been enjoying my time with my new friends and spending time in my little hut, I had been feeling restless the last few days. I was used to being on the go and traveling by airplane nearly every week. It was not like me to stay in one place for any length of time, and I'd been here for almost eight weeks. I was finding it nearly impossible to explore the area—the heat makes it difficult to do any extensive walking and I didn't have a car to easily get around. The buses only ran until 6 p.m.. To really go somewhere, I had to borrow Pedro's car and have either him or Carlos drive me.

I needed more flexibility and freedom.

As luck would have it, I had scheduled a quick trip to San Francisco this week to take care of some paperwork and get my hair done. I packed a few things in my suitcase that I hadn't really used in Guatemala, asked Marta to watch Juan Carlos and Lupe, and started my trip back home. It felt wonderful to be at an airport again. I have always loved the options that airports give you: pick any place in the world and there was a way to get there.

It took about twenty hours to get to my hotel in San Francisco, between my flights and layovers. I got to my hotel almost exactly 24 hours before my flight back to Guatemala. I slept for a few hours and then got up, ready to tackle a busy day.

Part of me had been concerned about whether I'd be able to adjust being back in the hustle and bustle of airports and a big city after being in the slow-paced jungle for so long. It ended up being a non-issue. I adapted easily back into my previous lifestyle, but I noticed that I was far more relaxed about everything. Pretty much everything rolled off my back—people's emotions and anger over delays, the noise and the throngs of people—and I just did my thing with a sense of tranquility that I hadn't had before. I found myself connecting more with people than I had in the past, which may be why the flight attendant on one of my flights had brought me a free glass of wine.

I started my day by taking a bus to my storage unit to drop off some things and pick up a few copies of my book since people had been asking for them. I boarded the bus, and without thinking, greeted the bus driver by saying *"Buenos días"* instead of "Good morning."

"Buenos días! You speak Spanish?" he replied.

I laughed. "Not very well. I've been in Guatemala for the past month and a half or so. My Spanish has gotten better since I've been speaking it every day, but I have a long way to go."

"I'm from Guatemala City," he said. "Where have you been staying?"

"Up in Peten, near Tikal. I've rented a small hut with a thatch roof in the jungle and am really enjoying it."

"Are you living there alone?" When I nodded, he continued, "A woman shouldn't live alone there. It's not safe."

"I haven't had any problems," I replied. "The people there have been very nice and have welcomed me into their family."

He smiled broadly. "Guatemalans are the nicest people in the world."

I agreed. We had reached my stop. I wished the driver a good day and walked over to my storage unit to get some files I needed.

I wrapped up my errands with a stop at See's Candies to get some gifts for my Guatemalan friends before heading over to my friend Alan's salon for a much needed hair appointment. It was great catching up with him, and after my hair was styled, we went out for a Thai dinner before I went back to the airport to fly back to Guatemala.

I was tired but happy when I got back. My trip further confirmed that I needed more freedom and the ability to go places easily. I decided to rent a car for the month of May. It cost a bit more than I wanted to spend, but I realized that it was worth it for the freedom it was going to provide. Besides, I had three events in May that required a car: a shamanic ceremony in Chuarrancho, a two-day trip exploring ruins with Felipe, and a two-day trip exploring ruins with Carlos. And, as much as I appreciated the time that Carlos, Pedro and Felipe have spent with me to take me to the ruins, I felt a strong need to visit some of the ruins alone so I could fully absorb the energy there. When I am able to wander around a site by myself, my heart often leads me to a place in the site where I feel the energy strongly and can get messages and insights on whatever it is that I am looking for answers to.

◆ ◆ ◆

Tomorrow Carlos and I leave for Chuarrancho for two days of shamanic ceremonies. I had been counting down the days and going back and forth on what to wear. Fatima, one of the shamans I had met at the Spring Equinox ceremony in Uaxactun, had invited me and I wanted to make a good impression and be respectful of the ceremony and my host.

This trip would give me the opportunity to continue building the relationship with Fatima and others, and I knew that I would learn a lot. I stopped packing my backpack and, closing my eyes, asked, "What will help me most learn, grow and connect while I'm in Chuarrancho?"

Trust your heart and your intuition. Be true to yourself and walk forward confidently in who you are and in your abilities. Hold positive, loving thoughts. This is a positive development for you that signals more spiritual growth. Enjoy the ride!

The most difficult thing will be "walking forward confidently." I was certain of my abilities and have experienced so many incredible and miraculous things on this journey through my shamanic practice, but I also knew that these people have been living in a shamanic culture their entire lives. I was surprised that Fatima and the others accepted me when we were at Uaxactun and hoped that the people attending the ceremony this week would do so as well. All I could do was relax, be myself, and send love out to everyone there, including myself.

We left in the morning for Chuarrancho in my newly-rented

car. Our plan was to drive to Guatemala City and stay there for the night before heading out on Tuesday to San Juan Sacatepequez for some shopping, then to Mixco Viejo, a Mayan site, and finally to Fatima's house for the ceremony on Tuesday night and Wednesday.

I hadn't realized how poor the road infrastructure in Guatemala was until I started driving. There were no major highways, and most of the roads had just two lanes —one in either direction. In the villages, there were a number of really big speed bumps to ensure that motorists don't drive quickly. Add to that all of the potholes and the likelihood of getting stuck behind a slow-moving truck, and you had a very slow journey. What amazed me was how courteous the drivers were to each other. When a driver passed another car (or a line of cars!) and a car was coming in the opposite direction, the car coming in the opposite direction slowed down so that the car could get over. There were no honking horns or rude gestures.

I had downloaded a bunch of upbeat music to help pass the time and Carlos and I sang along to Michael Jackson and others and talked about the areas we were driving through and the things we saw along the way. After a quick lunch in Rio Dulce, we continued on our way and arrived in Guatemala City that night.

I was tired from a full day of driving, and, after a quick shower, crawled into bed and went to sleep. Carlos and I had made arrangements to meet for breakfast at 7 a.m. so that we could have a leisurely drive the rest of the way.

I had planned on sleeping until 6 a.m., but the universe had a different plan for me. Or more accurately, a yellow-winged tanager, a small blue and black bird with a yellow band on its wings, had a different plan for me. At 4:44 in the morning a tapping sound on the window woke me up. My room was on the 14th floor, so I couldn't imagine what was tapping. When I looked out the window, there was the bird. He continued tapping on the window and hopping around, his black eyes looking towards me.

Birds have always symbolized hopes and dreams to me, and are often considered messengers from the heavens. As the sleepy fog cleared from my brain, I wondered what message was he bringing to me. He continued to tap at the window as I asked my question.

Tap, tap, tap. Wake up! You are here living your dreams. Don't be fooled by the illusions of life, trust your heart and know that you are right now living the life you are meant to live. You are living your dream. Keep this in your mind and be present. There are many gifts that are coming to you as you are present and living your path.

Thank you, yellow-winged tanager, for reminding me that I am where I am meant to be. At breakfast, Carlos announced, "I have a gift for you," and pulled a large package out of his backpack.

"What is it?" I asked as I reached for the package.

"When I spoke with Fatima, she told me that you would need to wear traditional Mayan attire to the ceremony. So I made you an outfit," he replied.

I opened up the package. Inside was a white huipil (short-sleeved blouse) embroidered with a red, orange, green, black and purple design around the sleeves and neckline and a long, flowing corte (skirt) with green, gray, yellow, red, purple and white horizontal and vertical stripes of varying widths. Each was beautiful, although I had some concerns about the corte. It was one long piece of fabric, sewn together at the end so that it was a complete circle of fabric. The fabric could easily wrap around me three times and felt large to me. Carlos explained to me that this was the style for the indigenous Mayans who lived in the area where I lived, and showed me how we would use a cord to gather up the fabric at my waist. He then said that my outfit would be different from everyone else's since the style in Chuarrancho was very different.

I thanked him profusely for the gift, wrapped it back up and carried it to the car. We left Guatemala City and drove the winding roads to San Juan Sacatepequez, known for the wooden furniture and flowers that it produces. It was a larger city, filled with many side streets and alleyways. We found a place to park and walked toward the market. I wanted to buy a hostess gift for Fatima. The market was located in a series of alleyways. Tarps had been strung from the roofs of the buildings to create cover from the sun and rain. Vendors lined the sides of the alleys with tables showcasing their wares.

The market was a riot of colors—reds, greens, purples, yellows, blues, pinks, black—and filled with baskets and displays of traditional clothing, linens, food and supplies. People crowded the walkway, stopping to look and barter with the vendors. Women piled their purchases into large fabric squares called tzute and balanced them on their heads as they continued shopping.

We walked along, looking at the items. I wasn't sure how many people lived in Fatima's house, so I decided that buying something for the house that everyone could enjoy would be the best bet. We came across a vendor who had napkins and tablecloths for sale and I stopped to look. Carlos tried to barter with the vendor while I picked out a tablecloth and napkins, but he wasn't successful. I was certain it was because I was there. There is a general impression in Guatemala and other Latin American countries that people from the United States are wealthy. The vendor wasn't about to lose out on some income, and I completely supported that. I paid the full price and then Carlos and I were on our way again.

Our next stop was to a Mayan archeological site called Mixco Viejo. It is located at the top of a mountain. We drove through the windy, mountain roads, slowly climbing until we reached the site. Carlos explained to me that his grandfather had brought him to this site many times when he was a child and he had many fond memories of the site. There was only one other car in the parking area as we began exploring.

The site was spread out over a large area. There were several groupings of buildings with their respective pyramids, ceremonial buildings and altars. A number of large mounds of grass and small trees indicated that there were other buildings yet to be excavated.

As we walked to the first group of buildings, Carlos shared some of his childhood memories of his grandfather, a man that he quoted often and had the utmost respect for. We climbed a large hill to a second set of buildings, a ball court and a pair of twin pyramids. The buildings were distinctly different from others I had seen in that they were built with thin, flat rectangular slabs of rock, rather than larger more squarish stones. I didn't see any carvings or ornamentation anywhere, until we got to the ballcourt. At the midpoint of the ballcourt, on either side, was a carved stone head of a serpent, with the face of a man in the mouth. It reminded me of Chichen Itza, and I asked Carlos about it.

"Why aren't there any carvings at this site except for these?"

"I think there were many more, but they were stolen or destroyed. Any that were found during the excavation were brought to museums," he replied.

I sighed, slightly disappointed that I wouldn't be able to see the talented carvings of the Mayans who lived here. Carlos was a good guide and friend, but I realized that I just wanted to walk around by myself. My need to explore by myself came up again, and I promised myself that when I was back in El Remate I would visit Tikal on my own. I turned and walked toward a large tree in the middle of the Grand Plaza to give myself some space. The sun was out and it was getting hot. As I headed toward the tree, I looked over to the twin pyramids and saw the occupants of the other car in the parking lot. It was a family and a shaman…and it looked as if they had just finished conducting a ceremony at the altar in front of the twin pyramids.

I watched them discreetly as they packed up their things and wondered what the ceremony was about. Carlos joined me under the tree, and we relaxed in the shade and enjoyed the beauty and tranquility of the site. We talked a bit about the cultural differences between Guatemala and the United States before heading to the next group of buildings.

The site had been built on an area with steep cliffs off each side as a means of protection from potential invaders. As a result, the site had a breathtaking 360-degree view of the fields below and the mountain chain in the distance.

We worked our way back to the entrance area, when I started to get concerned about the time. It was mid-afternoon, and we still needed to purchase flowers and fruit for the ceremony and drive the rest of the way to Fatima's house. I wanted to do that in the daylight since neither of us knew quite where we were going.

It was a fairly quick drive to San Raimundo, a good-sized village on our way to Chuarrancho. Eric asked and was told where the town market was and we headed that way. The market here was different from the one in San Juan Sacatepequez. Here, there was a multi-story building with parking. Vendors had booths in the building and there were wide aisles that made it easier to navigate the crowds.

Fatima had asked that we bring flowers and fruit as offerings for the ceremony. When I asked what types and how many, she merely said to bring what appealed to my heart. With her words running through my mind, I began shopping.

We had seen a woman walking toward the market with bundles of dark pink roses perched on top of her head as we were looking for access to the parking garage. Her booth happened to be right at the main entrance, and our first stop. I bought several bunches of roses and watched as she carefully wrapped them in cardboard so the thorns wouldn't prick us. Carlos gallantly offered to carry them while we continued shopping.

We walked up a concrete ramp to the second floor of the market and were greeted by a large display of fruits and vegetables. I picked out a variety of fruits—grapes, oranges, apples, pineapples, mangos and plums. We started talking with the woman who was manning the display, and she mentioned that a lot of people were buying fruits today for the ceremonies this evening and tomorrow.

I asked, "What types of fruits are they buying?" "The ones you have bought as well as a couple others." When I asked what other ones, she mentioned two fruits that I had never heard of before, and pointed them out to me. One looked somewhat like cherries, but yellow, and the other resembled grapes. I added them to my growing pile and then paid for the lot of them.

We left the fruit and flowers there and continued to explore the market. Around the corner from the fruit vendor was another florist with a large variety of flowers. I picked out some big bunches white and yellow chrysanthemums, yellow roses, and purple statice. The resulting bouquet was so large that I could barely hold it in my arms. We walked by another vendor that had some Yucca flowers for sale. The edible, creamy white bell-shaped flowers were on a long stalk and looked pretty. I decided that I wanted to buy some of them as well for the flower offering.

Making our way back to the original vendor, I realized that I hadn't bought any bananas, so I purchased a large, crescent moon-shaped bunch, as well as a late lunch for Carlos and me. We loaded everything into the car and, amid the heavenly scent of the flowers, started the last leg of our trip.

Chuarrancho is located up in the mountains and has a population of about 10,000 people. While only about 20 miles away from Guatemala City, it's at least a 90-minute drive and it feels like you are in another world. Small houses painted bright colors line the sides of the street, and tiny tiendas or stores are tucked between homes. There are no chain stores or restaurants here, nor are there any hotels. We were going to stay at Fatima's house for the night.

Carlos called Fatima and she talked us through the directions to get to her house. She was standing outside, wearing a green patterned huipil and a coordinating corte, and smiled broadly when we pulled up.

Her house was on the main street and the front patio was filled with half a dozen people.

"Welcome to Chuarrancho and my simple home!" she said in Spanish and gave me a hug. "This is my family and these are some friends," she continued, introducing Carlos and me to everyone there. "I met Jennifer when I was at Uaxactun for the Spring Equinox ceremony. She is visiting from the United States and lives in El Remate. Carlos, her friend, is a tour guide at Tikal," she explained as way of introduction.

After the introductions, I turned to Fatima. "Do you need any help with anything?"

"Oh no. We have everything ready. Please sit down and relax. The ceremony won't start for a few hours."

I sat down and looked around. On the walls of the outside of the house that bordered the patio there were a number of large leaves pinned up in the shape of a cross. In the center of each were palm fronds. They were bright and cheerful decorations on the cinderblock walls, and I found myself admiring the simple beauty of them.

A young girl of five or six, with bright brown eyes, a long black braid down her back, and a purple sweater peered at me shyly from the doorway. I smiled and waved at her, and she smiled and waved back before disappearing in the house.

An elderly woman came out of the house to the front patio. She was diminutive, standing only as tall as my shoulder, with braided gray hair tied up in a wide blue ribbon onto the top of her head. Her eyes sparkled as Fatima introduced her to me. "This is Senora Miguel. She is one of the spiritual leaders of the community."

Senora Miguel took both of my hands in hers and greeted me warmly. "Welcome," she said, and indicted that I should sit next to her on one of the chairs. "I used to lead these ceremonies, but now Fatima does. It is difficult for me this year. My husband of 58 years passed away recently."

"I am so sorry to hear of that," I responded. "You were together for a long time. It must be very difficult for you." I gave her a hug. "

Yes," she said. "I am doing the best I can to move forward with my life without my husband, but I there are many times that I feel sad and lonely. I am fortunate, however, because my family is nearby and visits me often. The young girl you waved to is my granddaughter."

"I am so happy to hear that your family is with you," I said.

She nodded and squeezed my hand. We talked for a few more minutes. The sun was starting to set. I excused myself and made my way inside to ask Fatima if she needed anything.

The entryway hallway was filled with a marimba and several drums on one side. I squeezed by and continued in. To the right was a room, and I looked in, trying to find Fatima. Except for an armoire in one corner, the only other furniture in the room were chairs and benches that had been arranged around the perimeter of the room. Like the walls in the patio, the cinderblock walls were covered with crossed leaves and palm fronds. They were carefully and evenly spaced around the walls so that they formed a horizontal line of decoration that included all four walls. A huge basked sat on the floor just inside the door, with a variety of fruit in it. In the center of the room was a 5-foot tall symmetrical cross. Each arm of the cross was the same length and was covered with fresh flowers that aligned with the directions: white for the north, red for east, yellow for south, purple (black) for west, and blue/green for the center.

Seeing the fruits and flowers reminded me of all the things we had in the car, and I left the room in search of Fatima. I found her in the kitchen and asked her where she would like us to put the offerings. "You can bring the fruit into the front room and put it in the basket, and the flowers can go out back in the sink in water."

I grabbed Carlos and we went out to where the car was parked. He took the fruit and I brought in the flowers.

When Senora Miguel saw the flowers, she squealed in delight. "Come with me," she said, and took me by the hand to the back yard area to a large sink. She filled the sink with water and we began unwrapping the flowers together. I laughed when we unwrapped the package with the Yucca flowers.

"I know that these flowers are used as food," I said, "but I thought they were very pretty and wanted to include them with the other flowers for the offering. The color is so pretty."

She smiled at me and patted my hand approvingly. With the flowers in water, she led me back to the room with the cross in it. "Do you see that basket?" she asked, pointing to a huge basket on the floor. When I nodded, she continued, "Please arrange the fruits you brought in the basket. There are some others already in there, but it is important to make the offering look pleasing."

I happily unpacked all of the fruits we brought and added them to the ones in the basket, moving things around so that each type of fruit was showing. Senora Miguel nodded in approval. While I was doing this, a man was scattering pine needles evenly on the floor.

Finished, I sat in one of the chairs, next to Senora Miguel. Her granddaughter came in and sat between us, looking up at me inquisitively. "My name is Jennifer," I said. "What's your name?"

"My name is Anna, and I am six years old," she said, smiling.

"Have you started school?"

"No, not yet. But I do have one best friend, and we will go to school together next year."

"That will be fun for you," I replied. She smiled in agreement.

With the ice broken, Anna warmed right up to me and before I knew it she was sitting on my lap. I remembered that I had a braided butterfly bracelet in my purse, and I pulled it out and gave it to her. Her face lit up when she saw it and she immediately put it on her wrist. Even though it was adjustable, it was still a little too big for her arm, so I showed her how it could be worn as an anklet as well.

Senora Miguel motioned for me to follow her to the back of the house. In a side room there were five or six other women standing around a chair. Senora Miguel had me sit in the chair. Taking a comb, some water, and a blue and gold sash, she began styling my hair in a traditional Mayan hairstyle. The other women offered suggestions and helped to control my unruly, short (to them) hair. Somehow they managed to make two braids and weave the sash through it. The long ends of the sash were wrapped around my head a couple time and then tied together to form a knotted bow on my forehead. Senora Miguel handed me a mirror so I could see her handiwork. *I don't look anything like myself*, I thought to myself, *and I feel kind of silly wearing my hair this way.* As I looked at the other women, though, I realized that my hair was styled just like theirs. *This must be the traditional hairstyle here.* I remembered Carlos's words about the ceremony being an important one and that I needed to wear traditional dress. *I guess that extends to my hair as well.*

Fatima poked her head in and announced that it was time for the ceremony to start. I patted my hair in place and followed

Senora Miguel. We made our way back to the front room with the floral cross in it and sat in our seats. I didn't know what to expect or what to do. I looked around and did my best to mimic how people were sitting and what they were doing. There were about twenty-five people in the room, sitting in chairs around the perimeter of the room. In addition to Fatima, there were three other Guatemalan shamans there. Candles were lit in front of the cross, and small groupings of candles were placed for each direction: east, north, west, south, and center. Two incense burners had been lit and let out the scent of copal with their smoke. The musicians started playing the marimba and drums to signal the start of the ceremony.

We began by facing and calling in each of the directions. Each of the Guatemalan shamans aligned with a direction, and when it was his or her turn, called in and expressed gratitude to the direction. They then called in the ancestors and those living to come together for the purpose of ceremony.

With the ceremony begun, Fatima held the speaking stick, an 18-inch or so stick that had been decorated with colorful threads, beads and feathers, and began explaining the significance of the ceremony. "The ceremony of the Mayan Cross was celebrated throughout the Mayan region here and in other countries, but now is only celebrated in a few areas of Guatemala today. The cross is special to the Mayans and has been used as a symbol of the balance that exists in the world. You'll notice that the cross itself is balanced. Each arm of the cross is the same length as the other ones, indicating the balance between two extremes or differences. Among other things, the horizontal arms symbolize male and female, and the vertical arms symbolize Father Sky and Mother Earth."

"This ceremony is one of gratitude and is very powerful. We are thankful for the many blessings we have received from Mother Earth and Father Sky, such as the fruits, fire and flowers that we have placed around the cross. With heartfelt gratitude we give these gifts back to Mother Earth and ask that she provide more for us so all peoples around the world have enough to eat. With gratitude and open hearts, we ask Father Sky to bring sunshine, wind and rain to help food grow."

"And we pray that people around the world care for Mother Earth and Father Sky. There has been so much harm to the planet;

it breaks my heart." She paused for a moment, thinking, and a tear rolled down her cheek. She continued, "We must work together to clean the water, to clean the air, to clean the earth. The pain we have inflicted on Mother Earth and Father Sky has to be reversed or else they will stop caring for us."

Finished, she handed the speaking stick to another shaman, a man from Guatemala City. He took the stick and said, "We also need to care for ourselves so that our traditions and wisdom can be shared with the world. This is linked to caring for Mother Earth and Father Sky. Did you know that in the United States a lot of people drink water? Water is so much better for our bodies than soda. But here we drink soda because it is less expensive than water. Our water is contaminated and we have to buy expensive purified water. Soda is not good for our bodies, so when we poison Mother Earth, we end up poisoning ourselves. This is just one example of this." He then reiterated Fatima's comments about caring for Mother Earth and Father Sky before handing the speaking stick back to Fatima.

She looked across the room at me, and said to the group, "Today we have a guest with us from the United States who is also a shaman, Jenni. We met at Uaxactun during the Spring Equinox celebration and she and her friend Carlos drove here from Flores to participate in our ceremony. She is still learning Spanish, but perhaps she will say a few words for us about what she is feeling and her friend can translate?"

I hadn't expected to speak at all, and took a second to collect my thoughts before I reached for the speaking stick. Carlos came and stood next to me.

"I am so grateful to be here," I began, as Carlos translated. "I am grateful to you, Fatima, for sharing your home, your family, your friends, and this ceremony with me. I am grateful for this opportunity to learn from all of you. It touches my heart deeply, and, like you, I have the greatest respect for our planet. My hope is that I will be able to share your message and the message of this ceremony with other people in the world so that we can all work together to care for Mother Earth and Father Sky."

I looked around the room as Carlos translated. Some of the elders nodded in agreement. Senora Miguel smiled and clasped her hands together, and I could see tears of gratitude in Fatima's eyes. I bowed slightly and handed Fatima the speaking stick.

The ceremony continued. The men left the room and the women filed into the kitchen. We filled up bowls and cups with gifts of water, chocolate, soup, bread and alcohol. Fatima lined us up according to age, with the oldest first and gave us each an offering. Little Anna was last; her grandmother was first. We walked back to the ceremonial room and placed our offerings around the cross. Each direction received its own set of offerings, which were carefully arranged around the candles. With the offerings in place, Fatima began chanting and praying in the Mayan language, expressing gratitude and asking for balance and rain. The ceremony traditionally focused on asking for rain, but I had overheard one person say that the lake in town had dried up, and there was a real concern about having enough water for crops to grow this year.

A container of seeds was passed around and we sprinkled them on the offerings, asking for new growth and life. We began dancing around the cross and its offerings, sprinkling on more alcohol to continue the offerings. After about ten minutes, Fatima gathered us into a circle around the cross and led us in a final prayer of gratitude for the many blessings from Mother Earth and Father Sky.

Finished, we walked out of the room and the men walked in. The men replicated the ceremony that the woman had just completed, with the exception of bringing in the offerings of chocolate, soup, etc.

With the first part of the ceremony complete, we danced, talked and ate for the rest of the night. The musicians played until 5:30 in the morning. When the night sky began to lighten at dawn, they stopped playing and began breaking down the instruments. That was the signal for the rest of us to begin preparing for the next round of the ceremony.

The cross and all of the offerings were loaded into the back of one pickup truck. A second pickup truck held the musical instruments, completely reassembled, and the musicians. Fatima asked if I would drive my car and bring Senora Miguel and another elder.

I quickly changed into the traditional outfit that Carlos had given with me. The women helped me make a couple adjustments to the clothing and showed me how to tie the sash. Senora Miguel re-styled my hair into two short braids and wove the blue and gold sash through them and left the long tails hanging down my back, tying them together at the bottom. She gave me a necklace of green crystals, and another young woman there, Sarah, gave me one of clear crystals to wear with my new outfit.

With everything ready, we piled into the various vehicles. The backs of each pickup truck were full of people. At least twenty people were going, while a small group of people stayed behind at Fatima's house to begin preparing the lunch for later in the day.

We drove slowly to a sacred site about twenty minutes away. The site had a large tree that had obviously been part of many ceremonies—there were ribbons tied to a few branches fluttering in the breeze and remains of candles were at the base of the trunk.

Everyone except for the musicians got out of the vehicles and made their way toward the tree. As the musicians began playing from the back of the pickup, Fatima led us to the tree. We placed some candles and flowers at the base of the tree, and two of the other shamans circled around with their incense holders, letting the smell of copal fill the air.

Several villagers from nearby houses joined us. We kneeled and Fatima and another shaman led us in a prayer, asking for rain and water. While most of the prayers were in the local Mayan dialect, which I didn't know, I was able to understand the basic premise of each because of what Fatima and Senora Miguel had told me before we left. I bowed my head, grateful for my many blessings, and made a silent plea for water and the security for these giving people. We stood and each one of us sprinkled water on the base of the tree, asking for rain.

I was quiet as I walked back to my car, thinking about the lives of the people in this small community and the simplicity of their way of being. The contrast with my life in San Francisco was stark. Stripped of all of the things that had passed for trappings of success in the United States, these people truly lived each day. Without having to compete and purchase and keep up with the latest things, they were able to live in the moment and feel complete.

Our small caravan left the sacred tree and headed back in the direction of Fatima's house. We had three more stops to make before the ceremony was complete.

A short drive later, we were at the second site. The altar was located at the top of a hill, so we all carried something up. The altar was a pretty cement structure with a raised platform in it. Someone had placed four brightly colored piñata crosses across the back wall of the altar. Pink, purple, green, blue and yellow streamers hung from the ceiling and rustled in the breeze, while bright bouquets of flowers lined the walls. One large candle was already lit when we got there. The musicians set up their instruments near the altar and we conducted a similar ceremony as we had at the first stop, with each person lighting candles and placing them on the altar instead of sprinkling water.

Leaving, we began our way to the next ceremonial stop. I brought up the rear, after the people walking, and put my hazard lights on so that other cars would see the dozen and half people walking in the street. We were like a small parade going down the street, with the musicians announcing our arrival. People came out of their houses to watch and clap. Some people set off firecrackers, and others brought fruits and other donations and loaded them into the second pickup truck.

It was a couple miles from the second ceremonial site to the third one, so Fatima made the decision to take a break in front of her house. People got something to drink and relaxed in the shade, away from the relentless sun. Carlos asked me if I wanted water, and then went to get some for me. He came back to the car, carrying two bags of mangoes and laughing.

"Why are you laughing?" I asked as I put the car in drive.

"I was walking back to the car and a man came up to me. He gave me two bags of mangoes and said, 'Give these to the gringa.' I told him that you weren't a gringa and that your name was Jennifer. He tried to say your name, gave up, and said, 'Yes. Give these to the gringa.'"

I laughed and Carlos continued, "He didn't say it meanly or anything, he just really wanted you to have these mangoes."

"Did you happen to say thank you to him for me?" I asked.

"Yes I did."

More people had joined the procession as we neared the third ceremonial site. The area was filled with people, waiting for us to arrive. I carefully navigated my car into a parking spot and then looked around.

The site had an atmosphere of a large party. A cement altar with a cross on it stood to one side. Both the pedestal and the cross had been painted a vibrant blue. Boughs of leaves and evergreen needles had been tied to the pillars at each corner, and red hibiscus flowers were tucked into the greenery and at the base of the cross. A large bouquet of white and red flowers had been placed in front of the cross. Bottles of water and burning candles were on the ground in front of the pedestal.

Nearby a second marimba and drums were being played and I watched as our marimba player and drummers joined them. A group of men stood in front of the musicians, and I noticed that one man had what looked like a box with a paper mache cow head on it over his head. He was dancing to the music and the other men were cheering him on.

We made our way to the altar and, after giving thanks, prayed for water. We added more water to the bottles that were already there, and then lit candles and placed them at the base of the pedestal.

People were dancing with the music. Anna was standing next to me, and I took her by the hands and we danced together. Senora Miguel joined in and the three of us danced together. When the song ended, one of the men in our group asked me to dance to the next one. I laughed and nodded. As he whirled me around the site, I realized that, just like in El Remate, the people here in Chuarrancho had fully embraced and accepted me into their lives and customs.

I was grateful to get into the air-conditioned car after all the dancing. We drove to the last stop and everything was unloaded from the cars for the last time. We walked down a steep hill to a large ceremonial site.

Several of us started preparing the altar, while others began preparing the feast for the villagers. Anna was with me and wanted to help, so I invited her to help me prepare the copal and flowers. She happily sat among the woman, smiling and working as fast as her little fingers would let her. We prepared the altar in a similar manner to the one at the Spring Equinox ceremony at Uaxactun and then waited for the ceremony to start.

A small group of us sat, knelt, or stood by the altar while the rest of the villagers, easily 50 or so, spread out and sat on the hillside. Children laughed and played, adults talked with one another, and I could see some of the women starting a fire to cook lunch.

Fatima started the ceremony and those of us near the altar knelt and called in the directions. The people sitting on the hill watched or continued talking. It surprised me that not everyone participated, but then I realized that the people on the hillside were participating and supporting by their very presence. They too wanted rain and were lending their petitions to ours, but also trusted in the shamans to do the "heavy lifting" of the ceremony.

I wasn't ready for the chicken offering. I had seen them in Fatima's house the night before and had an inkling of why they were there, which was confirmed when I saw them at the site as we were preparing the altar. I understood at a mental, emotional and spiritual level why the chickens were being sacrificed and recognized the love and respect that Fatima and the other shamans provided to the chickens. Each chicken was blessed and then given alcohol to sedate them. Once the chickens were in a semi-paralyzed, near-sleep state, each was held by a shaman and beheaded. The chicken blood was sprinkled on the altar and then the chickens themselves were. I had never seen an animal killed before, and the shock of it made me dizzy and nauseous. I had to sit down because I felt like I was going to faint. Carlos quickly brought me some water when he saw how pale I was. I drank and breathed deeply, trying to get my physical reaction under control.

Fatima must have seen my reaction as well, because after the chickens were offered, she spoke in Spanish to the group. "I want to explain about the chicken offering for those who have never seen this before. The chickens are a gift to Mother Earth and Father Sky and are given with great love and reverence. We need to give back to Mother Earth and Father Sky with gratitude, and these chickens are a symbol of our gratitude. We place them on the altar and offer them to them."

I nodded, and Fatima saw that I understood her message. The fire was lit and the ceremony continued with many petitions and offerings of bread, candles, sugar, and chocolate. Occasionally one of the shamans would walk around the fire with a large stick and stoke the fire to keep it going.

We knelt, stood and bowed for over an hour, asking for rain and sharing our blessings with the fire. Anna sat near me, leaning on me. As I knelt for the last time, she put her head on my lap and fell asleep. I picked her up when we needed to stand again and held her as we finished the ceremony.

After a communal lunch and some joyful dancing, Carlos and I began loading up the car for our long drive back to El Remate. Senora Miguel stopped me and asked me to follow her to her home. She led me into her living room and she showed me a photo of her deceased husband. "I miss him greatly," she said, "but I know I have to keep going."

"He is a handsome man with very kind eyes," I replied. "He and his love lives on in your heart, and you can connect to him anytime through your heart."

She took both my hands in hers, squeezing them tightly. "Thank you. I think you should come and live with me."

I stammered, because I could see that she was serious in her offer. Before I could respond, her family members joined in, saying, "She has plenty of food. What more could you want?"

"Thank you for such a generous offer," I responded, "however, I have promised my mother that I would return to the United States."

She nodded, understandingly. "I have a present for you." She pulled out a large box and opened it. Inside were two handmade and hand embroidered ceremonial huipiles. "I made both of these, and I would like you to have one." She took them both out so I could see them.

I knew each represented many, many hours of work and her talent was immediately evident. I couldn't even begin to imagine what I had done to merit such a beautiful gift. Is this part of the culture here, I wondered silently. It seems like everywhere I've gone people have given me gifts. When I first went to Maria's house, she gave me a gift of a scarf and a small woven purse. Her daughter-in-law made me a hat. Marta gave me a hat, and Oscar gave me two pieces of Mayan pottery after we completed the ceremony at Uaxactun. Felipe has brought me flowers, plants, and a variety of small gifts, and Julian has brought me flowers. And in addition to the beautiful traditional outfit, Carlos has brought me food and offered to help me anyway he can.

"Why would she want to give me something so valuable?" I silently asked the universe.

She sees an interest and spark within you for their traditional ways. She knows that times are changing. She has seen it happening, and she wants the beauty of her culture to live. She hopes that by sharing with you, you will share with others, and part of her way of living will not only stay alive, but also grow and be understood by others. She also sees your heart and the care you have for her granddaughter Anna and the other people here, including herself. This is her way of saying thank you.

I thanked my guides for their wisdom.

Oh, and one other thing: this is also a life lesson for you. Learning to receive—and believing that you are worthy of receiving these gifts—is something you need to work on. You are great at giving. Now it is time to learn to gracefully receive without expectation.

I mentally nodded and then turned my attention to the huipiles. The first one was a solid geometric design of bright colors— oranges, reds, fuscias, greens and blues. The pattern covered the entire garment, with just a few small patches of white showing through, and was similar to the one my new friend Sarah was wearing. The second one had wide bands of embroidery that ran vertically down the front and the back of the blouse. The middle band was filled with red, navy blue, purple and magenta rearing horses and flowers, while the two outer bands had red, green, navy and magenta flowering trees surrounded by a border of flowers.

It was a difficult decision, but I decided to accept the second one. We put my new huipil in a bag, gave hugs all around, and headed back to the car. Given the distance we needed to drive, and the fact that Carlos and I wanted to stop at Quiriguá, a Mayan site a few hours outside of Peten, I wanted to get a few hours of driving in before it got dark.

We spent the night in a hotel in Guastatoya, a town a few hours outside of Guatemala City, and continued on our way early Thursday morning. As we neared Quiriguá, I slowed for a stop sign.

"Why are you stopping?" Carlos asked.

"There's a stop sign," I replied, pointing to the sign on the side of the road.

"That's just a decoration. You don't need to stop."

I turned and stared at him, and then we both burst out laughing before heading into Quiriguá.

CHAPTER 9: EL DIA DE LA MADRE

El Día de la Madre—Mother's Day—is observed on May 10 in Guatemala. Pedro, Enrico and Maria's mother invited me to celebrate with her, Maria and her other daughters and daughters-in-law. I hesitated before answering.

Since 2001, Mother's Day has been difficult for me.

In 2001, my then-husband and I decided to adopt an older child from the foster care system. Before we married, we talked about having a family. He wanted children and I didn't, so, after several discussions and a visit to a marriage counselor, we decided to not have children. But then, after we had been married for several years, as fate would have it, a distant relative's toddler needed a home and we were asked if we would be her parents. After some discussion, we said yes. Ultimately, things worked out for the toddler and she didn't need a home with us after all, but the seed of interest had been planted. We started exploring our options to adopt a child in the US foster care system.

To be deemed eligible for adoption, we had to attend three months of classes, get background checks, pass several home visits, get references, and go through several individual and couple interviews. But we were committed to doing everything by the book, and we checked off every step on the list, slowly but surely.

Then we waited.

We had filled out forms indicating that we were open to adopting one child and were told that it might take some time to find a child for us. The state-run agency kept us advised on children in the system and upcoming events. One day, we received an email about an "Adoption Fair" event with a game night theme and decided to attend.

"Adoption Fairs" brought together children and prospective adopters in some type of social activity. Part of me rebelled at the idea of having children showcased like animals in a pet shop, but part of me also realized that making these children "real" to people, instead of a story on a piece of paper, could increase adoption rates.

Children who were available for adoption wore a special color name badge, and I was appalled to see prospective parents fighting over the children. I was about to suggest that we leave, when two girls caught my eye. My husband had already noticed them, and we quietly watched them. They were obviously sisters, around 9 and 11 years old. I consulted the printout we had received that listed the children available for adoption and saw that the goal was to find them a home together.

Our profile indicated that we were interested in adopting one child, not two. Before I could say anything, my husband said that he would be willing to adopt both of them. I looked up from the printout, surprised, to confirm what he said. When he nodded, I smiled, and we walked over to our adoption specialist and let her know that we were interested in being considered as adoptive parents for the two girls.

The wait while the state went through the process to determine the best family to place the two girls with felt like an eternity. I tried to go about my day-to-day, but I kept thinking of them. Our adoption specialist said that she would call us as soon as the decision was made.

I was sitting at my desk working on a client issue when my phone rang a couple weeks later. "Are you sitting down?" It was the adoption specialist.

"Yes."

"Congratulations! The team unanimously selected you to be the parents of the two girls."

I babbled a thank you as tears rolled down my face. I had to force myself to listen to what the adoption specialist was saying.

"As you know, we normally give you a few months to get to know the children (and vice versa) through visits, weekend sleepovers and other activities before they are placed fully in your home, but unfortunately we have a problem with the foster home they are in and need to shut it down as quickly as possible. We would like you to spend time with them this weekend and then have them move in with you the following weekend or, at the latest, the week after that," she explained.

I had let my boss, a huge teddy bear of a man, know that we were being considered as adoptive parents, and he had told me that whatever the timing ended up being, that he would work with it. I relayed this to the adoption specialist and we made arrangements for my husband and I to visit the children in a couple days.

I hung up the phone and immediately picked it back up to call my husband. He wasn't at his desk and didn't have a cell phone. I was full of energy and emotions and needed to share my news with someone. I walked over to my boss' office. The door was closed, but through the window I could see that he was on the phone. I started to turn away, but he saw me—and the look on my face—and quickly motioned me in, while excusing himself from his call.

"What's wrong?" he asked.

"I just found out that I'm going to be a mom!" I exclaimed as more tears spilled out onto my cheeks. He gave out a loud whoop that brought other people running to his office and gave me a huge hug. His smile went from ear to ear and my coworkers crowded around to congratulate me.

"Have you told your husband yet?"

"I tried calling him, but he's not at his desk."

"Well, what are you doing here? Get in your car and go tell him in person. I don't want to see you back here until tomorrow morning."

We spent the night calling our family and closest friends to tell them the news. My mother, father and stepmother were excited and couldn't wait to meet their new granddaughters. My dad actually started crying on the phone, although he claimed that it was allergies.

Most of my husband's family was excited for us as well, although one of his sisters responded to the news with "Why would you want to do that?" in a very disparaging tone. I tried to shake off the negativity of her comment, and we ended up calling my mother back so that we could bask in her excitement and release the lingering energy of my sister-in-law's rude response.

The next couple days dragged on, but it was finally the day to meet the girls. We had received some vouchers from the state and planned on taking them shopping for some new clothes and shoes, show them the house and let them pick their bedroom decor, and take them out for pizza.

I changed my outfit three times before we went to pick them up, trying to find something that said trustworthy, friendly, warm, and, most of all, "mom." Their foster mother opened the door and invited us in. The girls hung back, looking at us cautiously. I debated between giving them a hug, shaking hands or just saying hello before deciding that a simple hello might be best. I smiled at them, and introduced myself.

"Hi, I'm Jennifer."

My husband followed suit. The girls mumbled an answer, but gave small smiles with their responses, before asking what we were going to do that day.

"Well," I said, "I thought we could take you to our house so you can see it and meet our dog and cat." They brightened up and looked interested at the mention of our pets. Encouraged, I continued. "And then, once you take a look at your bedrooms, I thought we could go shopping for clothes for you and bedspreads for your beds."

The girls nodded enthusiastically. "Do you like pizza?" I asked. They jumped up and down and said yes. "Okay, then, let's go."

The girls nearly ran to the car in their excitement and we started our day. The shopping trip ended up being a necessity—both girls' clothing was too small and worn and the older girl's shoes were so small that she could barely walk. My co-workers had quickly pulled together a shower for me, and the house was filled with gifts for the girls, which they squealed over excitedly. They also loved that we had a swimming pool and a dog and cat. I could see us being a family, and knew in my heart that these were the children for me.

With the weekend visit over, I set to work. I had a lot to do in one week! The girls had each selected her own bedroom and we stopped by Bed Bath & Beyond and I let them pick out the comforter set they wanted for their respective beds. Using the comforter designs as my starting point, I painted, stenciled and decorated each room that night, pulling an all-nighter to get it done. The next morning I picked up new curtains, lamps and a few other items for the finishing touches. I was flying out to a client site later in the day and wouldn't be home until Thursday night, the night before the girls moved in. I wanted their rooms to be completely ready for them so that the girls felt like they had their own space in their new home.

We had made arrangements to pick up the girls on Friday after they got home from their last day of school before the summer vacation. On Friday morning, as we were discussing the day, my husband told me that he wouldn't be able to be there to pick up the girls. I was surprised, since we had made plans a week ago that we would both take the day off from work. He had decided that he needed to go to work instead. A concern about my husband's interest in and commitment to the girls started nagging in the back of my head, but I ignored it. Maybe a big meeting had come up and he needed to go to work.

I drove to the foster home by myself in my small car to pick up the girls and their stuff. The state was shutting down the foster home the next day, so we had to get everything out that night. I didn't realize how much stuff they had until dozens of Hefty trash bags and a pile of toys and two bicycles greeted me at the house. How was I going to fit all of this in my car, plus two children?

I had just resigned myself to making multiple trips when a red Jeep Cherokee pulled up into the driveway. It was my husband. He told me that he was sitting at his desk and realized that the most important thing was for him to be here. The concern I had been carrying around with me all day dissipated and we set to work loading up the cars. By some miracle, we are able to squeeze everything, including the girls, into the two vehicles and began our new life together.

My work gave me eight weeks of maternity leave, which I happily took. I wanted to give the girls some time to settle in and start feeling like we were all a family before I went back to working full-time.

The weeks flew by. My family members were so excited that I finally had to beg them to stop buying the girls gifts for when they met them. The girls and I bonded, something that the state wasn't sure could happen given the long time that they had been in foster care. I made huge envelopes and put them on each girl's bedroom door and would leave little love notes and stickers for them while they were sleeping. They loved this so much that they made one for me and one for my husband and filled them daily with drawings, notes and little gifts.

I wanted the girls to learn responsibility, so I created weekly chore sheets. When they did a chore, such as setting the dinner table or cleaning their room, they would earn a star. The number of stars they each earned would dictate their weekly allowance, up to $5. It became part of our nightly routine to award stars for chores done that day. I was surprised at how quickly they took to it and how they both competed to earn the full $5.

They were anxious to get involved, and we talked about their joining the Girl Scouts and playing basketball when the school season started. We went shopping for back to school clothes and supplies. The youngest applied to be an altar girl at church. One sunny day, they set up a lemonade stand in front of the house. I, of course, was their first customer. I even brought them to my work and my husband's work so they could see each of our offices.

Most importantly, I made sure that I had one-on-one time with each of them. They both had a lot of pain and bad memories from their childhood, and I encouraged each one of them to write a letter to release the pain. When they did, I held a small ceremony with them where we burned the letters in the fireplace. As the letters burned, I explained that that part of their life was past, and now they had a new life and a new family going forward. After the ceremony, I noticed a change in both girls. They began talking about the future with more confidence and were quick to give me hugs or hold my hand. They wanted to be with me all the time and began mimicking my actions. When they saw that I used a laptop computer for my work, they made their own out of cardboard and began playing "consultant."

While we were definitely in a honeymoon stage, it wasn't all roses.

One day, I set up two easels with paper, paint and brushes on the deck so that the girls could paint. With them happily occupied, I went into the house to take care of some things. Not more than ten minutes later, I heard yelling and went out to investigate. They were fighting and had thrown paint all over each other, the table and chairs, and the deck. After talking with them about what had happened and helping them come to a resolution to the initial cause of the accident, I had them clean up the mess they had made and then sent them both to their rooms for an hour or so.

On another day, the younger of the two started crying while we were in her room putting away her clothes. When I asked her why she was crying, she asked me if I was really going to be her mother. I assured her that I was, and held and rocked her like a baby for several hours while she released years of fear and abandonment through her tears.

Around the same time, the older of the two went through a brief phase where she didn't want to interact with anyone. Like her younger sister, she was processing the change in her life and family status, and went inward. I learned to give her space while still letting her know that I was available to her. At one point I sat with her on the floor of her room, not saying anything while I held her in a hug. Within a couple days, she began confiding in me and shared some of her dreams with me.

Throughout each of these moments I did my best to come from my heart and love them unconditionally. I knew that I had broken through years of uncertainty and hurt when they called me "Mommy" for the first time six weeks after they had been placed with us. Our adoption specialist was amazed at the progress of the girls and started calling us a success story and telling others about us.

My heart was completely open to the girls, and for the first time I understood what was meant by "mother's love." I felt like a mother bear protecting her cubs...and knew I wouldn't tolerate anyone hurting them. We were starting to feel like a family.

And then it fell apart.

I walked into the bedroom one day to find my husband on the floor, curled into a ball on the floor. "What are you doing?" I asked.

"I don't know. I don't think I can handle this," he responded.

"Can't handle what?"

"Being a parent. I keep thinking about what my sister said. Why do we want to do this?" he asked.

"We both wanted to do this, and you have wanted children since I met you. I'm here to support you. We are here to support each other. We can do this."

He took a deep breath, uncurled and got up off the floor.

The second time I found him curled up on the floor, our conversation was similar but I wasn't as patient. A few days later, right after the girls first called me "Mommy," he began having difficulty breathing and chest pains. I loaded him and the girls in the car and we drove to the emergency room. After a tense wait, the doctor came out and said that my husband was suffering from anxiety attacks and prescribed him some medication to help.

"I think we should have a meeting with the adoption specialist," he said, "to see if we can figure out a way to make this work.

I agreed and set up the meeting. While the girls watched "Mary Poppins" in the family room, we sat at the kitchen table with the adoption specialist.

"I'm nervous about having to care for the girls," he began. "Jennifer works further away than I do, so on the days that she couldn't work from home I would have to pick them up from the afterschool program and start dinner. And when she's traveling, I would have to care for them myself."

I explained that when I wasn't traveling I could easily work from home, as I already did every Friday. I shared that I had arranged for an afterschool program for the girls so that they had a supervised place to go to every day until 6 p.m.

The adoption specialist listened carefully and then suggested that we hire a nanny to cover the afterschool time and help with dinner prep. I looked at my husband.

"Will that remove your concern?" I asked. He said yes, and I immediately started looking for a nanny. Within a couple days I had found and hired one.

In spite of having the nanny and action plan in place, my husband's anxiety continued to increase—so much so that within days, he called up the adoption specialist and requested that the girls be placed in a different home, and then told me of his decision and that he had made the call.

I felt as if my heart had been ripped out. I stood staring at him while my mind tried to make sense of his words. A split second later, I grasped what he was saying and knew immediately the impact it would have on the girls. They had come so far and truly trusted us and believed that they were in their "forever home." The tears that were forming quickly turned to anger and I screamed at him. "How could you do this? We had a plan to address your anxiety. These girls are not like a piece of clothing that you can just discard because you no longer want them."

The pain that I was feeling over the loss of the girls paled in comparison with the pain I knew they were going to feel. The thought seared my conscience as I stood there, crying. My husband stood by awkwardly for a moment, until I told him to get out, and then he left.

When the adoption specialist came over the next day to tell the girls that they were going to a new home, I asked her to tell them that it was because my husband was sick. I didn't want them to think that they had done anything wrong. I knew the minute she told them. The girls' loud cries and wails filled the house and brought me to tears.

The girls and I slept together in my room that night. I held them both close and told them that I would always love them. They weren't moving to their new home for a few days, and I begged the adoption specialist to find a way that they could stay. Unfortunately, their policy was very clear on this: if the couple is married, both parents had to want the children. No children would be placed with someone who was separated; the person had to be divorced.

I packed up their belongings like a robot, unable to focus on anything except trying to find a way to adopt them. I called in as many favors as possible from friends and family members to see if they could help me keep the girls, but nothing worked.

The day that the adoption specialist and the new family picked up the girls was the worst day of my life. I wouldn't help put any of their belongings in the car. Both of the girls were crying and begging to stay, one on each side. I held each fiercely, refusing to let them go, with my tears joining theirs. Eventually, the girls were loaded in their new family's car and they left.

The pain of losing—and hurting—the girls aged me a hundred years.

I went back to work right after Labor Day but didn't care about the job that I had once been so passionate about. I was going through the motions, and nothing, not even the September 11 attacks that happened about a week after the girls left, was able to break through the deadening numbness in my body.

Deep in my heart, I knew that my marriage was over, but I was unable to connect fully with that reality for a while. It was all I could do to make it through the day and pretend to care about my clients' issues, focus during a conversation, or even eat. I knew that even if I did get a divorce, it wouldn't be done in time for me to get the girls back before their new family adopted them. I was barely functioning, but I did find the strength to tell my husband that he needed to move out. He agreed, and moved in with a relative.

I held out hope through the end of the year that a friend who was related to a politician would be able to help me get the girls back as a single, separated mother. I sent a box of Christmas gifts to the girls that were returned by their new parents, unopened and with a note that broke my heart even further. The state agency forbade me to talk with the girls, so that they could have a chance at bonding with their new family as tightly as they had with me. The notice from the agency caused me to double over in pain and anger as I realized that the girls were gone from my life forever. At the time, I was very angry with the agency's decision, but now that some time has gone by, I realize that it was designed with their best interests in mind.

After the holidays, with the news that the politician couldn't do anything, I gave up hope and tried to move forward with my life and my own healing from the pain. The process took several years. It took me over a year to mourn the loss of the girls and get to a point where I started to feel a glimmer of life in me. During that first year, I tortured myself with "what if" and "I wish" scenarios for every holiday, birthday, and daily life event and I mourned each possibility that could have been. I read and reread the notes that the girls had written to me until they began to get worn from so much handling.

As I came out of my deep grief, I slowly began making some changes in my life. My husband had moved back in, convinced that we could work things out and insisting that because the house was in both of our names he had every right to be there as well. He stayed in a different room and I did my best to avoid him and started looking into what it would take to buy him out of his half of the equity.

Armed with information on how I could buy him out, I hired a divorce lawyer and began the process of separating my belongings from his. He moved out again, permanently, after we had come up with an approach to calculate his equity that he agreed with. Once the divorce was final, I took a month sabbatical from my work and really looked at my life. It had been a little over three years since the girls had left and been adopted by another family. As I assessed my life and decisions, I realized that I had been holding onto the house in case the girls decided one day that they wanted to visit me. They hadn't, and I knew that it was probably for the best since it meant that they were fully integrated into their new family.

With that insight, I grasped that it was time for me to move on and really start living my life. I packed up all of the notes and gifts from the girls and put them in a box, and began going out with friends again. That year, for Christmas, I threw a huge holiday party in the house for my family, friends and coworkers. It was a combination thank-you party for them and "coming out" party for me. I sold the house right after the New Year and moved to San Francisco.

Since then, Mother's Day is the only day of the year that I allow myself to open up the box with the notes from the girls and re-read them. A few years ago, on Mother's Day, I impulsively typed their names into the search bar on Facebook and found them. I cried that day as I looked at their pictures and status updates. They were all grown up and I was overcome with how many years of their lives had passed. I debated about sending them a friend request or a message but ultimately decided to not intrude on their lives. I had already hurt them once and didn't want to cause them more pain by reappearing in their lives.

My family never talks about the girls, which I'm sure is because they don't want to remind me of that time and the pain, so I try to do something nice for myself on that day. I avoid places where people are making a big deal out of mothers—which is pretty much everywhere on Mother's Day—and count down the hours until the day is over.

Now, in Guatemala, here was the Senora, inviting me to her house on Mother's Day to celebrate. I had thought that I had moved through and healed the pain of losing the girls, but from the moment I came to Guatemala, motherhood had been at the forefront of my consciousness. Every woman I met had children, and the culture here venerates mothers. People asked me if I had children and then told me that I would be a great mother. As with the questions about whether I had a husband or boyfriend, I had a couple standard responses when asked about children. Usually I would simply say that I hadn't met the right person to start a family with and thank them for the compliment. Every once in a while I would bring up my niece and nephews and say that I was an aunt. Even so, there were several times where I left events with my new Guatemalan friends feeling sad and as if I had missed out on something special. Once or twice I even went back to my little hut and cried.

The last thing I wanted to do was pretend to be happy on Mother's Day while inside my heart was breaking. I opened my mouth to politely decline, but instead found myself accepting Senora's invitation. Immediately afterwards my brain screamed silently to me: *What the fuck did you just do that for?*

As soon as I got home I went to Marta's house and invited her out for dinner on Mother's Day. Her son lived in Europe and I didn't want her to be alone. *Plus*, I rationalized to myself, *if things get too difficult for me emotionally at Senora's house, I have an excuse to leave.*

Renee's words from the reading she gave me as my birthday gift about me having a limited perception and definition of a mother kept coming back to me. What does that mean, I wondered. And how does it impact my relationships?

I got my answer to the first question on Mother's Day.

The night before, I had invited Pedro, his wife Camila, and their four children—Rosalio, Jorge, Sofia, and Esteban—for dinner. I'd had Pedro's siblings Enrico and his family and Maria over for dinner, but it was going to be the first time I'd hosted Pedro's family. I really liked his wife Camila. She is a very warm person, with an easy smile and a wonderful sense of humor.

Since the next day was Mother's Day, I wanted to make a nice dinner for her. Even though I was a bit limited with only a stovetop and no oven, I'd made Chinese, Moroccan and Italian meals for Pedro's siblings, which were really well received. I decided to make a French meal for Camila and Pedro. I kept the menu simple: cheese, crackers and grapes for the appetizer; rosemary chicken and spring potatoes and ratatouille for the dinner; and strawberry crepes for dessert. I knew that there weren't any baguettes in the jungle, so I fudged a little and made garlic bread instead to go with the dinner.

I had purchased small Mother's Day gifts for Senora, Camila, Maria, Isabel and a couple other family members, and gave Camila her gift, a brightly colored beaded necklace, as we sat down to dinner. I told her that the dinner and the necklace were her Mother's Day gifts, and recruited Jorge to help with the serving and cleaning up. She must have said thank you to me a dozen times, and asked that I stop by the restaurant where Pedro was working for lunch the next day, to celebrate the restaurant's grand opening. It was only the second restaurant in the town where they lived. I knew that it was the low season for tourism in the area right now, so I was glad to hear that Pedro had another job.

Wednesday, May 10 was a bright sunny day. Senora had asked that I come to her house at 2 p.m. I spent the morning doctoring up a bundt cake I had purchased with some whipped crème and strawberries and filling the leftover crepes from last night's dinner with bananas foster and a tiny drizzle of chocolate sauce. I loaded everything into my car and dropped the food and gifts for Senora off at her house before heading over to the new restaurant.

Pedro was waiting for me. He had told the chef that I was a vegetarian, so the chef made a special plate of pasta primavera for me. Camilia stopped by and sat with me while I ate. She had just finished having lunch with her mother, and wasn't hungry. The three of us were chatting, when Maria showed up. She was going to an event in another town and was not going to be at Senora's house, but had heard that I was coming to the restaurant. In her hands was a small cake, decorated with strawberries and peaches. "Feliz dia de las madres!" she exclaimed, while putting the cake down on the table in front of me.

"What's this?"

"It's a cake for you for Mother's Day."

"But I'm not a mother," I replied.

"No matter. Enjoy!"

I got her gift and gave it to her. She quickly put on the wooden bangle bracelet, smiling. And then, with a quick goodbye kiss on my cheek, she was gone. I looked at the cake and took a deep breath. *It's just a cake,* I said to myself. *She probably heard I was going to be eating here and, when she realized she had some leftover batter, made it into a small cake.* With the gift thus justified in my mind, I looked over to Camilia and asked her if she'd like some. Pedro got a knife and I cut up the cake and shared it with everyone at the restaurant. By the time we finished eating the cake, I was stuffed and barely had the energy to move.

I made my way back to Senora's house. She was there with a handful of daughters and daughters-in-law, and asked if I would drive them all to El Remate to do some shopping. Somehow we all fit into the car and drove to two towns over.

They had me stop in front of a store that I would best describe as a general store. It had dried and packaged food, housewares, craft supplies, cleaning supplies and clothing in it. For Mother's

Day, it had a large table and display set up with brightly colored plastic housewares—storage containers, cups, pitchers, etc.—that had been wrapped in clear plastic and tied with a bow.

Senora and her family swooped into the store, clearly on a mission that I didn't understand. I tried to follow them as they fanned out throughout the store, but eventually gave up and found a place to sit near the cash register. Within a few minutes they came back with their treasures—silk flowers, cooking utensils, colanders, mugs, and some of the wrapped housewares.

I couldn't understand why they wanted to buy all this stuff, but good-naturedly helped carry and load it into the trunk of my car. Senora stopped me and handed me a white silk hydrangea blossom and wished me a happy Mother's Day. I was surprised by the gift and thanked her, carefully placing it on the dashboard of the car. As I was smiling wistfully at the flower, one of Senora's daughters handed me one of the wrapped housewares packages. Inside was a clear plastic pitcher with a green lid and two green plastic tumblers, nestled in a green plastic salad spinner.

"Feliz dia de las madres," she said as she handed it to me. "We wanted you to have this gift."

My hand trembled a little as I reached for the gift and, after saying thank you, I put it in the trunk. I got into the car and was grateful for my sunglasses, because the tears were starting. It was a simple gift, yet it went right to my heart. I drove the short distance to Senora's house with blurred vision, trying not to sniffle to attract any attention to me. Luckily, everyone else in the car was excitedly talking to each other. I felt like I was driving a party bus.

After we unloaded everything from the car, Senora handed out gift bags to all the women there, including me. Inside mine was a mug with blueberries on it, which happened to be one of my favorite fruits. Enrico and Senor were the only two adult men there. Senor was manning the small store that they had built into the front of their house, and I soon learned that Enrico was the master of ceremonies for the rest of the afternoon.

Enrico explained to me that the mothers were about to play some games. I was very happy sitting on the sidelines, watching, but Senora wouldn't hear of it.

"But I'm not a mother," I protested.

"You are a mother in your heart," she responded, and pulled me to the chairs where the rest of the mothers were.

We spent the next couple hours playing a variety of games—hot potato, musical chairs, guessing games, etc.—for all the things the women had purchased at the general store. It didn't take long for me to start laughing with the rest of them as we battled for a pair of tongs or coffee mug. Even so, I did my best to not win, feeling that somehow I didn't deserve to be sitting with these women who still had their children. When we were playing "hot potato/pass the prize" I made sure to quickly hand it over to the woman next to me so that I wouldn't be holding it—and winning it—if the music stopped.

However, my "bad" luck ended when we played a game where we each picked a piece of paper from a basket. My paper said "si," indicating that I had won the royal blue food strainer. The other woman cheered and clapped for me as Enrico handed me my prize. Soon after, I won 20 Quetzales during the same game. I initially felt guilty, but then realized that my guilt was negating my (short) role as a mother. Even though motherhood didn't go the way I had planned, I still had been a mother and still was a mother. No one, not even my ex-husband, could take that away from me. I may not see my children, but I know that in some way I helped them on their journey...and they on mine. As we continued playing the games, I started to wonder if I was doing myself, and the girls, a disservice by not talking about them. Maybe it was time to start sharing this part of my life.

After all the prizes had been handed out, it was time to eat. Two large sheet cakes were removed from the refrigerator, and Senora asked me to cut the cakes and put the pieces on small plates. Each plate was then completed with two tostadas, one with black beans and the other with chow Mein noodles and vegetables. I wasn't hungry and wasn't planning on eating anything, but Senora noticed that I didn't have a plate. My protests that I had just eaten pasta primavera and cake at Pedro's restaurant fell on deaf ears.

"You don't eat enough and are too skinny," began Senora. "I made the chow Mein noodles especially for you, because I know you like them."

There was no doubt in my mind that Senora was a mother. You only get to that level of guilt inducing expertise when you have children! We ended up compromising: I piled food on a plate and promised to eat it later (which I did).

The party ended and I headed home with my Mother's Day

gifts. I found myself looking at them repeatedly. They were special to me because of the spirit in which they were given, and at some level I felt that I had finally celebrated my first-ever Mother's Day. I was still feeling sad and teary-eyed, but the tears and sniffles were interspersed with smiles as I remembered the afternoon's activities.

I met Marta at 6 o'clock at her house and gave her the Mother's Day gift I had bought for her: a necklace with carved animals on it to replace one that she had had like it that had broken. She thanked me and then handed me a wrapped package with a bright red bow on it. I looked at the card she had attached to the package and read the words:

For Jennifer, who gives birth to so many! Thanks for being in my life.
Marta

That was it. That was the answer to my first question about having a narrow definition of mother. I stared at the words for a while, lost in thought. There are so many different ways to be a mother and to give birth. Through my work and my interactions with people, I help them discover and rebirth themselves. I help birth people into healing, deeper soul connections, higher consciousness and authentic living. Wow.

I went to dinner feeling lighter and happier than I had on a Mother's Day in a long, long time.

The next morning I called my friend Arthur. He had texted me to see how I did with Mother's Day and I was anxious to tell him everything that had happened, including the insights that I had had at the party and from Marta's note. We chitchatted for a little bit, and then I told him about my day. When I shared my thoughts about how I might be negating my time as a mother by not talking about it, he surprised me with his answer.

"You know, we have been friends for over seventeen years now and I still don't know the full story of the girls and what happened. I know just bits and pieces. I think you think I know more than I do. "

"Really?"

"Yup. And I do believe that you are hurting yourself and the memory of the girls by not talking about it."

I let this sink in. Here was a person that I had been friends with for a long time, trusted explicitly, and even asked to watch my car and some of my possessions while I was away on this trip. When I was hit by the minivan, he stopped by my apartment a couple days after the accident while he was in town for a business meeting to make sure I was okay. Our visit was a short 15 minutes because I couldn't focus much more than that at that time. I found out much later that he didn't have a business meeting in San Francisco, and that he had driven a total of nine hours to see me for 15 minutes. And yet I had not shared the details of one of the most painful and defining moments of my life with a friend like him.

Before I could respond, he continued.

"I don't think you're ready to tell me the entire story yet. When the time is right for you, you will. But I do think that this is still impacting you today. My sense is that the loss of the girls has impacted your ability to be in a deeply intimate and personal relationship with a prospective life partner. I think you unconsciously keep any man who shows interest in you at arm's length to prevent yourself from getting hurt like that again."

"Hmmm," I replied, reflecting on what he had just said. "I'm not sure about that. Part of me thinks that it's more because I am too much of a nomad and that makes it difficult for me to be in a relationship. I haven't yet met a man who is comfortable with a woman who is on the road all the time. But, I will think about what you said. And I really appreciate you sharing your perspective."

We talked a bit more and then hung up.

Arthur's words swirled around in my head. Do I keep prospective men away? My friend Alan teases me all the time that I am a commitment-phobe. Maybe I do. My mind went back to the last guy I had dated, Dan.

We met through an online game. He lived in the South and was a couple years older than me. He was separated and father to two daughters. We started chatting through the game's chat capability and moved to chatting through Kik and talking on the phone and through Skype. We both traveled a lot and shared our favorite travel stories with each other. As we continued talking, we both recognized the sparks that were forming and decided that we should meet in person. As luck would have it, we were both going to be in Las Vegas at about the same time—him for work and me for fun with friends. He extended his stay by a day and I came out a day earlier so that we could have two days together.

I told only a few friends that I was going to meet a complete stranger in Las Vegas, but those that I did tell were understandably concerned. I did everything I could to mitigate the risk to me: I had reservations in a different hotel than Dan, made arrangements to meet him in public places, and promised Alan that I would text him every 30 minutes until I was safely back in my hotel room.

Dan and I joked about the craziness of what we were doing, but he also did what he could to allay my concerns, including sending me pictures of his driver's license and other personal information so that I could see that he was who he really said he was. My intuition told me that he was "safe," but I gave his full name, address and contact information to Alan, just in case. His goal, he said, was to have me be able to report back to my friends that he had been a perfect gentleman. He also told me that he would understand if I decided not to meet him.

I knew I would regret it if I didn't meet him and counted down the days until our encounter. He suggested that we meet at his hotel, the Mandarin Oriental. I agreed, since his hotel was significantly nicer than The Luxor, where my friends and I would be staying. I would arrive at the Mandarin a few hours before his meetings ended. A day or two beforehand, he sent me a message, telling me that there would be an envelope waiting for me at the front desk. "Your mission, should you choose to accept it, will be outlined in the envelope." A smiley-face emoji followed his message.

When I got to the hotel a couple days later and asked the front desk clerk if she had an envelope for me, she smiled broadly and said, "We have been waiting for you all day!"

Curious, I took the envelope and opened it. Inside were a room key and a note from Dan: *Jen, SO glad you made it! I have a gift for you! Something to hold you over till I get back! Dan.* The note was the first note of a scavenger hunt that eventually led me to his (empty) room and the mini-bar. Inside was a bag with two large chocolate-covered strawberries and two handcrafted truffles. I smiled at the gift, remembering that I had mentioned to him on one of our many calls that berries were my favorite food, with chocolate a close second. At the time, I had said to him that heaven is when they are combined together. He had obviously been paying attention. I took a picture of the gift and sent it to him to let him know I found it and thanked him for the fun. For good measure, I included the photo in the next "check in" text message to Alan as well. I freshened up and made my way to the hotel restaurant/bar to meet Dan.

The restaurant/bar was near the top of the hotel and had sweeping views of the strip. Dan had suggested that I try to find a table near the window so we could watch the lights of Las Vegas. I had told him once that I loved being in hotel rooms that were high up so I could look out at the lights of the city where I was staying, and I knew that this request was because of that. In fact, he had mentioned to me on a prior call that he had started turning out the lights in his hotel rooms so he could look at the skyline lights of whatever city he was in better.

My phone buzzed. Dan had texted to say that he would be there in about 5 minutes. All of a sudden I was nervous. I texted Alan to tell him that Dan would be there in a few minutes and get some encouragement from him. "You've got this!" he texted back.

I saw Dan the minute he walked in. He scanned the room, and then smiled the biggest smile when he saw me. As he walked over to me, I stood up. We stood about a foot apart, awkwardly, to greet each other, each privately unsure if we should shake hands or kiss on the cheek. Dan made the decision and gave me a big hug and a kiss on the cheek.

My nervousness disappeared. Within a few seconds we were as comfortable as we had been on the phone. We sat and shared a glass of wine and looked out at the lights, talking and laughing. At one point, I unconsciously rubbed the back of my neck. Dan moved his chair behind mine and gave me a quick neck and shoulder massage.

Time flew by and before we knew it, the bar was about to close. Neither of us wanted the night to end, so we decided to continue talking in his room. He promised me again that he would be a gentleman, and I trusted and believed him. I texted Alan and gave him my 30-minute update before heading to Dan's room with him.

We shared the strawberries and chocolate as we kept talking. We walked, hand in hand, over to the window to admire the view from his room. Dan turned to me and kissed me, softly and gently. I moved my arms around his neck and returned the kiss. He was a good kisser. We made out in his room for a good thirty minutes, and then he said to me, "How can I make it better?"

I didn't understand the question, since I thought he was a good kisser already. "It's good," I replied, kissing him again. We ended up falling asleep together and he held me through the night.

The next day was a workday for both of us: I had calls with my publisher and publicist about my book that was coming out later that year and he had meetings for the conference. We agreed to meet for lunch at his hotel, and he encouraged me to stay there for my calls. With a last kiss, he left.

I finished up my calls and then headed over to my hotel to freshen up before lunch. We hadn't figured out what we were going to do that afternoon, so I tossed on some jeans. I could always come back and change depending on what we decided to do.

At lunch we decided to "glam" it up and go to the old Las Vegas area to gamble a little and have dinner. We stopped at my hotel so I could get changed and had a good laugh at the difference between his room and mine. I put on a dress and heels, and slipped a pair of flats in my purse. After 14 months of wearing a cast and then a brace because of the accident, I had finally gotten the green light from my doctor to go without one. I had been practicing wearing and walking in heels in my apartment, but this was going to be my first time walking outside in them. I didn't want to push it if my foot started to hurt.

We spent some time exploring Fremont Street and the sights there. As we walked around, Dan kept scanning the crowd and pointing out interesting aspects of the people we saw around us.

"Notice that guy there? Five minutes ago, he had a backpack. Where did he put the backpack? And look at that woman over there. We saw her when we were over on the Strip, but she was wearing a different outfit."

I hadn't ever met someone who was this observant before, and I marveled at his memory for people's faces and attire. "How do you do that?"

"I used to work as a police officer. We were taught to scan the crowds to look for threats. It's something I keep doing."

We made our way into one of the casinos. Dan had budgeted $100 to gamble and played blackjack, explaining the rules and rationale for his actions at the table. My job was to hold his winnings so that he didn't gamble it all away. I didn't take my job too seriously, though – when Dan said he had decided to gamble with his winnings, I handed it over. He ended up losing it all, but felt okay about it since he had stayed within his original budget.

141

After dinner at one restaurant and dessert at another, we headed back to the strip and found a bar to hang out in for a bit so we could keep talking. When it got too loud, we made our way back to his hotel room to continue talking. We started kissing, and he said again, "How can I make it better?"

"Dan, I don't understand why you keep asking that. You're a great kisser."

"No," he said. "That's not what I'm asking. When I kiss you, I feel your fear. What are you afraid of? How can I make it better?"

Holy crap! Does he really sense that? I stared at him, assessing him. He looked back at me, and I could see the care and compassion in his eyes. I thought about what he had shared with me about his daughters and the level of care I had surmised from those conversations. And then in a flash it hit me. He was a Protector. His life purpose was to protect people and keep them safe. That explained his work and even why when we were walking around Fremont Street he not only was constantly scanning the crowd for possible threats (and sharing what he was seeing with me) but also noticed immediately when I started to walk more slowly and encouraged me to change my shoes. I decided to tell him, since I really had nothing to lose at that point.

We sat on his bed, and he held my hand while I started talking. I told him everything: about how the guy I gave my virginity to broke up with me the next day after we had been dating for a couple years, saying that he had just wanted to bag a virgin; about how I was raped at 19 and sexually assaulted at work when I was in my 20s; about the girls and losing them; and about my failed relationships. I didn't leave anything out. My voice quivered as I told him, and he pulled us down on the bed and held me close in his arms. A tear rolled down his cheek as he listened to me. I rested my head on his shoulder as I finished and he stroked my hair.

As I relaxed into his embrace, he told me he couldn't believe that I had come to meet him given everything that had happened to me. I fell asleep in his arms, surrounded by tenderness and care.

We started dating regularly...or as regularly as you can when you live 2,500 miles apart and both travel for work. We met up in Chicago the following month for his birthday and then again in Las Vegas a few weeks later for my birthday. The following month we managed our schedules so we could see each other in Boston.

As much as I enjoyed being with Dan, and felt that he cared

about me, I found myself holding back from fully feeling or expressing my emotions. I realized that from the get-go I had suppressed my naturalness to, for example, reach out and hold his hand or give him a spontaneous kiss in public. I purposely tried to keep our interactions light and somewhat less emotionally intimate after the intensity of our conversation in Las Vegas that first time. I was still raw from the conversation and worried that somehow my honesty would come back to haunt or hurt me.

It was during the trip in Boston that he looked at me and said, "We need to talk. I like you a lot, but I can't give you what you deserve right now. The situation with my daughter is demanding my time, and you deserve someone who is fully able to be with you."

I nodded, trying to hold back the tears that were threatening. His daughter had recently had some serious health issues and he was understandably focused on what was most important in his life right now. I thanked him for being honest with me, and we agreed to stay in touch. He reached out to me nearly every week for eight months to see how I was doing and whether or not I had found someone. When I told him I was going to Guatemala, the protector in him came forward again, and we talked quite a bit about what I would do to be safe while there. We both wanted to see each other again; so a few weeks before I left for Guatemala, we met in Dallas.

It was as if no time had gone by and we slipped easily back into our deep conversations, joking and togetherness. But this time it was me saying goodbye, and he knew it. Like before, we agreed to stay in touch, and since I'd been here we texted every other week or so. And we still play an online game together. It has been a nice feeling knowing that we still care about each other. I had no expectations that anything would come of the relationship, and was okay with whatever happens.

My mind went back to Arthur's words. On the one hand, I was more open with Dan than I had with any other man I had dated. I realized that I had also trusted him. But on the other, I hadn't fully opened up myself to be in the relationship, and kept a protective shell around me. As wonderful as Dan had been, I didn't allow myself to open up my heart to him. And Dan had felt it, when he asked me how he could make it better. Even though I cared for him, I was glad for the 2,500-mile distance between us since it meant that my dating him would have minimal impact on my day-to-day life, and would make it easier for me to not fully engage with him. There was a bit of a trend there, since prior to Dan, I had dated two men who did not live near me. One lived in Mexico, the other in the South.

I closed my eyes, sighing. Arthur was right.

CHAPTER 10: GETTING BUSY

lthough I knew this new personal insight needed more exploration, I didn't feel ready to dive into it just yet. Instead, I kept myself busy by going on trips to different Mayan sites, having people come over for lunches and dinners, and eating tons of comfort food. Basically I got busy keeping myself busy so that I didn't have to deal with it. I rationalized to myself that I needed to maximize the rental car.

And did I get busy!

The day after the Guatemalan Mother's Day, Enrico, Isabel and Valentina visited me. We ended up going to a local restaurant that was located right on the lake and had a beautiful dock and swimming pool. We sat on the dock, under a thatched roof, talking and watching the water. I had told Isabel about the girls about a month or so ago, when we were chatting one day. She was the only one in the family that I had mentioned it to, and I found myself wondering again if I should talk more about the girls, when it was appropriate to the conversation. But I wanted to be able to do it in such a way that I not only honored the memory but also didn't come across as someone to be pitied. Even though I knew that I was still working through some of the issues around the failed adoption, I also knew that I was strong and had come to accept the things the way they are.

"Yesterday was a lot of fun, wasn't it?" asked Enrico. "You don't celebrate that way in the United States, do you?"

"No, we don't. While there aren't any set traditions, a lot of mothers get breakfast in bed or are taken out to a restaurant," I replied.

I decided to take the chance. "I don't know if Isabel told you, but I used to be a mother to two girls," I said matter-of-factly. "Yes, she did." "Yesterday was a great way to celebrate and I really enjoyed it."

"I'm glad," he said and gave me a hug. Just then, Valentina asked for help coloring in the coloring book I had brought for her, and our conversation finished as we picked up crayons.

I thought about the conversation later. It was short, but, much like the celebration the day before, helped me honor myself as a mother, and honor the girls. Feeling good about how it went, I turned my attention to packing. Carlos and I were going to explore a couple more Mayan sites south of El Remate. As much as my soul was still screaming for time alone at these sites, the roads were so confusing and poorly marked that I didn't dare try to find the sites by myself. They were far enough away that we were going to stay at a hotel.

We left early in the morning and made our way towards Ceibal, a Mayan site used twice by the Mayans—from about 300 B.C. to 250 A.D. and from 830-950 A.D. It took us about two and a half hours to get close to the site. Because the site is not accessible by car, we hired a boat to get us there.

A weathered, hand-lettered sign that looked as if it was about to fall over greeted us at the site. "Siteo Archeological: El Ceibal," I read out loud. The sign was attached to two very tall posts that were at least six feet tall. Before I could ask about it, Carlos said, "We are in our dry season right now. When we are in the rainy season, all of this area will be filled with water and the sign will be barely visible over the top of the water."

"Wow! That's a lot of rain!"

We made our way across a marshy, muddy tract of land that would normally be covered with water to a set of stone stairs that went up a very steep hill. It was hot, humid and muggy, and the mosquitos were out in full force. We stopped to liberally spray ourselves with bug spray before continuing up the stairs.

The hike through the jungle took about thirty minutes but felt like an eternity to me. In spite of reapplying the insect repellant every five minutes or so, I was covered with a swarm of biting mosquitos. Amazingly enough, they were only bothering me; Carlos didn't have a single mosquito on him. We both were taken aback, and I started thinking. What message is there for me in this situation? Is mosquito trying to tell me something?

Yes! You've got this! I know that you think that what you need to do to heal and move forward is overwhelming, but in the grand scheme of things, it is a small and annoying task (similar to us mosquitos) for you. You are stronger than you know and can work through this. Connect to your emotions and let them flow. Don't keep them stagnant and don't bury them. As your emotions flow though you and you release them, you will heal.

Thank you mosquito. I appreciate the message and the insight…just please stop biting me!

We stopped at the first building, a temple and altar. What set this one apart from the others I had seen was that the building was circular rather than a pyramid. We climbed to the top and looked around before going back into the jungle—and the mosquitos—to the main plaza.

At the main plaza area, I signed in and paid the admission fee while Carlos went to talk to the groundskeepers. He came back with a metal bowl filled with wood chips. The wood chips were smoking, reminding me of the incense holders Fatima had used at the ceremony earlier in the month.

"Here," he said, as he handed me the long handled bowl. "The smoke will keep the mosquitos away far better than the insect repellant."

He was right. Carlos went to the top of the temple, and I used the opportunity to walk around the site by myself, looking at the beautifully carved stelae, lined up as if they were in an art museum. I swung my bowl gently around me. Not a single mosquito came near and interrupted me.

After a while, I went to the top of the temple and meditated for a few minutes with Carlos before starting back down to the boat. The smoke made the walk back much more enjoyable. One of the groundskeepers was waiting for us near the marshy area. I gave him the smoker and began picking my way through the marsh and walking on the boards that had been placed there.

As I walked through one area where there weren't any boards, my foot sank about a six inches into the mud.

"Oh no!" I called out, as I tried to prevent myself from falling completely into the mud.

Carlos ran over. "Let me help you," he said, as he held his hand out to me. I grabbed hold and used it to steady myself and then tried to pull my foot out. With a loud sucking sound, my foot came out...without my sandal.

I stared at my muddy foot for a second, and then started laughing.

"Why don't you go stand over there, where it is a bit drier, while I try to rescue your shoe?" suggested Carlos. I watched as he fished around in the mud, and then, with a triumphant smile, pulled out my shoe. "I found it!"

"Thank you!" I was still laughing as I took my sandal. "I think I'm going to take off the other one, and walk barefoot to the boat."

Carlos very gallantly washed my shoe once we got to the boat and I began preparing lunch. We had stopped at a grocery store in the morning, and bought some things that would be able to handle not being refrigerated. Our food was waiting on the boat.

"What are you making?" Carlos asked.

Peanut butter and jelly sandwiches."

"What are peanut butter and jelly sandwiches?"

"You've never had a peanut butter and jelly sandwich?" I asked. At his negative response, I said, "You are missing out on one of the most beloved traditional lunches in the United States. Here, try one."

I watched him and the captain take a bite. "Well?" I asked.

"They're good!" Carlos said. The captain nodded in agreement. "Is there enough for another?"

"Of course," I said, and quickly made a couple more.

We docked and got back into the car. We were going to Chiminos Island Lodge, about an hour away. It was situated on an island and on a Mayan archeological site named Chiminos. Carlos knew the owners and had taken care of all the arrangements for our stay.

The owner met us at a small docking area and brought us over to the island. The resort was beautifully rustic, with a large common room with a thatch roof. The dining room was on one side; on the other were hammocks for lounging while looking at the lake. Five bungalows were spaced around the island. Each was quiet and secluded and had beautiful views of the lake. I was in Bungalow #2.

"Do you want me to show you around the island?" Carlos

asked.

"That would be great," I replied.

"This island used to be a Mayan civilization, and the ruins are in the middle." We walked along a narrow path through the jungle, as Carlos continued. "The buildings haven't been restored, but you can see where the temples and ball court were," he said, as he pointed to vegetation-covered mounds.

Howler monkeys swung from the trees overhead as we continued to walk along the trail. One stelae was standing, and we stopped to admire it before continuing on our way.

At dinner I discovered that we were the only guests and that we had the island to ourselves. After an excellent vegan dinner, I talked Carlos into going back to the Mayan site at night. We took some flashlights and a small votive candle and made our way carefully through the jungle back to the site.

It was pitch black. There was no electricity on the island; the lodge used a generator and only had electricity for a few hours each day. The jungle growth hid any sign of the moon. In the trees I could hear the howler monkeys, frogs, cicadas and some sounds that I couldn't define the source of. There were no sounds of human habitation—no music, no traffic, no voices. It felt as if we were the only two people in the world.

We lit the candle and placed it in front of the stelae. During the day, it had been difficult to discern the carving on the stone. Time had eroded many of the finer details. But with the candle flickering at the base of the stone, the carving came to life. We could clearly see the face and attire of the man pictured, and when the flame moved gently in the breeze, the man almost appeared to be moving.

It was magical.

We sat on stones in silence, watching the stone man come alive and listening to the night sounds of the jungle. The candle cast a small, but warm glow and we imagined that the ancient Mayans who had lived here over a thousand years ago had built a fire and sat where we were sitting. Beyond the reach of the flame was blackness that somehow felt welcoming rather than scary or threatening and I took it as a sign that the people who had lived here were happy we were there. I felt a peacefulness descend throughout my entire body and down to my core.

A small bright light flew by. The fireflies were out. When I was a little girl...and even an adult...I loved watching fireflies. I was surprised and disappointed to learn that there are no fireflies in California when I moved there. I pointed out the firefly to Carlos and we followed its path through the dark jungle. Others joined it and we watched them crisscross the area for several minutes before blowing out the candle and making our way back to our respective bungalows.

I lay awake in my bungalow, listening to the sound of the water. Tomorrow we were going to Aguateca, another Mayan site that is only accessible by water. I realized that I had been surrounded by water all day long. To shamans and others, water is associated with the feminine and emotions. With a start, I recognized that the water had a message for me too. As I work through this next level of healing, I need to emulate water. I need to recognize, feel and release the emotions that come up, knowing that they are in the past. In short, I need them to roll off like water.

I smiled as I thought of all the wisdom that had come through to me and drifted off to sleep.

The owner took us in his boat to Aguateca. Aguateca was built on top of a natural plateau that has steep ravines on the sides to prevent the inhabitants from being attacked. To get to the actual site, we had to follow a steep path up to the entry area. From there, we had two choices: we could climb a long set of rickety stairs up to the site or we could follow a path through the jungle. Since there was another couple there that was taking the jungle path, we opted for the stairs, figuring we could take the jungle path back down.

In spite of my regular workouts and exercise, I was out of breath by the time we reached the top of the stairs. The site was spread out over a large area, with a number of the original stelae lying on the ground, broken and covered with moss. Carlos played tour guide, bringing me to the various pyramids and temples and explaining their significance.

We walked over to where the chasm was. It was extremely deep, and Carlos told me that people had tried to climb down but had not been able to reach the bottom. As I looked at the dizzying depths I could understand why the Mayans would build here. It would be very difficult for other tribes to sneak up and attack them.

The site had a number of residential buildings and a large palace and private area for the royalty to conduct business. Carlos explained how the residential buildings had space in them for the people to conduct their business—the first home offices! One of the larger ones belonged to a banker. The long rectangular stone building had a room in the center that was used for business. A hole in the raised platform floor was used to capture and store payments made. Rooms opened up off of each side of the center room that were used for sleeping. Smaller rooms were on the back that might have been used for storage or sleeping.

After exploring the palace area we started down the path through the jungle to the waiting boat. At one point, Carlos stopped for a moment, looking around and then started walking again. We walked for about five minutes in silence, and then he asked me, "Do you remember the snake we saw that day when we were walking in El Remate?"

I sure did. The snake was easily six feet long and was making its way across the road when we came across it. I had immediately freaked out. The snake wisely decided to turn around and return back to the brush on the side of the road. I had made Carlos cross over to the opposite side of the road with me so that we could put as much distance between the snake and us as possible.

"Yes, why?"

"Well, we just walked by one just like that one."

"Thanks for letting me know. Next time, please don't tell me...or at least don't tell me until we are several kilometers away from it. I'm much happier pretending that they aren't there," I said, doing my best to not freak out. I've been afraid of snakes for as long as I can remember. Through my shamanic work and journeys, Snake shows up often, but nicely makes himself look like a cartoon character to minimize my fear. I've been working on overcoming my fear of them. My shamanic teacher, Antonio, told me repeatedly that I had to stop fearing them and I knew that he was right. I took a couple deep breaths, told myself that I was fine and the snake was five minutes back, and continued down the trail to the boat.

After lunch at the lodge, we headed back to El Remate. I was going to spend Sunday in my hut and then head out for two days with Felipe to explore some other ruins.

Sunday happened to be Mother's Day in the United States. My box of letters and gifts from the girls was in my storage unit in San Francisco, but, for the first time since I lost the girls, I didn't feel an overwhelming need to reread the letters. I had already honored them. I got up early and called my mom from my hut. As we were talking, a movement overhead caught my eye. There, on the rafter, was a gray tiger-striped cat. I had no idea how he had gotten in—the doors and windows were closed—or how long he had been living in the rafters and the storage space over the outside living room. He took one look at me and ran along the rafter until he got to the thatch roof. Ducking under the roof line, he jumped down into the yard and ran off.

Well, I thought to myself, *at least it wasn't a snake!* There had been a stray cat around the house the other day when Pedro, Camilia and their family came for dinner. In fact, the cat had eaten all of the cheese on the cheese and cracker tray when we weren't looking. *Poor thing must be starving.*

I finished my call with my mom and went out to the living room. The cat was laying in one of the chairs and hissed at me when it saw me. I went and sat in one of the other chairs, studying him. He was extremely thin and looked like he had been in at least one minor scuffle. As I sat there, he stood up, stretched and then walked right over to me and curled up on my lap. Obviously I had passed whatever test cats have when assessing a human. I pet him, feeling all of his ribs.

I guess I have a cat and some chickens now. I'm getting quite the zoo. I picked up the cat, put him back on the chair, got my purse and drove downtown. I wasn't certain the local stores had cat food, but I did remember seeing canned tuna fish and sardines in Las Gardenias' store. I bought three cans of tuna and drove back home, hoping that the cat was still there.

He was, and he devoured the can of tuna fish that I gave him. I was surprised to see that the tuna had gravy and some vegetables mixed in, but that didn't dissuade the cat. He ate it all and then jumped up onto my bed and went to sleep like he had done that for every day of his life.

I posted a picture of him on Facebook and asked for name suggestions. My friends and family had a lot of great ideas, and I eventually settled on Rayas, which is Spanish for "stripes."

The next morning I left food and water for Rayas and for Juan Carlos and Lupe. I drove over to El Arbol restaurant and picked up Felipe. We loaded up the back of the SUV with camping supplies. Our plan was to drive to Nakum, another archeological site, and camp there. However, I was concerned about whether or not my SUV would be able to make it there. Several of my friends had told me it wouldn't. When Felipe's father looked at my car and said that it wouldn't be able to drive to Nakum, we quickly changed plans. We decided to drive to La Blanca and then to Yaxha, and camp at Yaxha.

La Blanca is known for its "graffiti," pictures scratched into the stone walls of the buildings by the original inhabitants. The site was used by the Mayans about 900—600 BC, and archeologists are currently working there. Only two areas have been restored: the temple used to track the movements of the sun and the equinoxes/solstices, and the palace building, which is where the graffiti is.

There are very few street signs in Guatemala outside of Guatemala City, but Felipe said he knew the way. After driving for a couple hours, he said that we needed to look for a dirt road on the right. We stopped in a small village and asked one of the people walking along the road for directions. We had missed the turn, so I turned the car around and we made our way back the way we had come, looking for a red house by an intersection.

Of course, there were several red houses, and we stopped to ask an elderly couple standing by the side of the road near an intersection with a red house.

"Is this the road to La Blanca?" asked Felipe.

"Yes," the man replied. "It is a few kilometers down this road."

"Are you going to La Blanca?" asked the woman. When Felipe said yes, she asked if they could get a ride, adding that their homes were on the way to the site. They were waiting for the bus, but the next bus wouldn't arrive for several hours. It was easily 100 degrees out, and I would never leave two elderly people out in the sun like that. They each had to be at least 80 years old. I nodded.

The trunk of the SUV was filled with camping supplies and we had a large water bottle and cushions in the back seat. In my mind, I was thinking that we could just push the things over to one side and the couple could sit on the other side. And then the man stepped forward, holding a small rope.

"Oh!" I said, surprised. "You have a pig." For a moment I was speechless, trying to grasp the fact that the pig needed to come along with them. I looked at the pig, thinking. It wasn't full grown, but it wasn't a piglet either. It was probably a teenager. If we could move some of the stuff in the back seat to the trunk area of the SUV, it might work.

"OK," I said. "I think if you both sit in the back seat, with the pig lying across your lap, it will work."

The woman got into the car, and then the man pulled out a huge burlap bag, placed the pig into it, and got in. He laid the pig across their laps and we got started. The pig was not too happy about being in a bag and being in a car and started squealing loudly. I cranked up the air conditioning. The car got very hot very quickly, and the AC helped with the pig smell.

Fortunately, the roads were in decent shape and we got to the man's house in about twenty minutes. We let him and the pig out. Then we continued on to the site. When we got to the site, I asked the woman where she lived. She said she lived just two kilometers past the site.

We followed her directions along the paved road through two small villages and finally got to her house 25 minutes later. I dropped her off, glad that I was able to do a good deed, and drove back to the site, laughing with Felipe about the whole incident.

"Only in Guatemala," he said.

I chuckled and agreed. But as I thought about it, I realized that he was partly correct. When you're in a different culture, you have to let go of your expectations about how things should be...including about time and distance...and you never know who might get in your car!

The site was empty except for an attendant. Because we were the only ones there, the attendant gave us a tour of the site, pointing out the different pieces of Mayan artwork carved into the walls: Mayan gods, fertility symbols, animals, and depictions of people hunting. Each was stunning in its own right, and I took dozens of photos of them.

Once the tour was over, Felipe and I made our way back to the car and retraced our route to go to Yaxha, stopping to eat at a local restaurant on the way. The road to Yaxha is also a dirt and gravel road, with many potholes. I carefully navigated the car around them and made my way to the site.

I had been at Yaxha before, but this was going to be the first time that I had ever camped there. In fact, it was going to be my first time ever really camping. I had had a tent when Carlos and I went to Uaxactun for the Spring Equinox ceremony, but didn't sleep because the celebration went all night.

We spent time walking around Yaxha before going to the camping area. The previous times I had been there, I had only an hour or so before the site closed, so I appreciated the extra time to fully explore. Yaxha is one of the larger Mayan sites in Guatemala. It is estimated that nearly 42,000 people lived there. Many of the 500 buildings have not been restored, but the ones that have are impressive. The tallest building, one of the pyramids, stands about 100 feet tall. From the top, we had beautiful views of the jungle and the river.

Felipe pointed out toucans and monkeys as we walked through the archeological site and back to our car. It was a short five-minute drive to the camping area. The area was quite nice and had bathrooms, showers and raised platforms with thatch roofs to sleep on. Felipe quickly set up the tent for me and a hammock for him and then lit a fire in the fire pit. We made a simple dinner of spaghetti and, after cleaning up, headed down to the dock. One of Felipe's friends had agreed to take us for a nighttime boat ride around the river so we could see crocodiles.

The moon wasn't yet out, so the sky was a dark blue-black with thousands of stars. There was a slight breeze and not a single man-made sound except for the boat motor. We spent a few hours canvassing the lake and its little lagoons. I drank in the peacefulness of it while Felipe and his friend shone their flashlights along the shoreline, looking for the telltale glowing eyes of crocodiles. We saw several and Felipe's friend caught a baby crocodile so I could hold it. Its skin was so soft! Once we finished taking photos, we carefully returned the baby crocodile to the water, headed back to the dock, and went to sleep.

After watching the sun rise and eating a leisurely breakfast, we headed back toward El Remate. I took care of some errands and went back to my little hut.

I barely had the energy to unlock the gate to my driveway and open the doors so I could drive my car into the driveway. I dragged myself into the hut, collapsed on the bed, and was asleep in seconds.

I woke up a few hours later, feeling horrible. I felt feverish, had a headache and was nauseous. The nap hadn't helped me regain my energy, and it was an exertion to even lift my arms. *Well this isn't good*, I thought as I drifted in and out of sleep. I rarely get sick, so I started to get a bit concerned, trying to figure out what was going on. *A lot of mosquitos bit me while I was at Ceibal. And then there's that scratch that Rayas gave me. Oh! And I've been swimming so maybe I accidently swallowed some of the lake water. Or maybe it's heat exhaustion—I did spend an hour chasing after Juan Carlos after he escaped from the yard yesterday…*My mind went through the potential causes of my sickness and I realized that it might be a good idea to see a doctor. I reached for my cell phone and texted Carlos: "Where is a good doctor?"

After asking what was wrong, Carlos told me to stay put and sent Pedro over to drive me to the hospital. Pedro was there within minutes, with his oldest son, Rosalio. I sat in the front seat and slept as we drove the forty minutes first to pick up Carlos and then to the hospital. Pedro later told me that he was very worried because he had never seen me like that before.

When we pulled up to the hospital gate, I woke up and looked around. Everything was dark. "Is it open?" I asked.

"Yes," said Pedro as he drove through the gate and parked by an unlit door. We got out of the car and knocked on the door. A nurse opened it and admitted us. I looked around. We were the only ones there. I had never been in a hospital emergency room where there hadn't been any other patients there. The admitting room was much smaller and set up very differently than any other hospital I had been in. In three of the corners of the room were hospital beds; the fourth corner held the admittance desk. A hallway in the middle of one wall was darkened and quiet. We were the only ones there. Carlos came with me to the desk to help with translation while Pedro and Rosalio waited outside by the door.

After asking my symptoms and taking my vital signs, the nurse asked me to lie down on one of the beds while we waited for the doctor. I dozed a bit, but was feeling agitated and couldn't get comfortable. Carlos paced around the room, doing what he could to help me get comfortable and keeping Pedro and Rosalio informed about what was going on.

The doctor spoke English. After reviewing everything, she decided to run some blood work. About thirty minutes later we got the test results. My white blood cells were slightly high, and the doctor thought I was fighting some type of infection. It could have been from the mosquitoes, the cat, or even being overtired. My whole body relaxed, including my mind, which had been going through scenarios of multiple rabies shots, treatment for typhoid fever and rounds of drugs for malaria—all at the same time. I let out a deep breath as she explained that it wasn't anything to worry about. She prescribed some antibiotics and we were on our way.

CHAPTER 11: SLOWING DOWN FOR NEW INSIGHTS

I spent the next day sleeping and woke up in the afternoon feeling much better.

Both Pedro and Carlos had texted me earlier to see how I was feeling. I responded to both and suggested to Carlos that we get together. He had paid for my prescription since I didn't have enough cash on me for both the hospital visit and the antibiotics. I knew he was leaving to visit family, and I didn't want him to not have the cash he was going to need for his trip.

He was in Santa Elena, about a half hour away. I needed to go out that way anyway, since the doctor wanted me to eat a lot of fresh fruits and vegetables and avoid meat...not too difficult for a vegetarian...and I needed to go to the grocery store. Carlos was very relieved when he saw me and how much better I was doing. It was nearly sunset and he asked me if I wanted to go to Tayasal before going to the grocery store. Tayasal is a Mayan site located on an island near Flores. I said yes and we drove over to Flores. Carlos quickly found a boat that ferried us over to the island.

We walked up the hill, following the trail, to a set of steep stairs. At the top was a small plateau with a large tree. Someone had built a platform on the tree, which Carlos said was an excellent place to watch the sun set. There were several people already on the platform as we made our way up the stairs to the platform.

The platform gave us a birds-eye view of the lake and the island of Flores. The city buildings were a mix of bright, happy colors—yellows, greens, pinks and blues—that were glowing in the setting sun, while a golden stripe rippled on the water from the sun's reflection. I closed my eyes and breathed a quick prayer of gratitude for the friends I had made in Guatemala and their help last night.

◆ ◆ ◆

After relaxing for a few days to give my body time to heal, I found myself wondering if there was a reason why I had gotten sick, and I turned to my spirit guides for some insight.

> *You need to slow down! You've been running from one place to another, and from one gathering to another. These are all good, but you've been neglecting your spiritual growth and the things you came here to discover, learn and incorporate into you life. Your recent understanding about a different way to be a mother and how it your past has impacted your ability to be in a relationship is a great example. The only way you are going to work though this insight is if you spend time in meditation and with your own feelings and fears.*

They were right. I had been avoiding exploring deeper, worried that I would not be able to handle the emotions that came up. I was getting more clarity on the new definition of "mother" but wasn't quite sure how to bring that forward in my life.

I decided that finally taking some "alone time" at one of the nearby Mayan sites might help me and headed out to Tikal early the following morning.

The parking lot was fairly empty when I arrived, and I counted my blessings that I would be able to have some time to meditate while I was there. I made my way through the site, avoiding the pathway to the Gran Plaza, which I knew would have a lot of tourists, and, instead headed to the left, toward Temple VI. There was no one on the path, and I enjoyed a leisurely walk. My plan was to meditate in the Plaza of the Seven Temples, but I wanted to explore a little first.

Temple VI was completely secluded and free of other people. I looked up the tall expanse of the stone building, trying to see the inscription for which it is known, but couldn't see it. I considered climbing up the hill and the stone steps, but decided not to. It was getting warm in the sun and I didn't want to exert myself.

I followed the pathway and circled around the temple before

heading toward the Palace of the Grooves. The Palace is a large rectangular complex with many rooms. I walked through a narrow, dark tunnel through the structure to get to the interior plaza, and sat on a rock in the shade while I looked at the building. There were many rooms on the interior as well, and some had some timeworn carvings in the stone.

I breathed in deeply, listening to the sounds of the jungle and then continued walking west toward the Plaza of the Seven Temples. I entered the plaza from the back, admiring the four large buildings aligned in a row as I passed them. While there were no tourists here either, there were several workers using their machetes to clear the vegetation in front of and on the various buildings. I watched them for a moment, amazed that they could do such physical work in the heat and humidity of the jungle, and then walked to a bench under a tree in the middle of the plaza.

Closing my eyes, I turned the rest of my senses over to the Mayan site. I could feel the heat and a slight breeze on my skin, smell the freshly cut grass, and hear the insects, birds and monkeys going about their daily business and filling the air with their individual music. I cleared my mind and began meditating.

With a start, I realized that I had had a dream where I was sitting in this exact place. I haven't been dreaming much here in Guatemala, and the dreams that I had had have evaporated quickly when I wake up. But this dream was coming back to me in bits and pieces. I felt myself sitting in the same place, but was not alone. There were many people there with me. I recognized that they were the ancestors of this place, and they were walking with and celebrating with me. I felt their support and knew that I was not doing this alone. I had an invisible—and a visible—network here with me.

I sat there for a while longer, but knew that this was the message I was meant to receive. I could feel my "team" with me as I walked back through the site and to my car. Glad that I was finally able to get some "alone" time at one of the site, I silently thanked the universe for the wonderful vision and message I had received by doing so.

◆ ◆ ◆

I spent the next few days reveling in the gift from my visit to

Tikal. I let the feeling of the ancestors' support really sink into my being, and found myself connecting with them as I started to think about and integrate the insights I had received over Mother's Day. As I did so, Marta's words kept coming back to me. *For Jennifer, who gives birth to so many!*

I was meditating on those words one day when a memory came up that I hadn't thought about in years. It was 2004 and I was at a soul retreat in upstate New York. Our guide had told us a story just before we broke for lunch about how one of her cats had died that morning, and how horrible she felt that she wasn't able to save it. When we were sitting around the table at lunch, I took the opportunity to talk with her.

"I'm so sorry about your cat. I'm sure you did everything you could. It's difficult to lose a pet. " In my mind, I was thinking about the girls and how I felt after losing them.

Before she could respond, one other woman in the group, an older woman, looked at me sharply and said coldly, "You can't fix everything, you know."

Her words were like a verbal slap across my face, and I had no idea what had caused her to say that. We hadn't had any real interactions and to my knowledge I hadn't done anything that would cause her to dislike me so much. I was the youngest member of the group and had formed a friendship with the oldest woman there, Sue.

Both Sue and the guide immediately started talking. Sue came to my defense, and the guide thanked me for my concern. I did my best to smile and then excused myself from the table.

I later found out that the woman was dealing with her own personal issue and was projecting it on me. But before I knew that, I went to "my" sacred space on the land and thought about what she had said.

I know I can't fix everything, I thought. *But that doesn't mean that I can't show care and compassion to other people or beings. And who is she to say whether or not I can help others? I've always helped others...*

That realization led me to do a private ceremony at the retreat to release and reframe parts of my being, including the caretaker role.

And then the mental light bulb went off in my head that there was even more to this message than I had thought in 2004. I had been taking care of others, not necessarily helping them. At that time, I had been acting like a mother, in the traditional sense of the word "mother," and doing things for people rather than helping or guiding them to do for themselves. That is the difference that I need to be fully aware of. Sometimes that means letting someone feel and work through the pain and grief that they have in their lives instead of trying to fix it for him or her. I had been making some shifts with this through my shamanic work, but needed to be more conscious of it. My "mother" role is one of helping others see their true selves so that they can then move forward and evolve consciously. I can be caring and compassionate and guide him or her during the process of "rebirth," much as a mother instinctively guides a baby through the birth canal, but ultimately, they need to do the work.

Wow. That is a major shift in thinking and doing and being. I took a deep breath and let the wisdom of this insight settle into my being.

◆ ◆ ◆

One of my former work colleagues, Roger, reached out to me. Roger and I had worked together on one of my toughest client engagements; he had been my boss and had coached me through a number of situations. We had spent many hours together at the client site, in restaurants, and in airplanes because of our work, and a strong work friendship had developed before we each went our own separate ways when the consulting firm shut down. We hadn't spoken in over ten years, but had been keeping up with each other's lives on Facebook. He had seen my posts about my book and about moving to Guatemala and wanted to get more details. After some chitchat, he got right to the point.

"How did you do it? How were you able to walk away from everything that had defined you and follow your dream?"

In that moment, I realized that our roles had flip-flopped. Now I was the coach. He was asking me the million-dollar question, something that I had been thinking about for a while. "Well, I'm not going to lie to you. It wasn't easy. But I knew it would be harder for me to stay as I was than it would be to make the changes," I began. "I knew that if I didn't take this chance, I would regret it for the rest of my life."

"I think," I continued, "that we go through life with these limiting beliefs that trap us into a role and life that may not actually bring us joy. How many people do you see in your life that are truly living joyful lives?"

"Practically none," Roger responded.

"I think that most people are going through life on autopilot and just going through the motions. They aren't finding and living from that place of joy inside of them; instead they are like zombies because they feel dead inside. They don't realize that the boundaries and complications they see in their individual lives are self-created—either consciously or unconsciously—and can be broken down and through." "I started questioning everything in my life; all the things that I had taken at face value as being 'right,'" I explained. "For example, the idea of home ownership. That's the dream, right? To own a house and build some type of security for your future while also creating a home. I've owned four houses and lost money on three of the four. And, at the same time, I always felt stressed and weighed down by the unending responsibility of home ownership. People told me I was crazy when I decided to move back to apartment living, but, for me, an apartment removed a bunch of stress and ended up giving me much more time to do what I wanted. I gained freedom by releasing the limiting belief that I needed to own a house."

"And," I continued, "it was the logical next step to start questioning whether or not I really needed to live in one place...or even to have a set home to live in. I mean, let's be real here. I worked as a consultant and traveled nearly every week of the year and was home on weekends. So my rent (or mortgage before I sold my homes) was really just for the weekends. I was paying a lot of money to have a place to go on the weekends. What if I hadn't had an apartment? I could have traveled to other places, visited friends, you name it for probably about the same that I was spending on rent and utilities."

"I get that," Roger said. "But why now? What made you decide to do this now?"

"Well, there were a couple reasons," I said. "For starters, I didn't have anything holding me to my life in San Francisco. I'm not married. I don't have a boyfriend or children. I don't even have any pets. My shamanic, coaching and writing work can be done anywhere as long as I have phone and Internet access. It was really eye-opening when I realized that I was keeping myself 'locked' in one location."

"And then the second reason is a bit more woo-woo out there," I continued. "When I started doing my shamanic work, I decided to just dip a toe into that area of my life. My rationale was that by keeping my consulting job I had a fall back, a safety net. And yet, deep down inside, I knew that my shamanic work had the potential to reach far more many people than it had been. But I ignored that and continued down my 'safe' path. My accident was a wake-up call for me, and, ultimately, a message from my guides to quit being afraid and jump into the deep end. I knew in my heart that if I didn't jump in, the universe would give me another little 'love tap' to get me where I needed to be."

"Well I know that you aren't woo woo or crazy," Roger said. "Actually, you are inspiring to me. I mean when we worked together you wowed me, but now, you're off the charts. All of this is very interesting. I think we need to talk again because I have more questions, but have to run to a meeting now."

We made plans to talk again and then said goodbye.

I thought about our conversation for some time after we hung up. While making the decision to change careers and move to Guatemala was not the easiest decision to make, I didn't think it was particularly courageous or inspiring since everyone has the potential to make changes in their lives that help them become more happy and alive. Sure, it may take some trust and a leap of faith, but courageous and inspiring? What is courageous about following your heart?

I suddenly remembered a quote from Nelson Mandela that I had read a few years ago and did a quick Google search to refresh my memory about the exact wording:

"Our deepest fear is not that we are inadequate. Our deepest fear is that we are powerful beyond measure. It is our light, not our darkness, that most frightens us. We ask ourselves, 'Who am I to be brilliant, gorgeous, talented, fabulous?' Actually, who are you not to be? You are a child of God. Your playing small does not serve the world. There is nothing enlightened about shrinking so that other people won't feel insecure around you. We are all meant to shine, as children do. We were born to make manifest the glory of God that is within us. It's not just in some of us; it's in everyone. And as we let our own light shine, we unconsciously give other people permission to do the same.

As we are liberated from our own fear, our presence automatically liberates others."

That could be the reason why so many people don't follow their heart. We are afraid of our own personal power and what it requires. It is far easier to give our power away to another person or a situation than it is to be fully responsible for our lives—our actions, our mistakes, our successes and failures, our words and our interactions with others. Claiming and living in our individual personal power requires complete accountability to ourselves. We cannot blame others, our employer, the government, our religion or race or gender or sexual orientation for a less-than-ideal life that doesn't bring us joy.

In my opinion, power is misunderstood in our world today. Many people think power means having a lot of money or being stronger than someone else or being able to boss a bunch of people around. I don't define those things as power. As an example, think of a dictator. Some people would say that a dictator is powerful. I would disagree. Dictators are not connected to their own personal power. Instead, they increase their perception of their own personal power by forcibly removing personal power from other people through threats, abuse and domination—all designed to wear down people to comply while making the dictator appear to be more powerful. This is not power. This is controlling and limiting other peoples' power.

When we step fully into our own personal power we are stepping into our connection with our soul, Source and love. We see that we are limitless in our power and that there is more than enough power to go around for everyone. We do not look to take power away from others because we recognize the inherent strength in each other when we are filled with our own power. From our place of personal power, we are then free to make the decisions—or not make them—that help us align more with our life purpose. We become a beacon for others who are looking to tap into their own personal power, and then can serve as a guide to help them find their own power and live joyfully with it, without our own personal judgments, expectations, or point-of-view getting in the way. We let the other person define what brings him or her joy and best aligns with their life purpose.

That's an important point, I thought. *When we tap into our personal power we actually move away from ego, which has an inflated and inaccurate sense of where true power comes from.*

I also think that when we are coming from our own personal power, we are able to better employ acceptance as a means of living from moment to moment. What is acceptance? I define acceptance as the peaceful acknowledgment of how things are at an exact moment in time.

This doesn't mean that things can't change or that you cannot take steps to make a situation different. On the contrary, acceptance of a moment in time gives you the space to determine whether or not you can change the situation, and if you can and want to, the type of action you will plan to take. The amazing thing about acceptance is that it helps minimize personal suffering. By accepting what is in any given moment, we are not expecting what we think the moment should be. Imagine how much less stress, worry and pain you could carry through life by removing expectations on how things should be!

As I reflected on this, I realized that I had practiced acceptance when I was hit by the minivan. So many of my family members and friends were angry that I was hurt and tried to bring me along with them in their anger. Some of them focused on all the things I couldn't—and might never be able to—do, and wanted me to join them in their sadness. In both cases, I chose not to. I knew I was lucky to be alive, I was grateful that the man that hit me stopped and tried to help me, and I trusted the healing process that my body needed to go through. I had no promises that I would be able to walk again unaided, but I didn't allow myself to think about something that might be. Instead, I focused on what I could do and the small gains I made each week as I healed.

Ultimately, the only thing we can change with 100% certainty is ourselves and how we respond to a situation. We may take actions, such as taking an injured baby to the doctor, but even then, we have no guarantee that we will get the outcome that we desire. By embracing acceptance, we can continue moving forward in our lives with a connection to our own personal power and a peaceful, joyful heart.

CHAPTER 12: INCREASING PERSONAL POWER

The idea of personal power and acceptance stayed with me for several weeks and the universe gave me several examples of people realizing and tapping into their personal power to help shape and reinforce my thinking. The first was with my shamanic work and the clients that came to me. Over a period of a few weeks, I had a number of clients come to me asking for help figuring out their life purpose.

For each of them, I journeyed to speak to my and their spirit guides to get some insights to share with them. I really enjoyed doing these types of journeys; the messages I brought back from the spirit world usually helped open up my clients to a more authentic way of living.

One woman reached out to me a couple weeks ago for a shamanic session. She had been feeling a calling to be a healer for a while, but wasn't certain if this was really her life purpose and path, or even what "healer" meant. She was currently working at a corporate job and was trying to figure out if she should quit that work or not.

After talking about the questions she had—and the fact that I had been through a similar discovery process—I started my shamanic journey. Specifically, I wanted to help my client discover what is next for her and the steps she should take, get some more insights on her corporate job, and learn more about her personal guides at this time.

As the drumming started, I closed my eyes and connected with my sacred "starting place." My power animal, which has asked that I refer to him as 444, met me at my sacred space and I shared with him the purpose of the journey. We traveled together to the Upper World, a spiritual place similar to how people think of heaven. It is filled with clouds, beautiful architecture, angels, ascended masters and ancestors.

My guides were waiting for me. In addition, there was a young man there with dark curly hair who said he was there to help as well. Since the Upper World only has loving helping spirits, I welcomed his presence. I asked about my client's life purpose. They spoke directly to her, through me, as I captured their message.

You are a healer of souls. This is your life purpose. Right now, this is a time of learning and growing, exploring and integrating new concepts and new ideas. It is important for you to be open to everything. When we limit our thinking we limit our potential. Your first step is to believe that you can do this—that you can heal others and yourself at a soul level and that you are capable of this. The teachings and learning will come to you to help you do your soul work if you are open. You have hidden talents waiting to come to light, and being creative can help you find them.

This is not the right time for you to leave your corporate job. There are lessons to be learned there as well. Right now, your next step is to be open and learn from many different modalities. Soul healing requires an understanding of why souls are here, the life lessons they are to learn, and the things that cause our soul pain. Saying "no" to joy is the biggest one. Read, study, and join groups to learn more. But while you should have an open mind, we also ask that you take everything with a grain of salt. Question the teacher. Read opposing viewpoints. Look at things from a broader, wider perspective. (At this point in the journey, Juan Carlos, my rooster, jumped up on the roof of my little hut and started crowing. I could see how he was visually and physically demonstrating the message I had just received.)

And then, once you have looked at things from the broader perspective, determine the truth in your heart. Do not be afraid of rejecting anything that doesn't feel right to you. Do not believe people that say you need to spend a lot of money or even purchase things in order to do your life path. You may decide to take a course or to buy something that has spiritual significance to you, and that is OK. Check in with your heart for the truth, your truth. As you learn, opportunities will present themselves. You will be guided to develop your own way of healing souls.

The young man who had joined the session stepped forward and told me that he was there to help my client on her journey. *I am an ancestor of yours on your mother's side. I am to give and help you enthusiastically find and live your life path. Call on me when you are feeling discouraged or tired.*

I thanked them for their insights for my client and then traveled to the Lower World to find a power animal for my client that would help her at this time. The Lower World is a nature-based world filled with all kinds of animals, trees, plants, flowers and water. An Andean Condor, a large black bird with a white ring of feathers around his neck and an incredible wingspan, came forward and said he wanted to work with my client. I asked him what type of message or gift he would bring my client and he responded. *I will help bring you vision and help you birth and transform your life. I can help you soar and ride the currents of life.* I thanked the Andean Condor and integrated his spirit into the spirit or soul of my client.

After I called my client back and we discussed what happened during the session, I realized that what typically happens during these "life purpose" sessions is that my guides give me insights into how my clients can connect to and increase their personal power. In the case of this client, she was told that by opening her mind more she would be able to connect to her personal power, her life purpose and her authentic self.

I also realized that this guidance from my guides was similar to the guidance I had received from them when I first started down my shamanic and living courageously path, and was still relevant to me—and anyone looking to discover and live their life purpose—today. I need to continue to check in with my heart to discover the truth for me, and continue to live it. That is where my personal power lives.

The second example of personal power came while I was in El Remate. Marta had introduced me to a friend of hers, Angela, who was originally from Canada. Angela and I hit it off, and made plans to have lunch and visit while Marta was away on a trip.

During one of our visits, Angela offered to give me a tour of the local junior high school, the health and dental clinic, the town library, and the women's center. I jumped at the chance to see more deeply into the lives of the people who lived here. It turned out that each one of these places was an example of personal power, and of how Angela was giving back to the community that she now called home through work she was doing with a nonprofit organization, Ix-Canaan.

The townspeople had built the school with donations from individuals and a grant from Ix-Canaan. It was a simple, cinder-block structure with one room each for 7th, 8th and 9th grade students. A separate cafeteria sat across a grassy walkway from the main building. Angela pointed out the solar panels on top of the cafeteria and a newly constructed computer center next to the classrooms.

Angela knew all of the students. One of the things that she did for the female students was to match those students who were at risk of dropping out of school due to lack of funds with donors who sponsored them and their school expenses for a year, through an organization called Globe Aware. Unlike in the United States, public elementary, middle and high school is not free in Guatemala. Parents of children have to pay an annual registration fee and monthly stipends to pay the teacher's salary. When money is needed for basic survival things like food and water, school ends for these children—especially the girls—with the hope that the child can go back to school the following year. As a result, classrooms may have students of many different ages. It is not uncommon, for example, for there to be 16, 17 and 18-year olds in seventh grade.

Time and time again, it has been shown that when girls are educated, they bring that learning and the income they earn through their work back to both their families and the community they live in. Education is one way that young women, especially in third-world countries, begin to become aware of their own personal power and opportunities in life that they would never have even considered if they hadn't been educated.

The program that Angela had instituted at the schools here in El Remate was doing exactly that. Young women were given the chance to complete school, and a number of them that I spoke with were considering going to University to get some type of professional degree. Armed with knowledge, these young women were able to lift their heads above the poverty they were living in and see a different type of future that benefited all members of their family.

The Women's Center was doing the same thing for the adult females in the community. At the center, women planted gardens to provide for their family. Excess food was sold to help support the center and each of the women's families. Women learned basic cooking and food service skills and then used these skills to cater events for tourists in the area.

The impact of these programs has been incredible. More women (and men) are encouraging their daughters to complete school, and the families are no longer living in basic survival mode. Instead, there is adequate food and even some extra monies to help offset the household expenses. Each program is helping its participants to realize their personal power and begin to live with it.

The final example of personal power came when Carlos and I visited Livingston, a seaside community known for its Caribbean culture from the Garifuna people who had lived there since the 1600s. The Garifuna were ex-slaves who were brought over from Africa, and then were, according to some people, set adrift on a large boat to die after their owners had no more work for them and didn't want to care for them. Luckily for the Garifuna in Livingston, the boat drifted and beached on the shores of present-day Guatemala, and the ex-slaves began creating a life for themselves there. They had been isolated for many years, but now that Livingston has become a tourist destination, more and more Guatemalans are moving into the area.

There is no road access to Livingston; you have to travel by boat or helicopter. We parked the car in Rio Dulce and boarded a boat for our 90-minute trip to Livingston. I was excited; when I was in San Francisco I would often walk to the beach and meditate with the ocean. It wasn't until we boarded the boat that I realized how much I missed the ocean. Our first order of business was to find a hotel to stay in. I wanted a room that overlooked the ocean so I could listen to the waves at night and watch the sunrise in the morning.

After looking at a couple, we settled on the Hotel Villa Caribe, which was situated right on the bay side of the ocean. Carlos and the boat driver were going to stay in one room and I was in another. It had been about ten years since Carlos had been to Livingston, so we were anxious to explore—him to see what had changed, and me to see the area for the first time.

We followed the main road away from the bay, past a small

market area and homes to the ocean. Small wooden and cement houses lined the shoreline, and while the occasional resident walked by, the beach area was deserted. We found a place to sit next to a blue and yellow painted wooden boat named Geni Fernanda and I put my feet in the sand, watching the waves lap up against my toes and the sun sink lower in the sky.

On the horizon, to the left, was a large statue on a small island in the Amatique Bay. I asked Carlos about it and he told me that it was a statue of the God of the Sea and that the Garifuna people had placed it there.

"Let's walk along the shoreline toward the statue," I suggested.

Carlos hesitated. "When we are trained about doing tours in Livingston, they caution us to not go to this part of the town."

"Why not?"

"They say that it is dangerous."

I looked around the sleepy town. There weren't any people about and it was peacefully quiet. From where we were standing, I could see a number of small, modest casitas that ran along the shoreline. *These people have the best location in the entire town*, I thought to myself. Then I closed my eyes and tuned into my inner sense to see if I detected any threats. Nothing came up for me, so I opened my eyes and said, "I don't think it's dangerous. Let's go." And before Carlos could respond—or try to stop me—I started walking down a very worn path along the beach.

Carlos followed a bit reluctantly. We were heading into the part of the town where the Garifuna people lived.

We walked past a small house. In the doorway was a woman with a couple small children. I smiled warmly and said, "Buenas tardes." Her face lit up with a huge smile and she returned the greeting. We passed by more people as we walked along the shoreline, and I greeted each one. They in turn responded as warmly as the first woman had. We made our way to the only hotel on this side of the town, the Flamingo Hotel. Several friends had suggested that I stay there, but when I suggested looking at the hotel earlier, both Carlos and the boat driver had said that the hotel wasn't easily accessible.

I peered through the gate to the hotel, noting the many people in the reception area who were talking and laughing. There was a road that ran perpendicular to the ocean on one side, and I suggested that we walk up the road and then cut over to the main street.

"No, it is too dangerous," replied Carlos. I looked up the dirt and grass road, with its small casitas lining either side, and didn't see anything that would cause me to think that it was dangerous. I looked back at Carlos and could see the tension on his face. I sensed that the issue was less about the actual street and more about an unconscious bias against the Garifuna people in general, but didn't push the point. I sighed and reluctantly turned back. I really wanted to see this part of town; it felt like this was far more authentic than the main street lined with gift shops and restaurants.

As we picked our way back along the shoreline, Carlos shared his thoughts about Livingston with me. "This town is completely different from how it was when I came here ten years ago. Ten years ago, there was a lot of music and dancing in the streets. Now there is none of that. Ten years ago, all the houses were small casitas made out of wood. Now," he said, gesturing to the houses that lined the main street, "there are these big houses that look more Guatemalan than Garifuna. I don't know if this change is a good thing or a bad thing."

"Well," I mused aloud, "if the new homes belong to the indigenous people, I would say that it could be a good thing, because it shows that the people here have a better quality of life and more income."

Carlos agreed. "Maybe the music and dancing is in the evening in the town square."

We decided to eat dinner at the hotel and then walked over to the town square. When we got there, it was filled with vendors and people playing basketball, but no music or dancing. I was disappointed. Everything I had read about Livingston was that it was a Caribbean town with lots of reggae music and a culture unique to Guatemala. Aside from seeing a few African American people walking about, I didn't see anything that different—and certainly nothing that matched what I had read about the town.

Silently we walked back to our hotel, which was built right next to the junction of the river and the bay. I decided to explore the town more by myself in the morning so that I could have more freedom and flexibility in where I went. My intuition told me that there was nothing to fear about walking around the town alone, and I wanted specifically to connect more with the locals to better understand the culture in this part of Guatemala. By exploring alone, I knew I would have the chance to do so. I told Carlos that I would see him later in the morning and went to bed.

I got up early the next morning and watched the sun rise from my balcony. The sky was filed with oranges, reds and pinks as the sun came up over the horizon. I got dressed and went outside. My feet took me back to the ocean where Carlos and I had sat the afternoon before. I meditated with the sun, sand, wind and ocean for over half an hour before making my way back toward downtown.

I decided to walk over to the town square before going to the hotel. An African American man with dreadlocked hair and a beard streaked with gray struck up a conversation with me. His name was Philip, although he went by Polo. He told me how he met and befriended Jerry Garcia from the Grateful Dead, and that Jerry Garcia had even given him a guitar. He had lived his entire life in Livingston, except for time in the United States at a university, and had seen a number of changes.

"Look around you," he said in his Caribbean accent. "How many African Americans do you see?"

"Three."

"The town plaza used to be filled with Garifunas," he said. "Now, it is all Mayans. There used to be drummers lining the streets, and women would dance. There was music everywhere. Not anymore. We have been pushed to one small section of town to make room for hotels, restaurants and shops. None of these places hire Garifunas. We are struggling to find work."

"Look at that man," he continued. I looked in the direction he was pointing. An African American man was walking from the dock up to the square. "He is looking for work. He will walk up and down this street, hoping to get an odd job."

"It is a real problem here. The women have it the worst. Our culture honors women. Any children are hers. And women will do whatever it takes to feed their children. If the father doesn't provide, the woman will take things in her own hands to make sure her children are taken care of. When money was tight and there were no other options, the women here would turn to prostitution. Because of this, I started a program that provides food for the children. No woman should have to do those things to feed her children," he explained.

"Now, let me ask you this: did you see my town, where the

Garifunas live?" he asked.

"I saw a tiny bit of your town," I replied, and told him of the walk I had taken the night before with Carlos. "

You haven't seen my town. Come on, I will take you there."

"Okay," I responded. I had seen Carlos walking by as I talked to Philip and I waved him over. After quickly introducing him to Philip I said, "We're going to explore the traditional section of town. Want to come with us?"

Carlos hesitated and then nodded. I could almost read his mind: he was thinking that he couldn't let a woman go off to a dangerous area alone. Before he could change his mind or try to talk me out of it, I turned to Philip and off we went. Philip took us right into the part of town that Carlos had told me was too dangerous to go into. He led us down dirt roads and paths, and continued to explain about the plight of his people.

"At one point, we lived all over this town. But now, we are in one small corner of the town. But, as you can see," he gestured to the right, where the ocean was, "We have some beautiful land. The problem is that now other people want to force us out of here so they can build large hotels and restaurants right on the beach."

We walked past a number of small wooden houses and the inhabitants poked their heads out to say hello to Philip. A group of small children began singing a song, and Philip joined in. Within seconds they were dancing together. With the song completed, he continued. "I have been encouraging everyone to stay put. This is our land, our culture, and we have to work to protect it."

He stopped in front of a white wooden structure made of large sticks placed upright into a cement foundation. A large thatch roof covered the building. "Have you seen our temple?" he asked.

When we said no, he brought us over to the side doors and let us peer into the space. There was one large room, with a smaller room running the length of one of the short ends of the building. Benches with blue tops lined the walls, while red and white pendants ran across the ceiling. A hard-packed dirt floor housed a small altar in the middle of the room; candle stubs and a container of Tang were placed in the altar. In the ceiling rafters were drums, carefully covered with blue tarps and waiting for the next ceremony to be used.

"This is the oldest building in Livingston. It was built in the 1600s. The dirt floor was made by hundreds of dancers. My grandmother danced here. Today, we use the temple for ceremonies. There are shamans in the small room to the left that are preparing for a ceremony now."

As Philip continued to explain about the significance of the building to his community, I felt my heart expanding. I realized that I was exactly where I needed to be, and that this meeting with Philip gave me an opportunity to further trust my intuition. There was nothing here that was dangerous or threatening to me. I would have missed out on a wonderful experience if I hadn't gone with my gut. And, I also realized that this meeting was giving Carlos an opportunity to reframe some potential stigmas he may have had about the Garifuna people and see first-hand the beauty of their culture.

We took some photos and continued on our way. Philip wanted to show us the site where he was organizing the building of a new school for the Garifuna children could go to school. The building was partially complete, although construction had slowed down due to a recent hurricane.

"Our vision is to create a school where our children can go to and learn without having to worry about the expenses for school uniforms. Today, many of our children's families do no have the money to purchase the uniforms, so the children cannot attend school."

I realized that Philip was working to help his people find and claim their personal power. By providing the basics for children— food and education—he was giving the next generation the ability to stand on their own two feet and claim what is rightfully theirs. The work he was doing with the adults to help save their community and land was also helping the people see that they don't have to be downtrodden.

Why does it have to be this way? Why do people feel that they have to increase their power by taking away from others?, I wondered. The unfortunate thing that I had realized was that the darker the skin, the more likely to be robbed of personal power. The Spanish came to this country and conquered the Mayans by force. The Mayans, who have lighter skin than the Garifuna, have now been trying to forcefully remove the personal power of the Garifuna. It also appears to be a cycle. Those that are oppressed look for others to oppress so they feel more in control of their own lives.

Philip finished his impromptu tour, and I gave him a donation for the school and food programs, thanking him and asking that he continue the work he was doing. As Carlos and I rode in the boat back to Rio Dulce to get my car for the drive back to El Remate, I mused about personal power. *What would the world look like if everyone came from a place of personal power?*

Well, for starters, there would be no persecution of anyone because of race, skin color, religion, financial value, etc. A person who is in their personal power recognizes that true power comes from within, not from external factors. There would be no need to try to control others because such control actually diminishes personal power rather than enhancing it.

In addition, people who have tapped into their personal power have the internal strength and self-esteem to follow their life dreams. They know that there may be some bumps in the road, but they have the confidence to overcome those as they arise. More importantly, they know that if they *didn't* follow their dreams and live their life purpose they would ultimately end up limiting themselves and others by not sharing their gifts with the world.

As I thought more about it, I realized that if all people recognized and were leveraging their personal power, they would be more likely to collaborate with each other to help each other live their life purpose because there wouldn't be a fear that someone else would do something better than them or that their power would somehow be diminished. Competition for personal gain would no longer resonate. They would know that helping others would only help increase their own personal power.

I had definitely tapped into my personal power when I made the decision to quit my job and move to Guatemala. While most of my friends and family were supportive and even excited for me, there were some that brought up their personal fears and projected those onto me and my journey. Reviewing my trip and time in Guatemala so far, I realized that I had rejected their and my fears. Because it felt right, I had extended my time here by an additional six weeks. And even now, with just about a month left in Guatemala, I wasn't feeling any concern about where I would be living. Granted, I was going to head over to Asia when I left here, but I hadn't once regretted my life changes and was trusting that somehow a perfect home would manifest for me when I was ready to settle back down in San Francisco.

I closed my eyes, feeling the wind from the ocean and bay on my face as the boat continued its journey, and asked my guides if there was a lesson I needed to learn about personal power.

> *When you are in your personal power, you can accomplish anything. You are aligned with the universe and the energies to manifest flow easily to you because you are being true and authentic to whom you are. Old ways of being will fall by the wayside, some easily and some not so easily, but as you continue to drop these ways of being, you will move closer and closer to your core self, the true person that you are. All of these experiences were shown to you to show you the potential that exists within each one of us. Every person on the planet can be authentic. Every person had personal power and can use that power to build the life that resonates most with their soul and life calling.*
>
> *This is the lesson for you. The more you—and others—are coming from personal power, the more positive change can occur on the planet. Each person that is living authentically is a beacon for others. Their light helps others discover their own. Be the beacon and help others become beacons as well.*
>
> *For you personally, as you settle more deeply into your personal power, you will attract the people, things and situations you need and desire in your life. This includes your life partner. He will come when you are fully authentic. Continue to take action toward this way of being. Look at those things in your life that are not part of your authentic being or that try to rob you of your personal power and release them, with love. Continue to set the boundaries you need for your life. Call on us to help you with this and with manifestation. We are here for you.*

I opened my eyes. I had been releasing a lot in my life, but it was a good reminder to examine all areas to see what else might be holding me back. Perhaps there were some lingering limiting beliefs that needed to go. I vowed to spend some time on this as the boat pulled into the dock.

CHAPTER 13: COMPLETING A CYCLE

Carlos and I made plans to go back to Uaxactun, the Mayan archeological site that we had gone to for the spring equinox ceremony, for the summer solstice on June 21. He explained to me that there wouldn't be a big celebration like there had been for the spring equinox, but I still wanted to go.

The Mayans, like many other cultures around the world, believed that the annual cycle of the sun represented a spiritual path of enlightenment that could be followed throughout the year. The solar year began with the fall equinox, a time of death, darkness and going within. The winter solstice, the longest night of the year and a time of birth, creation and awakening from the darkness, gave way to the spring equinox's time of growth and resurrection. Finally, the solar year culminated with the summer solstice, where the light of the day overcame the dark of night. It is viewed as a time of spiritual initiation, renewal and transformation, and I wanted to honor it—and my journey thus far—at a Mayan site.

We left in the early afternoon of June 20. It had been raining quite a bit for the past few days, so we weren't certain that the car would be able to navigate the dirt road up to Uaxactun. After some conversation, we decided to stop in Tikal, on our way to Uaxactun, and get a report on the road. If it was impassable, we would stay at one of the hotels at Tikal and do our summer solstice ceremony at dawn in Tikal. Fortunately, we got the green light to go through to Uaxactun, which made me happy. I had been secretly hoping we could get to Uaxactun, since it would be relatively empty of tourists.

Carlos and I were the only people to travel to Uaxactun for the summer solstice. After a slightly white knuckled drive to the village, we made our way to the hotel that we had camped at during the spring equinox and got our rooms. The sun was just beginning to set, so we took our flashlights and walked over to Group A and B of the site. A small herd of horses was bedding down for the night in the ball court as we passed on our way to the temple.

We climbed to the top and watched the sun set. As it set, I silently asked the ancestors and spirits of Uaxactun and my helping guides for permission to conduct a summer solstice ceremony on the altar in Group E. I felt a resounding "yes" in my heart and thanked them for letting me be here. The fireflies were starting to come out as we made our way back to the hotel for dinner.

I woke up at 4 a.m. and got ready for the ceremony. At 4:30, I knocked on Carlos' door and a few minutes later we were on our way to the astronomy center of the archeological site. It had rained during the night, and the clouds still covered the moon and stars. It was just starting to get light when we got to the altar.

Using my hands, I cleaned out the leaves and debris that had collected on the altar stone. Carlos and I gathered some long, pointy green leaves and I arranged them in the form of a Mayan cross in the center of the altar, with each leaf point aligning with a direction. Taking some smaller leaves, I placed them on top of the center, where the bases of each pointed leaf met, making a pretty design. Finally, I took my crystals and put the appropriate crystal on the appropriate long pointy leaf: red for East, white for North, black for West, yellow for South, blue for above and green for below.

I lit a candle and placed it in the exact center of the leaf cross. We were ready to start the summer solstice ceremony.

One of my new Guatemalan friends had given me a clay whistle in the shape of a bird. I had brought it with me for the ceremony. Turning, I faced the east, blew the whistle, bowed and called in the spirits of the east. Making a quarter turn, I repeated the process for the north, west and south, before calling in the spirits of above and below. I faced east and began my silent prayers of gratitude for all that existed in the earth, sky and water.

Thank you, Universe, for all the gifts that you have given me and all the beings on this planet. Thank you for the earth that serves as our home and provides us with sustenance. Thank you for the wind that refreshes our day and the birds that fill the air with their songs. Thank you for the water that gives us life. Thank you for your guidance and support as we all make our way through our lives. Help us to recognize and appreciate the many gifts that you bring to us. Let us care for and protect Mother Earth, Father Sky and all of the beings that exist here. Help me to continue to love and respect you, and never forget that you walk with me through life.

As I prayed, the sky grew brighter and brighter. There was no sun because of the cloud cover, but I could see the glow of the sun behind the clouds.

I prayed until it was completely light and then closed out the ceremony. Carlos thanked me and then went off into the jungle for some bird watching. After cleaning the altar, I walked up the stone steps to where the three astronomical buildings were. To the left was the summer solstice temple; to the right was the winter solstice temple; and in the middle was the temple for the spring and fall equinoxes.

I spent time in each temple but was drawn to the center temple. Representing balance, it aligned most with what I wanted to achieve in my life. I sat on a stone seat in the temple and began meditating. My time in Guatemala was nearing its end, and I wondered if I had accomplished what I needed to while here. My mind went back to Arthur's guides' words before I left:

> *The circumstances for Jennifer are one of straddling the belief fence. To lean in the direction of fear is to attract disruptive energies and behaviors. Jennifer is in a place of shamanic vision, sight and understanding. The journey she is taking is to reinforce that sight and the language, practices and fullness of shamanic beliefs. By that very nature, Jennifer has aligned with experiences that will provide such growth… How much she lets go is her journey. How much she embraces the shaman of Mayan is her choice. In all of these choices, there is no precedent for life after this journey. There is in fact no precedent for the nature of shamanism Jennifer is and will live. As you say, Arthur, "taking the ancient and making it current" is the path and work Jennifer has chosen. Jennifer is gathering more experiences, more stories and more skills as a shaman on this journey.*

Have I been leaning in the direction of my fears? Have I been letting go of what needs to be let go so that I can grow, reinforce and embrace my shamanic beliefs? And, if I am releasing fear, how do I become love? I decided to journey while in the temple to get some deeper insights and answers.

I went to my sacred space and met 444, my power animal. I explained what I was trying to accomplish with the journey, and we traveled together through a burrow to the Lower World where we were met by some of my guides. We sat under a large tree and talked. They showed me how I had been releasing fears around rejection, homelessness and poverty by sharing my story and moving away from the typical ways of living (having a defined home, a 9-to-5 job). I realized that I had made some pretty big leaps but still had some work to do. The important thing though is that I was trusting that I would be taken care of by the Universe. This lesson of trust began with the accident and has become easier and easier for me to put into practice.

My guides continued, talking about love.

"To become love," they said, "You need to release fear completely. Stay open and spend time daily connecting to the heart. Feel the love we are channeling through you. It is always there. It never diminishes or runs out." They then reminded me that when I did my shamanic work with them, I was working with pure love.

I thanked them for their insights and guidance, and then 444 and I made our way to the ocean. I went into the water and swam through some beautiful colonies of coral and fish. Gold flecks of sunlight made their way through the water to where I was swimming. I swam deeper and deeper, following the colors of the coral until I was led to a beautiful huge clamshell. It was pink, and as I neared it, it opened up. Inside was a translucent opalescent pearl shaped like a heart. The clam spoke to me. "This will help you. Wisdom comes from the heart. Pearls of truth come from the heart. Take this pearl." As the clam said this, it put the pearl in my heart and I could immediately feel the energy flowing through me. I thanked the clam for the gift and then continued swimming.

A pod of dolphins came by and I swam and leapt through the water with them. Together we spiraled up and down in the water and then jumped out and into arcs. A whale swam by and asked me to dive with him. As we did, he sang his song for me. We stayed underwater in the deep ocean for a few minutes, and then he had me ride on his head up to the surface. When we reached the surface, he launched me to the shore with his waterspout.

I landed safely and easily on the beach and decided to visit the Crystal Cave, a cave filled with every type of crystal in the universe. 444 had shown me the cave years ago when I was recovering from my accident. I walked over to the cave with 444 and sat in it, feeling the energy of the many crystals there.

444, my guides and I walked from there through the forest to the den on the edge of the field where the big tree was. The den was very special to me, since it had been my "workplace" for many lifetimes. Along one wall were a variety of carvings. Each carving had been made by me during a lifetime; I had made my carving in the wall for this lifetime a couple years ago when I was fully initiated and accepted as a shaman. As I sat down, my guides asked me what I felt when I was in the den. I closed my eyes to better tune into myself and answered, "Total peacefulness." They nodded in agreement, and then said, "This is where you need to live, in this state. This peacefulness will help keep you open and increase love." I nodded and thanked them.

I opened my eyes and turned off the drumming mp3 that had been playing. The sun was starting to break through the clouds and I watched it light up the pyramid across the way as I thought about the many messages from the journey. *It all boils down to pure, fearless love*, I thought. *Can I tap into the love that I work with for my shamanic work for my everyday life?* I wondered.

I climbed down the temple and slowly made my way back to the hotel, thinking about love and how I could incorporate more of it in my life.

◆◆◆

A few days later, my friend Alan from San Francisco arrived. He had booked a trip to Guatemala specifically to visit me. Alan and I have been friends for almost a decade. I met him when a friend and I decided to do a "makeover day" in San Francisco. Our day included getting our hair styled, and Alan happened to be the hairstylist. We hit it off, and became nearly instant friends. Since then, we have supported each other through the ups and downs of our life. In fact, when I was hit by the minivan, Alan came to the hospital and brought me home when I was released. I picked him up at the airport, and, after dropping his stuff off at a hotel in town, brought him to my little hut so we could catch up. One bottle of champagne and some chocolates later, we had completely filled each other in on our lives and the hut was ringing with our laughter.

Over the course of the next few days we visited Tikal, went

horseback riding, and explored Actun Kan, a cave in Santa Elena that had been used by the Mayans for centuries. He had brought his shears and other hairdressing supplies and not only did my hair but also Marta's and Angela's hair. I introduced him to many of my friends in the area and had him meet Juan Carlos, Lupe and Rayas. I knew that the chickens had made an impression on him when he declared that he would never eat chicken again.

But I think the biggest impression was made when I showed him how some of the indigenous people lived in Guatemala. We drove by a few houses so he could see the thatch roofs, dirt floors and nearly empty homes. I took him to the school, health clinic and library so he could see the work that was being done to help improve peoples' lives here. Alan was quiet as he saw all of this, and I knew he was comparing what was here with his life in San Francisco.

The days went by quickly, and before I knew it, it was the last night of his trip. We went out to dinner and talked about his visit.

"So," I asked, "what do you think of Guatemala?"

"I love it! The people here are amazing. Tikal was incredibly spiritual. It is sobering to see how some people here live, but even so, they are so welcoming."

"I know what you mean. I am humbled by how accepting and welcoming everyone is here. I feel like I've made so many new friends in such a short period of time. That's why I ended up extending my stay by an extra six weeks. I couldn't bring myself to leave. I can't believe that the extra six weeks are almost over and I'll be leaving soon."

"This whole time has gone by so quickly," he responded. "When you first told me that you were going to come here for three months, it felt like an eternity. But it wasn't. I think it helped that you were able to stay in touch with me—and others—through email, texts and occasional calls. It was like you were in both places at once."

He was quiet for a moment, and then said, "Guatemala suits you."

I nodded. "Yes, in some ways it does."

We finished our dinner and I drove him back to his hotel. The next morning, I picked him up early and drove him to the airport. We hugged goodbye, happy to have spent time together and knowing that we would see each other in a couple weeks when it would be my turn to leave Guatemala. I was planning on staying at his apartment for a couple weeks before heading off on the next leg of my journey to Asia.

I thought about Alan's words about Guatemala suiting me. In so many ways it did. But at the same time, I missed San Francisco, my friends and my life there. I was attracted to two very different worlds. I definitely felt a connection to this land and this area, but wasn't quite sure what it meant or what I was supposed to do with that feeling.

Ever since I had seen that empty house when hiking with Felipe, I had been half-heartedly looking for a house. I had looked at a few but didn't see any that appealed to me. Someone had suggested that perhaps I should buy some land so I went and looked at some lots before Alan came to visit. None of them resonated with me either. I wasn't too concerned. In my mind, if it were meant to be, it would happen. I certainly wasn't going to stress myself out looking for something when perhaps it wasn't in my best interest.

But I couldn't deny my sadness about leaving my little hut, El Remate and all the friends I had met. I knew that I could always come back and visit, but I wanted more. I wasn't quite sure what "more" consisted of, since I knew I didn't want to live in Guatemala full time—and I truly missed my family and friends in the States and knew that I had no intention of leaving San Francisco.

All of these thoughts were going through my head as I began planning my going away/gratitude party for the following week. I stopped at Marta's house to invite her to the party. Angela was there as well, so I was able to extend her an invitation at the same time. I sat down at the kitchen table with them to visit.

"I hear you're looking to buy a house or land here," Angela said.

"Well, I'm considering it," I replied. "I haven't found anything I like, so it may be something that I do in the future."

"I am managing two pieces of land for some people who live in England. They are looking to sell it and are willing to sell it for the price that they bought it for years ago. Would you like to see it?"

"Sure," I said. We made plans to meet the next day.

Angela picked me up promptly at 10:15 in the morning and we drove over to the other side of town, near her house, and up a dirt road. The houses looked faintly familiar, but it wasn't until she passed by the empty house that had originally gotten me thinking about having a place here that I got my bearings.

She drove just a small bit past the empty house and turned right on an even more rugged dirt road before stopping her pickup truck in front of a fenced in lot. The land hadn't been cleared and it was filled with trees and brush. Monkeys moved overhead through the trees and I spotted a couple toucans. The brush was so heavy that we couldn't even enter the land…and wouldn't have been able to even if we wanted to since the fence didn't have a gate…but it didn't matter. I had heard a resounding *yes* in my soul that second I saw the land that continued as we looked at the land. With the *yeses* filling my heart, I knew that this was it. Every fiber of my being knew that I was meant to have this land and a house on it, even though I couldn't precisely say why. In fact, it wasn't until a few days later that the reason for me having a home on this land became clear to me.

We peered through the chain link fence, and Angela pointed out to me where the half-acre lot ended and the third-acre lot began. I walked the length of the land that ran along the dirt road, taking in the energy of the land. I kept hearing whispers from my guides in my head reassuring me that this was the right decision.

"I will have someone clear the brush tomorrow or the morning after so you can walk through it and take a closer look," Angela said.

"That would be great," I replied. "I'm going to ask Pedro to come with me to look at it. I'd love to get have another set of eyes look at it with me. But, I do want you to know that I am very interested in it."

I went back home, excited and filled with possibilities. I was going to see Pedro later that afternoon when I returned the rental car. He had offered to meet me at the airport and drive me back to El Remate.

He had barely pulled into the airport parking lot before I told him about the land. "I would love for you to look at it and give me your honest opinion about the land and the asking price. Angela is going to have some people clear it tomorrow or Sunday morning so we can walk through it, but do you want to see it today?"

My excitement must have been contagious, because Pedro laughed and said yes. I gave him the directions and we went straight there from the airport. He nodded when he saw the land and said that he thought it was a good piece of land. Then he asked a practical question that I hadn't thought of and didn't know the answer to. "Do you know if there is water or electricity up here?"

"That's a good question! Let's go ask Angela. Her house is near here."

We drove over to Angela's house. She greeted us and invited us in. I explained that Pedro and I had looked at the land, and that Pedro had asked about water and electricity. Angela sat with us for over half an hour and explained how to get water and electricity. Her answers made more sense to Pedro than me, and I knew it wouldn't be an issue when he smiled and said, "Good!"

On Sunday, Pedro and I went back to the land. Camila and baby Esteban came with us. There was a small work crew cutting the brush with machetes. When asked, they told us that they had tunneled under the fence to get in. They showed us the area they had used and then held the fence up as best as they could while we crawled under, passing the baby through to the workers.

Pedro was as excited as I was about the land. We walked through the entire lot, following the borders and looking at the trees and slope while Camila sat near the workers with Esteban. "This is good earth," he said, pointing to the rich dark soil. "You could easily plant fruit trees and a garden here."

I nodded. I would love to have some fruit trees and a garden. "I don't see any fruit trees here now, do you?" I asked.

He looked around and said no. "But you do have some Ramon Nut and Pimiento trees," he said, gesturing to them as we walked. We looked at the trees and then turned our conversation to where I would want a house to be built. I showed him the general area and told him that I had already started thinking of home designs.

"I would really prefer a two-story house to a one-story one," I began, "but I have no idea how much it would cost to build a house here. I know that you've built houses here and in the United States. Would you be able to give me an estimate on what it would cost? If I can afford it and you are open to this, I'd like to start building right away and have you manage the work."

"I can put together an estimate for you. Send me your home designs and I'll take a look at them. What are you doing on Wednesday? We could go to a couple stores and look at windows, flooring, and other things so that the estimate is more accurate.

And, if you're comfortable with the pricing, we could start building on Monday."

Wednesday is great," I said. "Let me finalize the floor plans and text them to you."

As we drove away, I sent a message to Angela and told her I would take the half-acre lot. She was thrilled and suggested that we meet with the lawyer on Thursday to do the paperwork. I agreed and we set a time.

Everything had fallen in place so quickly, and felt so right, that I didn't have time to stop and think. I sat in my hut, closed my eyes, and imagined myself at my land, with my house. A sense of peacefulness filled me, and I knew that my home here was going to be my sanctuary. In this house, I would be able to recharge and connect more deeply with the spiritual energy of the Mayan archeological sites. I smiled inwardly as visions of having my new friends over for dinner, hosting my family at my new house when they came to visit, and making Christmas gingerbread houses with Enrico's, Pedro's and Maria's daughters flashed before me.

With a start, I realized that it didn't have to be an all-or-nothing proposition. *I can spend part of my time in Guatemala and part of my time in San Francisco...or wherever I want to travel to. If I wanted to, I could have a home in both places and spend two weeks each month in each place. I could have the best of both worlds!*

Feeling good about my decision, I turned my attention to working on the floor plans and then called my friend Alan. He couldn't believe that I had found something and asked a ton of questions. When I mentioned that there was another lot for sale next to my lot, he said without any hesitation that he would buy it. I texted Angela and let her know so she could set up the lawyer appointment for both sales.

I have owned four houses, but none of them were built for me. I had no idea how much fun it would be. I spent hours working on the floor plans until I had it "just right." On Wednesday, Pedro was amazed at how quickly I picked out the windows, flooring, roofing and bathroom fixtures. I could already see the house in my mind and knew exactly what I wanted. We took pictures of everything and their respective prices so Pedro could create an estimate for me. I took extra pictures for Alan just in case he wanted to see what the options were.

The next day, Pedro drove me to the lawyer's office. Angela and her husband were waiting for us. The entire process took no time at all and only one signature—very different from a sale in the United States. In a matter of minutes, I owned a little piece of jungle in Guatemala.

With the design of the house and the land purchase behind me, I turned my attention to my going away party on Saturday. I had invited nearly 40 people to come for an American-style cookout to thank them for all their help and friendship. I had bought hot dogs, hamburgers, buns, chips, ingredients for pasta and tossed salads and condiments and spent Friday doing all of the prep work.

◆ ◆ ◆

The morning of my going away party dawned with a clear sky and a lot of sun. I was relieved, since the previous days had been rainy. I spent the morning doing some last minute preparations and setting up rented plastic tables and chairs in the garden and driveway areas of my yard.

While I finalized the details for the party, my mind raced with a mix of thoughts: *I can't wait to see my friends. I hope it doesn't rain. I'm really going to miss everyone, but I can see them again when I come back. I hope they like the party—it's going to be different for them.* I consoled myself with thoughts of the house that I would be building, telling myself that I would be back. *It's not so much a going away party as much as it is a thank you party to all my friends for all their help and friendship for the past four and a half months*, I thought to myself as my guests started arriving.

The food was a big hit, and I found out after the party that many of my guests were very excited about going to an American-style cookout, since most of them had not been to the United States. We sat around and laughed and talked about my time there. The afternoon flew by, and before I knew it, everyone except for Pedro and his family had left.

"We have something to show you," Pedro said. His son Rosalio pulled out a laptop and turned it on. He pulled up an architectural software tool and opened up a document. It was my house! He had taken the drawings I had made and plotted it into the software tool so I could see a three dimensional image of the house from every angle.

I pored over each drawing and made a couple minor changes.

Seeing it as a building instead of a flat drawing on graph paper somehow made it even more "real" to me.

As I finished looking at the drawings, Pedro told me he would pick me up on Monday morning for an 8:30 a.m. meeting with the master builder. With that, Pedro stood up and gave me a hug as they prepared to leave. "We are very excited about you being here more often. You are part of our family and we would hate to not see you." The rest of his family nodded their agreement.

My eyes blurred from the love and acceptance I felt from them and the rest of the people I had met in Guatemala.

◆ ◆ ◆

Pedro showed up at exactly 8:20 Monday morning and we took the quick drive over to my land, stopping to pick up the master builder as we went. Angela had hired someone to put a gate in the fence, so we no longer needed to crawl under the fence to get in. We walked around the land and discussed the pros and cons of building the house in different locations. Armed with that information I made my decision where I wanted the house to be. Based on my home design and the work required to build the house, they estimated that the house would be done by Christmas.

Pedro and the master builder immediately got to work, cutting down some small saplings and brush that was in the footprint area of the house. With the area better cleared, they began plotting out the exterior walls, using some string and stakes made from the saplings. I sat on a large, flat rock as they worked, answering their occasional questions and enjoying the energy of the space.

I hadn't expected them to begin working right away, and realized that I hadn't asked the land for permission to do the work. I made mental plans to come back early the next morning to do a small ceremony. Given how strong the pull and messages were when I saw the land, I was fairly certain that it was okay to build, but felt it was important to honor the land this way.

Finished with outlining the house walls, Pedro drove me back to my little hut and helped me bring my cat, Rayas to his new home. I had been worried about what would happen to him after I left and wanted to make sure that he had a home where he would be loved and cared for. As luck would have it, I had found his original owner, who was thrilled to learn that he was alive and immediately made plans to welcome him back in her home. It felt like the perfect solution. The fact that I could see how much she loved Rayas helped ease my sadness at saying goodbye to him. Juan Carlos and Lupe had gone to Maria's house just before the party. Maria had promised me that she wouldn't eat them, and I was hoping that at some point I would be able to have them move with me into my new house.

I had packed up some of my belongings and given them to Alan to bring back to San Francisco for me. With Juan Carlos, Lupe and Rayas gone, suddenly my little hut felt very empty. The energy that they and I had brought to the hut was dissipating. I spent some time organizing my remaining belongings and packing what could be packed up, before thinking through the ceremony I wanted to conduct prior to building the house.

I wanted to honor the Guatemalan Mayan customs with this ceremony, so I mentally reviewed the ceremonies I had attended. I would need to incorporate the elements into the ceremony—fire, water, air, and earth—as well as offerings of flowers and candles. I decided that a candle could do double duty as an offering and as fire when lit. I'd bring a bottle of water. Air was easy, since it was all around and was part of my voice when I spoke aloud. And the land would provide the earth.

At the same time, I wanted to incorporate aspects of myself into the ceremony as well, since it was for my house. I had made a small altar in the hut with some crystals that I travel with. The crystals were different colors that aligned with the colors of the directions. I had worked with them for years, and they were imbued with my energy. They would be a perfect way to bring "me" forward in the ceremony. I could also cut a small lock of my hair and leave that for an offering. Satisfied, I went to bed.

I woke up before the sun rose and pulled together the materials for the ceremony before walking through town to my land. The sky was light by the time I got there and let myself in. I walked into the staked out area of the house and set up a small altar on a rock in the middle.

Lighting the candle, I turned to the east, where the sun was just starting to peek through the trees. I bowed, and called in the energies of the east before taking a quarter turn to the north. I bowed again, repeating the process before turning to the west and south. Finally, I stood in the center and called in my guides.

Closing my eyes and facing east again, I raised my hands and began, speaking out loud.

"Thank you for bringing me here to this point in time. I am so grateful for the guidance you have given me through my life. I am grateful for Mother Earth and Father Sky and the many blessings they bring to all of us on the planet. Please bless this land and give me permission to make a home here." I paused, listening to my heart for the answer. The same feeling came over me that had when I first saw the land, and I heard a definitive "*yes*" in my heart.

I continued, "Thank you. I promise to honor and care for this land. I promise to replace any trees that need to be cut down with new ones. Please continue to guide me in working and living with this land."

I placed the flowers at the base of a tree as an offering to the land and a symbol of my promise. Blowing out the candle, I sat on the rock and breathed in the energy of the land.

That night, I had made plans with Pedro and his family to go to Flores. I was officially in my countdown to leaving Guatemala, and they wanted to take me out to dinner. Pedro was very excited when he saw me.

"Today we started digging for the foundation," he said, "And guess what we found?"

"What?" His excitement was so palatable that I found myself getting excited without even knowing what I was getting excited about.

He pulled out his phone, and, showing me a photo, said, "We found some small broken pieces of ceramic. Your land was once home to Mayan people. They were probably commoners, or maybe even slaves, but they had their homes where your home is going to be."

I looked at the picture. The handful of broken pieces were small and simple, but definitely were part of larger pieces of pottery. Julian had once said to me that there were bits of Mayan pottery all over the area and suggested that it wasn't valuable because it was so commonplace. While that may be true, I was still excited. *This is why I feel so connected to the land there,* I thought to myself. With a start, I made another connection. *That's why I was so attracted to that house around the corner from my land that I saw originally. It wasn't actually the house that called to me, it was the energy and spirit of the land behind the house that called to me. I was hearing the voices of some of the ancestors who had lived here.*

I smiled broadly at Pedro. "This is amazing!" I exclaimed. "I want to look at them tomorrow. In the meantime, let's buy a plastic container for you to put these pieces—and any others you may find—in. I don't know what I'm going to do with them, but I'd like to incorporate or showcase them in the house."

I paused for a moment, thinking. "Pedro, do you think some people might be buried on the land as well?"

He was quiet for a minute, and then slowly nodded his head. "Yes, there might be Mayans buried there. The places where we found the ceramic also have soil of a different color. That might be because it is a burial site."

I nodded and connected with my heart. "If you find any human remains, please put them aside with care. I will do a ceremony to honor them and bury them somewhere else in the property." "

OK, Jenny, we will do that."

"And I know this may sound crazy, but before you put the cement in for the foundation, I would like you to place flowers over the areas where you found the ceramic pieces. The cement would seal up any graves, and the flowers are a simple way to show honor and respect to them," I added.

"We will do that too."

I thanked him, and then we all got down to the serious business of eating dinner and challenging each other to arcade games.

I woke up early the next morning and made my way back over to the land. I had realized when Pedro told me about the potential graves that I needed to do another ceremony or at least make sure that any beings that had lived on the land were comfortable with my being there and disrupting things a little bit.

Laying out my crystals and the pieces of ceramic, I lit a candle, starting the ceremony in the same way I had yesterday. After calling in the spirits and guides from each direction, I turned and faced east and addressed the ancestors who had lived—and died—on the land I was standing on.

"Ancestors of this land: thank you for making your presence known to me through my intuition and the physical presence of the ceramic pieces. Yesterday I asked and was given permission to build and live on this land, however, I wanted to check with you as well. Do you welcome me to this land?"

I paused, listening to my heart. What I heard made me laugh.

They were laughing at me! *"Who do you think gave you permission yesterday?"* they asked.

I chuckled and acknowledged that they had spoken to me yesterday. *"We are here to help you grow in your shamanic abilities,"* they continued. *"We remain connected to the land, but are not connected to our remains. Those bodies served us many, many years ago but are not part of our spiritual beings. We will not be upset if the building of the house disturbs them. We heard your intention yesterday about honoring any remains with ceremony and burial, and that pleases us."*

"Were you calling to me when I first saw the house?" I asked.

"Yes. This land has been waiting for you. We have been waiting for you. As we said, we want to help you grow and evolve as a shaman. We will help you do that. We will speak to you through your dreams and through this land to share our wisdom with you. We can connect with you through your shamanic journeys as well and teach you that way too."

I bowed my head, grateful for the gift of their teachings. "Thank you. I am honored to share this land with you and the lessons you have for me."

After blowing out the candle, I spent some time looking at the ceramic pieces and reflecting on the conversation I had just had with the ancestors of this land.

For the rest of the week, I made daily early-morning trips to the land to watch the building progress. I was surprised at how excited I was about it. One morning I went and saw that the work crew had poured the concrete for the pillars the night before. The pillars would provide the strongest foundation for the house, so I carved hearts into the base of each pillar, asking that the house be built on a foundation of love. The next day, the rest of the foundation was poured, and Pedro sent me photos of the flowers placed in the foundation area before the cement was added.

Before I knew it, it was time for me to leave El Remate. I made plans to return in either September or October to see how the house was progressing, and then headed out to Guatemala City.

CHAPTER 14: WHAT DO YOU REALLY WANT?

I stood at the front of the line, waiting for United to begin boarding its flight from Guatemala City to Houston. It was 5 a.m., and I was feeling slightly zombie-like as I watched the gate attendants prepare for boarding. I was looking forward to getting into my seat and being a vegetable for the flight.

"Excuse me," a voice said behind me. "Do you mind if I go in front of you?"

I turned to see a man about my age standing behind me. He was holding his boarding pass and showed it to me. "I'm not trying to cut in front of you. I've been tagged for extra screening and I know that it will take some time for them to do it. Every minute would help."

I looked at his boarding pass. It had "SSSS" in large black letters on the bottom. I knew what that meant, having seen many instances of it on colleagues' tickets right after 9/11. He had been tagged as a Secondary Security Screening Selectee, which meant that he would have to go through another round of security screening, including a thorough review of his carry-on bags. Back in 2001, the SSSS code was given randomly to people, but also given to people who traveled to countries that were on a watch list or for those people that were on a watch list.

"Oh man, you got the quad S of death," I said. "I didn't even realize they still did that. I thought they did away with that a few years after 9/11."

"Nope. I get this at least a couple times a year," he replied. "I have no idea why I keep getting the extra screening. I'm Ernesto, by the way."

He didn't look like he was from Guatemala, but I couldn't quite place his nationality. I held out my hand. "I'm Jennifer. It's nice to meet you, Ernesto. Are you here on vacation?"

He shook my hand and then answered. "No, I am here for work. I have businesses and homes here in Guatemala and in the San Francisco Bay Area. How about you?"

"I've been here for about five and a half months writing my second book."

"You're an author?"

"Yes. A year ago I quit my job as a business strategy consultant in preparation of the launch of my first book, which came out about eight months ago. I'm also a shaman and a coach. What do you do?"

"I have a real estate business down here in Guatemala and a start up in San Francisco. Where were you staying while you were here?"

"Up in El Remate. I rented a small thatch roof hut by the lake there. Is your house here in Guatemala City?" I asked.

"No, I have a house in Antigua."

"Oh, Antigua is such a beautiful city," I replied. Just then the gate attendants began boarding. "It looks like we're about to board. Good luck with your screening."

"Thanks! Hopefully I'll see you on the flight."

Ernesto boarded just before the airplane door closed and sat a few seats in front of me. Just before he sat down he turned and scanned the faces of the other first class passengers. Catching my eyes, he gave a little wave. "They let you on," I said. He laughed, nodded, and sat down. I closed my eyes, relaxing as we took off.

The plane landed without incident in Houston and I gathered my belongings before heading to immigration. Ernesto caught up to me as I walked along. "Good flight?" he asked.

"Yes, I just relaxed and watched a movie. Normally I would have done some writing, but the battery on my laptop died so I was forced to relax," I said jokingly.

"I can never work on planes. Even in first class it is too cramped for me. I like to spread out."

"I usually find that my airplane time is my most productive time," I replied. "No meetings. No phone calls. Just focused time to think."

"I give you credit," he said. We had reached immigration. Ernesto explained that he had Global Entry, which I didn't have. I said goodbye to him and made my way over to the monitors to check in.

"Welcome home," said the immigration officer as I handed him my paperwork and he waved me through.

I made my way to the Club and watched some of the business travelers. Several were on conference calls, while others were jockeying for position about who had the worst travel nightmare story. *That used to be me,* I thought. I felt strangely disconnected from them and that lifestyle.

I decided to walk around the terminal while I waited for my next flight. I turned on my phone and began calling family members and friends. My three-hour layover went by very quickly, and before I knew it, I was standing in line to board my next flight.

"We meet again," said a voice behind me. It was Ernesto.

"Hey there. How was your layover? Do you have the quad-S's again?"

"No, not this time."

"Cool. Then you can't cut in front of me this time," I laughed. We chatted a bit and then boarded the plane.

Four hours later, the plane touched down in San Francisco. I was taking my bag down from the overhead bin when I felt someone touch my arm. I turned and saw Ernesto.

"Do you have a business card?" he asked? "I think I'd like to hire you to do some consulting work for my business."

"I actually gave my last one out yesterday," I said, "but let me give you my cell and email address." I took out a piece of paper, wrote down my contact information, and handed it over to him.

"I'll call you this week and we can talk about what I'm looking to do."

"Sounds great. Talk to you then!"

We said goodbye and made our respective ways out of the airport. I was staying with my friend Alan. I met him for dinner and we caught up over Thai spicy green beans and wine.

Ernesto called me the next morning, and we talked about his technology start up. He wanted help positioning the company to meet with venture capitalists. Specifically, he needed help putting together the pitch deck. I told him I'd pull together a proposal and we made plans to meet at the bar in the Fairmont Hotel in two days to review.

Two days later, we met. I had pulled together a proposal and brought copies with me. I was getting excited about the project. Given the scope and timing of the work that Ernesto had asked for, my project fees would equal the cost of the land and building the house in Guatemala. My income had decreased significantly, and a little bit of income would be refreshing.

We talked for two hours about pretty much everything except for the proposal. He told me about his businesses in Guatemala and the United States, his wife and his family. I was pleasantly surprised when he said that he doesn't believe in making work the only thing in life, and that it's important to make time to enjoy living. We shared travel stories, and I told him about my book, my shamanic work, and why I had spent time in Guatemala.

He asked me several questions about shamanism, and then said, to my surprise, "I work with a shaman in Guatemala. He has helped me with some health issues."

"Really? That's cool. So you know how impactful it can be."

"Yes. And I have to tell you that I feel as if we were meant to meet. I just know it. We are supposed to work together. I know you have to run to another appointment now but we can talk more about this later."

Given how we met, I was inclined to agree that we were meant to meet, but I wasn't yet completely sold on the idea that we were meant to work together. I smiled and said, "Take a look at the proposal and let me know what you think." We made plans to get together on Monday at a coffee shop, and then I headed out.

Monday was a beautiful warm day, so I grabbed a table outside for us to sit at. Ernesto arrived right on time and wasted no time getting to the point.

"I read your proposal, and I want more."

"More?" Mentally I reviewed the proposal contents, wondering where he wanted to expand the scope of the project.

"Yes. I want you to come work for me full time. I know you're thinking that you want a new way of life, but I think you are going to get bored with the lifestyle that you have right now. Hear me out. Here is what I'm suggesting: You come work for us full time. Your title would be Chief Customer Experience Officer, or something like that, and you would be a founding member of the company. You can tell me what you want your title to be. I would expect that you work full time until we get the funding needed for the company, but you can work wherever you want to work. I will pay for two first class tickets a month for you to fly to San Francisco from Guatemala. You will get a company laptop and a company phone that works in Guatemala."

"I also believe in compensating well," he continued, and shared a base salary with me that was more than acceptable. "In addition, I will give you options in the company. My goal would be to give you enough options that when we sell the company in a few years, you would walk away with $10-15 million dollars."

"You would be responsible for getting the funding we need to get the company off the ground. Once we got the first round of funding, I would expect you to take two to three months off to relax, recharge and do your shamanic thing and write. Then, when you're ready to come back to work, you can tell me what the terms are of your working engagement with us. I think you would be the best person to be the voice of the company."

I stared at him, trying to wrap my mind around what he had just said. I had not expected a job offer—especially one that seemed to address many of the things that were important to me, such as living part-time in Guatemala and having time to do my shamanic work. My mind was racing, but the one thing that kept going through my head was that I hadn't ruined my business career by taking this past year off.

"Wow," I said. "That's a very attractive offer." I asked a couple questions and then said, "Let me think about it and get back to you on Wednesday afternoon with an answer."

"Fair enough."

Our conversation turned to other topics, eventually touching on skydiving. "I love skydiving," I said. "I had wanted to get certified, but my work schedule was too crazy."

"I will throw in skydiving lessons so you can get certified. You can go with my wife. She has wanted to do that for a long time. And yes, you are probably getting the idea that I really want you to join my firm. Please don't take advantage of that!"

I laughed and promised I wouldn't.

When I left the coffee shop to meet a friend at the Ferry Building for dinner, my head was spinning. *Why has this job been brought to me at this time? Should I take it? How does it align with my shamanic work*? I could sense that the offer—especially the proposed financial security—was clouding my ability to tune in to my intuition, so I didn't have any clear answers.

That night, I had a dream that gave me more clarity about the job offer.

> *I am in Guatemala, at my new house. Juan Carlos and Lupe, the chickens, are with me. Lupe is sitting on an egg, and we are waiting for it to hatch. As the time gets closer, she encases herself and the egg in a giant sack, similar to a cocoon. It started to rain, and the water was coming up into the yard. I picked up the sack, with Lupe and the egg in it, and brought it into the house. It was translucent enough that I could clearly see Lupe in it. I sit down on a chair and hold the sack on my lap. As I watched, Lupe broke out of and hatched from the sack. She hopped down off my lap and started walking around the house. I felt something warm on my lap and looked down. The egg had hatched as well. Inside was a white rabbit. As I looked at the rabbit, I realized that there was something wrong with it. It was as if someone had taken the rabbit and cut it in half the long way. The rabbit, while alive, was only half of a rabbit. Even though the "cut" part was covered with fur and looked fine, I was afraid of touching the rabbit and hurting it in some way. I looked outside and the sky was black and red. The storm had gotten stronger and had blown my garage across the yard. I was glad my car wasn't in there! When I turned back, the rabbit was gone. I started frantically searching for the rabbit because I didn't want it to die. One of my friends was there, and she just shook her head at me sadly. I knew it was gone.*

I woke up and knew that I couldn't accept the full time job offer. In the dream, I was the white rabbit. In the Mayan spiritual calendar, the Tzolkin, I was born during the Lamat, or rabbit, trecena. If I were to accept the job, I would be literally cutting off half of who I am—the shamanic part of me that I had discovered fairly recently that was aligned with my life purpose. In effect, if I took my sight away from whom I was and what I was meant to do in this life, I would be killing myself.

As I thought more about it, I realized that the job offer was also a test for me. Ernesto had said all of the right things and had offered a number of things that made the job offer very attractive to me. My last day at the consulting firm—and my last day of having a regular paycheck—was just about a year ago. I had had to overcome a deep-rooted fear about the safety and security a regular job and home appeared to offer and jump without an apparent safety net into a lifestyle that was completely unknown to me and different from how most of my friends and family lived. To live authentically, I had to trust. Thus far, I had been taken care of. It was as if the universe was saying to me, "Do you really trust that you can have the life you desire or are you going to fall back into old habits and belief systems?"

I pulled out my pendulum and asked, "Is this full time job aligned with my best interests and life purpose?" As I watched, the pendulum began moving from left to right, indicating a clear *no*. Out of curiosity, I decided to ask about the consulting job. "Is the consulting job aligned with my best interests and life purpose?" The pendulum shifted direction and moved in a very solid front and back motion. *Yes*.

Well that's interesting, I thought. *Why would the consulting project be aligned with my best interests but the full time work not be?* A memory surfaced.

Years ago, as I approached the one-year marker of losing the girls, I was in the middle of selling a large global consulting project. The sales process was an especially complex one, since I was working with leaders from four different countries across several business units. I'd often be on phone calls late in the night with the client, trying to align all the different individuals around the project work. One such night, the prospective client was going around in circles about something. Bored, I opened up the Audi website and began configuring my dream car: an Audi TT convertible. I picked the engine type, selected a deep green color, and decided on the options I wanted, and then printed out the final product. I wrote a quick note to my boss: "When this project closes, this is what I want as a signing bonus." I was joking, since we didn't get signing bonuses, but I put it on his chair. The project closed right before Labor Day. As I looked at the newspaper that weekend, I saw an advertisement for Audi. They were having their annual sale. On a whim, I went to the dealership and there was my car, exactly as I had configured it online. Even with the sale price, it was a bit more expensive than what I wanted to pay. I asked the dealer if we could keep everything the same but change the engine to the standard engine rather than the performance one. He went online and looked. There wasn't another green car within over 500 hundred miles. I knew then that the car I was looking at was meant for me and I bought it. A couple weeks later I was at a seminar to learn how to communicate with angels. The woman leading the seminar saw my car and asked me if it was mine. When I said yes, she said, "The angels are telling me that the car was a gift for you to celebrate overcoming a difficult time."

I picked up the pendulum one last time and asked it, "Is the consulting project a gift for me?" Once again, the pendulum moved forward and backward, indicating a *yes*. I thanked the universe for the gift, even though it appeared that the consulting project was no longer an option, recognizing that I had overcome another area of my life in the past year. I was not going to take the job.

I sat with the insights I had just received and felt every muscle in my body relax. When thinking about the potential job, I had fallen into an "I can do this for a little while" mindset. I had even had a few passing thoughts about the fact that if I didn't like it, I could just quit. Neither of these is a good perspective for starting a new job!

Now comfortable with turning down the job offer, I turned my attention to packing. I was meeting my friend Arthur and his fiancée Ava in Sonoma for a couple days. I had called him right after Ernesto offered me the job. We had planned on talking about the job offer tonight, but given how I felt now, I didn't think we'd need to. We could spend our time on more important things, like talking about their upcoming wedding and drinking wine.

We had reserved a couple of rooms at a bed and breakfast in Healdsburg, near the town green. After checking in and walking their two Chihuahuas, we made our way downtown to have a late lunch. I hadn't seen them since January and was anxious to hear how they were both doing and how the wedding plans were coming along. We walked to a nearby restaurant, sat in an enclosed patio with flowered trellises, and ordered.

As we ate and talked, they shared with me the details of what had been going on in their lives and the marriage proposal and then surprised me by asking me to officiate their wedding. I immediately said yes. After a group hug of love and excitement, we continued talking and laughing until it was dark.

I woke up early the next morning and took a walk through the quiet streets of Healdsburg. In spite of my happiness for my friends, I had a knot in the pit of my stomach. I had to call Ernesto and tell him that I wasn't going to take the job. I had told him that I would call him in the evening, but as I walked around I decided that telling him sooner rather than later would be the better thing to do.

He picked up on the first ring. "Buenos dias, Jennifer. How's Sonoma?"

"Hola, Ernesto. It has been wonderful." I paused, and then said, "I wanted to thank you for an extremely generous job offer and opportunity, but I've decided to say no."

He let out a sharp exhale. "Why?"

"I am not ready to come back to the workforce full time yet." I didn't tell him that I didn't think I would ever be going back.

"OK, well, then, would you be willing to do the consulting project?"

"Yes, I would love to do the consulting project."

"Perfect. I will leave the full time job offer on the table for you in case you change your mind."

I thanked him, and we spent several minutes talking about what he wanted done first. I told him I would start the next day, and then we hung up the phone. I said a quick prayer of gratitude to the universe for the gift of work and how well the conversation had gone, and then made my way back to the hotel to meet Arthur and Ava for breakfast.

The next two nights I had dreams that further validated my decision to not take the full time job.

The first night, I am riding on a white horse. The horse is running freely through a field, but someone is trying to kill it and me. I try blindfolding the horse so that it doesn't see the person who is trying to kill us, but the horse doesn't like the blindfold and shakes it off as it keeps running.

The second night, I'm at an office. It's not clear to me whether or not I work there. Someone comes by and staples my hand to the table and then covers it with blue wax to prevent me from leaving and doing my spiritual work.

Horses symbolize freedom, inner strength and one's personal drive through life. White has consistently been associated with spirituality, which aligns with my shamanic work and spirit evolution. In the dream, I had been riding my spiritual life freely, but someone was trying to take that away from me. The blindfold represents deception, and my interpretation was that I would be deceiving myself if I thought I could work fulltime and still maintain my freedom and spiritual work.

This interpretation was hammered home in the second dream, where I was physically restrained from doing my life's calling.

◆ ◆ ◆

I started working for Ernesto and fell back into my old work routine fairly easily, with one notable difference: I set and kept boundaries with my time. I committed to working no more than thirty hours a week so that I could have a better work-life balance. Ernesto was great about that and honored and respected my boundaries. Because he split his time between Guatemala and San Francisco, and also took business trips, he was also very comfortable with me working remotely.

This was an added bonus since I was leaving in a couple days for Japan, Cambodia and Thailand for three weeks and then to the East Coast at the end of August for two weeks.

When I had first thought about taking time and traveling around, I had planned to be in Guatemala for about three months and then head over to Asia. While the cultures are very different, I sensed and had seen that there were more similarities than differences, especially if you looked back to the more ancient civilizations. I had felt this several years ago when I visited the ruins in Greece and Stonehenge in England. The temples in Cambodia reminded me of the pyramids in Mexico and Guatemala. While I hadn't visited Cambodia, the time I had spent previously in Thailand visiting some of the temples filled me with the same sense of peace and connection as I received at the Mayan sites. My intention was to connect with the spirituality of each location to further my spiritual development. I was going to start in Japan and visit my friend Sakura, and from there head over to Cambodia and then Thailand.

As I was getting ready for my trip, I received an email from Lyn Dalebout, who does astrological readings. She was writing about the significance of the upcoming total solar eclipse on August 21, 2017. She shared that it is a time to "courageously align the conscious light of Self (who you are becoming) with the subconscious depths of your Soul (who you've been) . . . as you commit to live more fully the totality of your Self." She then went on to explain that eclipses come in pairs, and the mate to this one was on February 26, 2017. Because they come in pairs, she said that it was a good time to think back about what you were thinking about and trying to manifest in February and then compare it to where you are now.

I found her insights interesting enough to look back and see what was going on then and now. February 26 was my second full day in Guatemala and I was preparing to move into my little hut the next day. But more importantly, it was a time where I was taking my first steps to creating a new life free from my personal limiting beliefs that were holding me back from living authentically. I was choosing to release the belief that I had to live in a prescribed way, and instead could live a very different life from the one I had been living.

As I reflected back, I realized that I had had some pretty deep-rooted fears designed to keep me living in a very "safe" and "constrained" life. I had to overcome a fear that I would somehow ruin my life and become homeless by releasing these things.

In spite of these fears, I took a leap of faith that it would all work out, and that somehow I would be able to have richer, more robust life. My intention at that time was to live more freely and spend six months or so traveling around the world while I wrote my next book.

I did some more research online to better understand the significance of eclipses. Spiritually, eclipses bring about massive changes, new waves of energy and open portals to new energetic pathways. Looking back, I did feel like I had made some significant changes to my life and was living far more authentically and freely than I ever had. I had overcome some limiting beliefs and had stayed true to my personal authenticity when others had challenged or questioned it. Interestingly enough, I would be wrapping up my international travel right around the time of the August solar eclipse.

The more I thought about it, the more I felt aligned to the cycle of this eclipse cycle. I started my journey with one and will be ending with another. With the August eclipse, I would need to define and manifest the next phase of my life. The big questions were: What do I really want? What do I need to be doing?

While I had some ideas, hopefully I will get more clarity while I'm in Asia.

CHAPTER 15: GETTING ANSWERS IN ASIA

The plane touched down in Tokyo's Narita Airport in the afternoon without incident. I had lucked out with an aisle seat and an empty middle seat next to me. I spent the eleven-hour flight relaxing—watching movies, reading and planning how I wanted to spend my time while in Japan, Cambodia and Thailand.

I also spent part of the flight debating about whether I should move all of my belongings down to Guatemala. Over the past few days I had started envisioning a different way of living; one where I didn't have a permanent address in San Francisco and instead would do some short-term weekly rentals of furnished apartments or even just couch-surf at friends' houses. My original goal had been to split my time between Guatemala and San Francisco, but now I wasn't feeling a strong pull to rent my own apartment in the city anymore. I had sent an email to an international mover to get a quote and was waiting for the response. They had sent me a rough estimate. It was a bit expensive but affordable—and would save me the monthly storage rental fees.

Every time I thought about moving my belongings to my house in Guatemala, I had two reactions: the first was a vision of how everything would look in the house. I could see everything there as clear as day: my new red couch against the long wall of the living room, with my favorite photo of redwoods hung on the wall above it; the dining room table and chairs arranged in the dining room with my grandmother's antique hutch along the back wall; and pictures of my family arranged along the wall leading to the upstairs. The second was panic. I would immediately start thinking

"What the hell am I doing?" and get stressed.

I decided to table the decision until after the trip.

I had been to Tokyo two times previously and had already seen the "must see" sights. My main objective for the visit was to spend time with my friend Sakura, an 86-year old Japanese woman who had lived on the same floor as me in an apartment building in San Francisco. She had just moved back to Japan this year after the death of her husband and I wanted to check in on her and see how she was doing.

We had made plans to meet in my hotel lobby to go to dinner. I jumped up from the chair I was sitting in when I saw her walk in. She looked great!

I gave her a big hug hello. "How are you? You look wonderful!"

"I am so happy to see you! Thank you for coming out to visit me. Are you hungry?"

I wasn't, but I also knew that I needed to adapt to the current time so that I wouldn't have jet lag for the rest of the trip. "Yes, dinner sounds like a great idea. Where would you like to go?"

"There's a really good Italian restaurant near here. Let's go there."

We walked over, talking, catching up and making plans for the three days that I was going to be there.

We ended up keeping very busy. We spent one day in Kamakura, admiring nearly forty-four-foot-tall bronze Buddha statue at the Kotokuin Temple, before walking over to the nearby beach and doing some window shopping. Another day we explored the old black market area of Tokyo and the Shinjuku Gyoen National Gardens before going to the department store basements, where they sell any type of food you can think of, and buying our dinner. On my last day there, we explored the park that used to house the military barracks where she lived after getting married and the Meiji Shrine. I had a wonderful time, but the best times were when we were sitting in her apartment or at a restaurant talking.

I had thought that I had known quite a bit about Sakura, but I learned so much more about her during my visit. Each place we went to stirred up memories for her that she shared with me. It was as if she needed to relive all these aspects of her childhood and young adulthood, and I was more than happy to listen to her. My sense was that by visiting places with me that she hadn't seen for over thirty years, she was reconnecting with them and herself. As she reconnected, I surmised, she was settling more and more into her new life back in Japan while also sharing a perspective that was, perhaps, fading from the Japanese culture.

I realized that there also was a lesson and message for me in this experience. Since the beginning of time, stories have been used to share ideas, educate each other, and fire the imagination. Stories can break our hearts, help us better relate to another person or culture, or teach us right from wrong.

But what is it about a story that is so compelling?

I think it's because we all have had life experiences that we can draw from to see ourselves reflected within the story. Stories allow us to connect not only with others but also with ourselves. We can put ourselves into the story. We can imagine what we would do in the same situation as the lead character of the story. We can even invent a different ending if we don't like the one in the story.

This is true of our "real" life too. We are the lead character of our life story. So many times we don't recognize our lead role in our lives and allow others to dictate how the story unfolds. Sakura was a perfect example of a person who took control of her life story early on and kept her personal power. Through the telling of her story, she inspires others and me to do the same.

We all have wisdom to share with others. Through the telling of our story, we can help others with whatever it is that they are working through at this time. Through the listening of another's story we not only validate the other person, but we also have the opportunity to learn something and apply it to our lives.

As I boarded my flight to Cambodia, I vowed to continue sharing my stories and listening to the stories of others and silently thanked Sakura for the gift of her stories and the insights from them.

◆ ◆ ◆

Cambodia was still hot, humid and sticky at 9 o'clock at night when my plane landed. I took a tuk tuk from the airport to my hotel, grateful for the breeze that blew over me as we made our way through the city of Siam Reap. Pulling down a narrow street, my driver dropped me off at the Golden Banana hotel, my home for the next week. The hotel was tucked back from the road and was surrounded by bits of jungle, giving it the feel of being a remote hotel even though it was within a five-minute walk to the river and Pub Street.

Cambodia hadn't been on my itinerary when I was planning the trip. A friend of mine, Donald, suggested that we meet in Cambodia. We would visit a few sites, go to dinner and just hang out. I was looking forward to seeing him. Donald was the first person I met when I moved to San Francisco in 2005 and we had remained friends in spite of both of us moving in and out of San Francisco multiple times.

Once I started reading more about Cambodia, the more I realized how perfect a place it was for me to visit. Siem Reap is home to Angkor Wat, the largest religious monument in the world and a UNESCO World Heritage Site. Built in the 1100s, the site is a representation of heaven on earth, with the large central tower representing Mt. Meru and the courtyards and moat representing the continents and oceans, respectively. The bridge is symbolic of man reaching the abode of the gods. Angkor Wat is actually part of a much larger a series of Hindu and Buddhist temples built over hundreds of years. The layout and design of the temple sites, with their many stone buildings and carvings, reminded me of the Mayan sites I had been to.

I wasn't sure how many sites Donald would want to go to. Since he wasn't arriving for another day, I decided to spend my first full day at Angkor Wat and some of the other sites nearby. I hired a tuk tuk driver for the day, and off we went. As luck would have it, there was a marathon that day, and the marathon went right through Angkor Wat. The site was a mob scene. There were runners, hundreds of people milling about, and tables and booths set up, plus all of the tourists that would normally be there.

The scene reminded me of the first time I visited Chichén Itzá, one of the largest Mayan sites, in Mexico. It, too, had been filled with tourists and vendors, and I had found it very difficult to connect with the energy of the site. I took one look and told my tuk tuk driver to keep going. I would visit Angkor Wat another day. Instead, I spent the day visiting a number of smaller sites in the area and the Angkor National Museum so that I could get more immersed in the history and culture there. I was hopeful that Donald wouldn't mind visiting Angkor Wat again.

That night, I got a text from Donald, saying, "I'm delaying

leaving right now. Things are hitting the fan here. My dog is sick and needs to go to the vet. My engine light is on. I'm going to see if I can come out tomorrow, instead of today."

"Wow. You've got a lot going on! I totally understand if you can't make it."

"I want to make it. Cambodia is my favorite place in the world. Have you seen the temples? How's the hotel?"

I told him about the marathon and how I ended up changing my plans for the day, about how relaxing the hotel was, and how much I was enjoying the food. We made plans to text the next day so I'd know what time his plane was landing.

Donald ended up not coming. I was initially disappointed, but quickly realized that this gave me the opportunity to spend my week in Siem Reap exactly as I wanted to.

The next morning I went to Kbal Spean, a river with the stone carvings. It was a 45-minute tuk tuk ride and then a strenuous hike through the jungle to get there, but it was worth it. Known as the "River of a Thousand Lingas," the phallic symbol of the Hindu god Shiva, the riverbed is filled with sandstone that was carved into nearly perfect identical circular bumps. Carvings of the Hindu god and animals are carved in the stones along the river.

The carvings served as a purification of the water. As the river flowed over the lingas, it was believed that the carvings removed any impurities and infused the water with the essence of the gods. My tuk tuk driver and I followed the river until it went over a ledge, forming a waterfall.

Even though the water was considered holy, it was permissible to go into the water after the waterfall. I took my shoes off and waded over to where the waterfall was, letting the spray of the water wash over me and cool me off. I spent a moment with my eyes closed, asking the energy of the water to clear anything that needed to be cleared from me before making my way back to where my shoes were.

Water was very important to the Mayans as well. In Yucatan, Mexico, water was scarce and formed in underground caves called cenotes. The Mayans viewed the water as sacred and would often make offerings to the cenotes to appease the rain god, Chaac. Archeological dives have discovered jewelry, jade, carvings and human remains in the Chichén Itzá cenote.

We visited two other religious sites in the area before heading

211

back to the hotel. It had been a long day and I was looking forward to relaxing. My tuk tuk driver Chet, a friend of Donald's, had suggested that I go to Ankgor Wat the next morning for sunrise, so I wanted to get to sleep fairly early to be ready to go at 4:30 a.m.

It was dark as we made our way over to the temple site the next morning. I looked out at the night sky and realized that it was a full moon. I remembered reading somewhere that it was also a lunar eclipse, which are associated with clearing out old emotional baggage, stagnant attitudes and habits. Like the solar eclipse, lunar eclipses come in pairs separated by six months. My personal journey felt as if it was aligning with the movements in the heavens.

Chet handed me a flashlight and I walked over toward the temple. In front of the temple were two reflecting ponds, where a small group of people had lined up. The sky was lightening slightly, and I could see why people were standing there. Even in the dim light I could see the reflection of the temple of the water. I stood with them, watching the sky change from black to dark purple to reds, oranges and pinks. Occasionally I would turn around and look at the full moon behind me.

I had a flashback to the morning I stood at Uaxactun, waiting for the sun to illuminate the middle temple at the spring equinox. While I didn't see any ceremonies here, the mood was equally expectant as we all waited for the magical moment when the sun would rise and bathe the temple in light. In spite of the many people around, it was quiet. People were meditating, standing and taking in the beauty of the coming day. As the sky became lighter, the reflecting pond began to be filled with the colors in the sky and the massive temple buildings. With one last look at the moon behind me, I greeted the day, thankful for the events that had brought me to Angkor Wat on this day at this time.

I spent the morning exploring the site. Since it was still quite early, there were not many other people there and it was possible to find a quiet place to absorb the energy of the site. It was still also relatively cool, so I was able to enjoy walking around without feeling overwhelmed by the heat.

I made my way over to the central tower and stood in line to climb the stairs to the top. The stairs reminded me of the steps at Mayan sites—they were carved in stone and were steep and narrow. I read somewhere that the stairs at Angkor Wat were built this way because it is not easy to reach the abode of the gods. I wondered if this was why the stairs at the Mayan sites were built this way as well as I climbed the stairs of Angkor Wat, willing myself to not look down until I got to the top.

The carvings in the central tower were exquisite. I took my time walking around admiring the asparas (celestial nymphs), historical events and mythological stories carved in the walls. The still-rising sun illuminated some of them, giving them dimension and life. I bowed to the four Buddha statues that were aligned to each direction and then carefully made my way down the stairs to the main plaza area.

Even though the style of the carvings was different, I thought, as I walked to the exit, *it is interesting to see how both the Mayan and Cambodian sites capture the religious and political history of their times. For the Mayans, they typically carved stelae, large upright stones, to document the site's history. Depending on the Mayan era, some of the buildings might have religious carvings on them. There is something so powerful about the capture of the "story" of a civilization in stone so that future generations can read and understand it. The big difference, I realized, is that the story here in Cambodia is nearly complete, whereas the Mayan story is almost completely lost. When the Spanish ruled over the Mayan civilizations and forced them to convert to Christianity, they destroyed many of the Mayan documents and buildings. By removing the physical evidence of the story, the Spanish were able to write a "new" story.*

I mentally mourned the loss of a rich culture and turned to the exit. Monkeys were running and playing on the grass as I walked out of the complex toward Chet's tuk tuk. We were going to visit the Kompong Phluk lake stilt houses next.

We arrived there just before lunchtime and hired a boat to take us through the mangroves to see the village. According to Chet, the area floods annually, so the villagers have built their houses on stilts to accommodate the rising waters. The boat took us through the village so we could see the different homes and businesses. Children laughed and shouted "hello" before jumping into the water to show off in front of us.

As we made our way through the village to the main body of the lake where fishermen were working to catch their dinner, a small boat pulled up next to ours. Inside was a woman and a variety of snacks, drinks and supplies. She asked if I wanted to buy anything and I initially said no. But then she pulled out some notebooks and pencils and asked if I wanted to purchase them for local schoolchildren. I was more than happy to do that, and she handed the school supplies over to me.

We drove back in the boat, looking for schoolchildren to give the gifts to. Two small boys were swimming near their house and we pulled up next to them. I gave them the notebooks and pencils, securely tied in a plastic bag, and their faces broke into wide grins. Saying "thank you" over and over, they swam back to their house with their new school supplies safely held above the water. They turned and waved goodbye as we continued on our way.

The week flew by. Over the week, I visited more temples and sites, the Banteay Srey Butterfly Centre and the Angkor Centre for Conservation of Biodiversity, which included a number of wild animals that had been rescued from people trying to sell them as pets. I also spent some time writing.

Before I knew it, I had only one day left in Siem Reap. I was debating on what to do on my last day and decided to ask Chet.

"I have a suggestion," he said. "My mother is so grateful for all of the work you have given me this week and she would like to meet you. Why don't you come to my house in the morning to meet my family? Then we can go to the primary school so you can see our school system. If we have time after that, we can go to the lake before you go to the airport."

"I love that idea!" We made plans to meet at 8:00 a.m. to start the day. I walked over to the night market and bought some fruit and a small gift for Chet's mother before turning in for the night.

The next morning Chet drove me to his home. His mother, father, three of his sisters and several young nieces and nephews were waiting to meet me. We sat outside, in a covered pavilion, on a raised platform and visited and enjoyed some beverages. I asked his nieces and nephews about school and they shared with me their favorite subjects.

After thanking Chet's mother and family for their hospitality, Chet and I went to the primary school. As his tuk tuk pulled up to the front gate a group of schoolchildren playing in the yard turned, saw us, and ran over, saying "hello, hello!" and smiling. I smiled and said hello to them as we walked into the courtyard.

The school director was waiting to greet us and invited me to walk around and see everything the school had to offer. We peered into classrooms, where the students would all call out "Good morning" or "Hello" when they saw us. I took a tour of the library, which was filled with books in both English and Sanskrit, and admired the many school trophies that were on display.

Chet and I were walking back toward the entrance when we passed by a third-grade classroom. The teacher saw us and invited me to come in. She had the students ask me questions, in English, and shared with me her lesson planning process and approach. I talked with her and the students for about 20 minutes, answering questions about where I lived, how old I was, and what I liked about Cambodia. I was surprised at the manners of the children— they would stand when asking me a question and bow a thank you for my response. When it was time for me to leave the classroom, all the students stood up and chanted their well wishes and blessings for me on my trip.

I had made it halfway to the entrance gate when the recess bell rang. My new third-grade friends came running over to me and asked that we take photos together, which I happily obliged. I watched as they then ran off to have some snacks, and then asked Chet, "Where is the school director's office?"

He pointed to a building near the entrance and we walked over to it. The director was out, but the manager was there. We sat and I said, "I'd like to make a small donation to the school to help pay for school supplies for the students—especially those students that can't afford to buy the materials." I pulled some money out of my wallet and handed it to her.

The manager was thrilled. "Thank you! We will use this money to buy pens and notebooks for the students, and perhaps some books for the library."

"That sounds great. I'm happy I can help out a little."

I stood to leave, and she had me stop. Getting a camera from her desk, she asked one of her assistants to take a photo of us. She then gave me a hug and asked for blessings on my travels and a speedy return to Cambodia.

I thought about her as we drove away. I hadn't given much money by American standards, but to someone in Cambodia it was a great deal of money. It's funny how a small gesture can ripple out and have a much bigger impact than you could imagine.

Chet then took me to the lake beachfront in the area and we relaxed in hammocks under a canopy until it was time for me to go to the airport.

What was the lesson I learned in Cambodia? I mused while waiting to board my flight. I thought about the things that hadn't gone the way I had originally planned them to—visiting Angkor Wat my first day there, spending time with Donald, and even the fact that Cambodia hadn't been part of my original plans when I was planning this trip—and realized that not only had I just gone with the flow without any stress, but also that what had occurred that was different from what I had planned was infinitely better than what I had planned. The universe had come up with something better.

That's the lesson, I thought. *It's okay to make plans, they can be necessary, but when they don't go exactly as planned, it's important to relax and see how things unfold. They may be even better than you could imagine.*

◆ ◆ ◆

My plane touched down in Bangkok. I had been here two years ago for just a few days, and felt as if I hadn't explored the city and surrounding area nearly enough. My list of things to do included visiting some new places as well as re-visiting a couple places that I had really liked from my last visit.

After settling in my hotel room and feasting on the chocolate covered strawberries waiting for me, I made my way to Wat Pho, a Buddhist temple. I had been to Wat Pho on my last trip. It had quickly become my favorite temple because of three things: the reclining Buddha, the fortune tellers and the on-site massage school.

The reclining Buddha is one of the biggest I have ever seen. It is nearly 50 feet tall and over 150 feet long. Built out of concrete, it is covered with gold leaf that gleams and fills the room with a soft glow. I spent time in quiet contemplation of the Buddha figure and what he stands for before making my way down and around his very large feet. On the backside of the Buddha is a row of 108 bowls. It is said that if you drop a coin in each, you will have good luck. I paid 20 Thai baht for a small container of coins and slowly made my way down the row of bowls, dropping one in each.

After putting my shoes back on, I walked over to where the fortune tellers sat. There was only one today, an elderly man who proudly proclaimed to me that he was 88 years old. I sat at his table and filled out a small slip of paper with my first name, date and time of birth and country that I lived in.

Armed with this information, he took out a piece of paper that had what looked like a red flower stamped on it. He began filling in the petals of the "flower" with different numbers. When he was done, he turned to me and started telling me my fortune.

"You are a fire horse in the Chinese zodiac," he began. "You have a good head for thinking and a good personality. You are also very direct when you communicate. You think first and then speak. Money for you is sometimes easy-come, easy-go, but you will have good support and good money in the future. You also have very good intuition.

I nodded my head to show my agreement. *I have often been told that I'm a very good communicator and presenter. And money does flow in and out of my life...but the universe has also taken care of me. I've never felt any real lack.*

"Now I am going to tell you about your past." He then gave me an overview of different time periods of my life, noting the general energy of each. "Twenty-six to 35 was up and down for you, with the end of this time being very hard for you."

That's right, I thought and nodded to him. *I was 35 when I lost the girls and it was one of the most difficult times of my life.*

"Thirty-six to 39 was better," he continued. "Halfway through 39 to 41 and a half was up and down. When you reached 41 and a half to 48, it was a lucky time for you. Forty-nine and 50 were up and down for you and difficult."

That's when I had the accident, I thought and nodded to him.

"Fifty and a half to 53 will be lucky and much better for you. This year, between April 8, 2017 and June 10, 2018 next year you will buy property in another country and build a house there. This will be an investment for you."

Wow! This guy is pretty good. I've already done that!

"Fifty-two and 53 will be a good time for your love life. You will meet a nice man and maybe even marry him. He will be from a different country than you."

Oh that's interesting. The last time I visited here and got my fortune told, the guy who did it also told me I would meet someone when I was 52. I'm not sure I want to get married, but meeting a nice guy would be fun.

As I nodded, he continued. "After December 1, 2017, it will be a good time for you to move to another city in another country. For the next two and a half years, it will be a lucky time for you."

Well that is interesting. When I requested the quote from the movers, I had put December 15 as the potential moving day.

"From 55 to 64," he said, "You will buy a house in another country and move there. Living outside will be better than living inside."

"I am going to move to different countries twice?"

"Yes, you are going to own two houses in two different countries. During that same time period, you will also have a very good surprise with the stock market and have a lot of money. Sixty-four to 79 will be a happy time for you," he continued. "When you are 80, you will stop work and spend a year or so taking a holiday around the world. After that, from 82 to 89 you will be happy. Ninety will be good for you too. I am going to stop there."

I nodded and thanked him.

He finished up the session by telling me my lucky numbers and associated colors. I thanked him again and stood up from the table, feeling happy about his predictions and hoping that they would come true.

The massage school was located on the far side of the temple grounds. I walked to the main building and added my name to the list for an hour-long Thai massage.

◆ ◆ ◆

I was up for most of the night, thinking about the house in Guatemala and whether or not I should move my belongings down there. There was something about an international move that felt so final to me, as if there was no turning back. Rationally it didn't make any sense to me, since I could always move everything back. I knew I wasn't stressed about moving. When I counted up the number of places I have lived and how many times I have moved, I averaged less than three years in one place. If there was one thing that I was good at, it was packing and moving!

I looked at my phone. It was about 8:30 at night in California. I decided to call Arthur to see if I could get another perspective.

He picked up on the second ring. "Hey there! How are you? And to what do I owe the pleasure of a phone call all the way from Thailand?"

"Hi, Arthur! Well, I'm freaking out a little about Guatemala. I'm really excited about the house. Pedro has been sending me weekly texts with photo updates. It's coming along very nicely…and really fast."

"I'm envisioning a life where I split my time between Guatemala and San Francisco," I continued. "I don't know the exact split, and maybe I don't have to right now, but at the very least I would like to be in San Francisco at least one week a month. Preferably two. Originally I had been thinking that I would rent an apartment in San Francisco and take all of my belongings out of storage and put them in the San Francisco apartment."

"But the more I think about it," I said, "the more that idea doesn't make sense to me. I don't have a 'regular' job and a steady paycheck, so if—and that's a big if—I were able to find a place that would rent to me, they would most likely want me to pay a year's rent up front. I have the money, but with rents being the way they are in San Francisco, that's a big chunk of change."

"What I do have," I continued, "is a lot of friends in San Francisco who have offered to let me stay with them. I started wondering if I could stay with friends and pay them a little bit of rent while I was there. I think I have enough friends that I wouldn't wear out my welcome at any one house. And the more I think about that, the more flexible and freeing it feels to me."

"This all makes sense," said Arthur. "Why are you freaking out?"

"I'm freaking out over moving my stuff to Guatemala. I know it sounds silly, but it feels very final to me, as if there is no turning back. And I'm worried about what I will do with Baby Car, my little Audi TT. She would not survive the roads of Guatemala but I don't want to sell her. "

"You definitely can't get rid of Baby Car!"

"I know, right? So I'm thinking that I would keep Baby Car in a secure monthly parking garage in San Francisco. That way I'll have transportation when I'm here. I feel comfortable with that solution. What I'm struggling with is the rest of my stuff. It doesn't make sense to keep it in storage and there is nowhere else to keep it there. And it doesn't make sense to buy an entire houseful of furniture, plates, and stuff when I have it all already. But it is still freaking me out. I feel like I am walking away from part of who I am."

"Honestly, Jennifer, I would be more concerned if you weren't freaking out. I think this is completely normal. Look at everything you've done just in the past month. You bought land. You bought a pickup truck. You designed a house and picked out all the materials for the house. You started building a house. You got and started a new consulting project. And you continued your world walk-about by going to Japan, Cambodia and now Thailand. That's more than some people do in years."

I laughed. "Well, when you put it that way, yes, I guess it is normal!"

"Everything you are doing is so aligned with who you are and the life you want to live," he continued. "You've been doing an incredible job of learning to go with the flow of life. This is just another test for you."

I thanked him. We talked for a while longer about things going on in his life and then hung up the phone. I had a full day planned between visiting Thailand's old capital and temples in Ayuthaya, a shamanic client call, a meeting with my consulting client, and a late-night Skype call with another friend who was also an energy healer.

Even though I felt better after my call with Arthur, I raised my concerns with my energy healer friend that night to get another perspective.

"Let me start by saying that you are looking younger and more open than I have ever seen you," he said. "You are more yourself and you have obviously released a lot of things that you needed to release while you have been on this journey. It shows and shines from you. What you have been doing is aligned with your purpose. In fact, for the first time, I can see the shaman in you."

I felt myself smiling from his compliment. "Thank you. I feel much more connected to myself and my shaman work than I ever have. My time in Guatemala really gave me some clarity about my life and my life purpose."

When I tune in to my guides," he continued, "all I keep hearing is 'why the fuck are you worrying?' You've been taken care of so far, why do you think this will be any different? Move your stuff to Guatemala. Guatemala is going to be your sanctuary and you will want to be surrounded by your personal things. My sense is that this is just the beginning of this phase of your journey. You're going to have many more adventures and you are going to need your own place where you can recharge."

"And as for feeling trapped there: why would you feel that? Worst case, you use your credit card and move everything back and stay with a friend until you get on your feet in San Francisco, or wherever you want to be. If you are ever over in the UK, you have a room here. If I didn't have the responsibilities I do now, I would love to be doing what you're doing."

I thanked him and hung up Skype, thinking. *No one said that being a shaman and living an authentic life was going to be easy. I've had to buck many norms while remaining true to myself. The most difficult times were the ones that taught me the most. In the grand scheme of things, moving my belongings to Guatemala is far easier than dealing with the lost of the girls or the accident. My mind is making this more stressful than it needs to. I need to remember to just connect with my heart. It never steers me wrong. And the excitement I feel in my heart about the house in Guatemala is strong.* I took a deep breath. *Okay, I'm going to do it. I'm going to move my stuff to Guatemala.* As soon as I stated my decision, a feeling of peace washed over me and I knew I had made the right decision.

I spent the next two days visiting a variety of sites and markets and treating myself to a couple massages. I decided to end my time in Bangkok with a visit to Wat Pho, my favorite temple. I spent a couple leisurely hours there, meditating and connecting with the temple cats before hailing a cab to go back to my hotel.

None of the cabs would take me. Several flat-out refused to drive me. Others quoted a price that was four times the standard fee. Eventually I found a police officer to hail a cab for me and I began my trip back to the hotel. After driving for a few minutes, however, the cab driver pulled over and refused to go any further, saying that he would only drive me if I paid an amount that was three times the usual fare.

I called my hotel. The concierge had told me to call if I had any problems with a cab driver, and I felt that this constituted a problem. I explained the situation, and the concierge asked to speak to the driver. After they spoke, the concierge recommended that I get out of the cab since the driver was trying to scam me. He told me that he had asked the driver to take me to a well-populated place so that I could get another cab. After wishing me luck, we hung up.

The driver refused to drive me to another area. I was angry and frustrated and on the verge of tears because of my emotions. I walked quickly away from the cab and waved down another cab and asked him to turn on his meter, which he did. I then called the hotel and the concierge spoke with the driver. I made it back to the hotel without further incident.

Back in my hotel room, I thought about it more. What was the message or teaching for me?

Well, the obvious one is that I don't like being taken for a ride, I thought. I decided to tune into my guides to see what they had to say.

> *Sometimes life brings you difficult things to teach you a lesson or reinforce a behavior. This cab driver came to you to show you that even when things are not going the way you want them to, even when things are "bad," you still have choice. You can choose how to respond and take control of the situation and help make it right. You also saw that everything worked out for you. We are always here for you. Don't forget to ask us to help you. We will help take care of you and help you get out of tricky situations. The important thing to remember is to continually come from a place of love. You can come from a place of love and still be firm in your convictions, as you were today. It is not necessary to point fingers or call names. As long as you stay firm and true to yourself and what is best aligned with your higher self and unconditional love you will be fine. Just as you were today.*
>
> *This entire journey for you has been one of learning to trust even when you don't know the plan. Even when things seem to be going badly. And even when you feel a bit scared. You have made so much progress in this area. We are proud of you.*

Thank you, guides. I needed to hear that and I needed the reminder that every incident in my life is an opportunity for me to hone and perfect coming from a place of love.

The next morning at the airport, I continued to think about the message my guides had given me. I realized that I didn't need to know exactly what I wanted down to the nth degree. It was enough to know the basics—I want to do shamanic work and teaching globally to help as many people as possible live joy-filled authentic lives—and let the universe help fill in the details.

It all boils down to trust…and being willing to jump in without being able to see the safety net that is there for you. As I thought about the last year, I saw the many times that I had jumped in to authentically live my life purpose and how wonderfully the universe had orchestrated things for me so that I could do so. The times that I had worried about something had become non-events. I had wasted time worrying about something that never even happened. With that insight, I vowed to trust my guides and myself wholeheartedly.

I boarded the plane, ready to head back to San Francisco and see where this amazing journey was going to take me next.

COURAGEOUSLY AUTHENTIC LIFE
WORKSHEET

Are you ready to start living your courageous life? One way to start is to answer some of the questions that I focused on during my journey. For more assistance you can visit my website (www.SpiritEvolution.co) and download my free report or email me at Jennifer.Monahan@SpiritEvolution.co.

1. What is your moment? What has caused you to sit up and take notice of your life?
2. What personas do you think you might need to shed in your life? Why?
3. What aspects of your life do you feel drag you down? What 'a-ha' insights have you had about your life that you haven't acted on? What limiting beliefs may be causing you to stay in those situations or doing those things?
4. What gifts do you have? How do you use them in your daily life? Are you using them consciously or unconsciously?
5. What do you think your purpose might be?
6. What does your heart want for your life?
7. What steps can you take today to make your life vision a reality?

ABOUT THE AUTHOR

Jennifer B. Monahan is a business strategy consultant, shaman and coach who helps people all over the world live courageous lives. Monahan spent 2017 as a traveling nomad, spending time in Guatemala before heading over to Japan, Cambodia and Thailand.

Her first book, *This Trip Will Change Your Life: A Shaman's Story of Spirit Evolution* (She Writes Press, 2016), has won six literary awards, including two Body, Mind, Spirit Book Awards and a 2017 National Indie Excellence Award. Monahan is a regular contributor to Medium.com and Sivana East and has had articles published on MindBodyGreen.com and Inc.com. Her podcast, "Living a Courageous Authentic Life," reaches people all over the globe and can be found at www.BlogTalkRadio.com.

Monahan holds a BA in Mass Communications from the University of Bridgeport (CT), an MBA in Marketing from the University of Connecticut, a Masters in Natural Health from Clayton College, and completed an accredited coaching program through Coach U. Her shamanic training began with a Mayan shaman in Mexico and then expanded to include shamans in Guatemala and her own personal guides.

She currently splits her time between the United States and Guatemala (where she has built her personal sanctuary to continue to connect with the magic and mystery of the Mayan ruins) and is in the process of writing her third book, a handbook for people looking to define, create and live their courageously authentic life. You can find her online at www.SpiritEvolution.co.

43564551R00139

Made in the USA
Middletown, DE
25 April 2019